NEW PLAYS
USA
4

New Plays USA Series

New Plays USA 1

Lee Breuer, *A Prelude to Death in Venice*
Tom Cole, *Dead Souls*
David Henry Hwang, *FOB*
Emily Mann, *Still Life*
OyamO, *The Resurrection of Lady Lester*
Adele Edling Shank, *Winterplay*

New Plays USA 2

Donald Freed and Arnold M. Stone, *Secret Honor*
Gary Leon Hill, *Food from Trash*
Franz Xaver Kroetz, *Mensch Meier*, translated by Roger Downey
Ronald Ribman, *Buck*
James Yoshimura, *Mercenaries*

New Plays USA 3

Allan Havis, *Morocco*
Emily Mann, *Execution of Justice*
Stephen Metcalfe, *The Incredibly Famous Willy Rivers*
Richard Nelson, *Between East and West*
Virgilio Piñera, *Cold Air*, translated and adapted by Maria Irene Fornes

NEW PLAYS USA

Edited by
JAMES LEVERETT
and **GILLIAN RICHARDS**

Introduction by
ROSS WETZSTEON

THE PLAYS

Theatre Communications Group   New York   1988

Contents

Selection Committee for
New Plays USA 4

New Plays USA 4 was supported in part by a generous grant from Home Box Office, Inc., and with public funds from the New York State Council on the Arts.

The playwrights whose plays appear in this volume are recipients of Playwrights USA Awards, also funded by Home Box Office, Inc.

Preface

Play publication must expand still more in this country if a national dramatic literature is to live both on the stage and in our imaginations. The fragile, inconstant lines of communication that keep the ancient, intimate art of theatre going on this gigantic continent still must get special care. Along those lines writers' reputations are made; down them plays travel from reader to reader, theatre to theatre, production to production, as they develop and become part of our creative capital.

More than eight years ago, these concerns—publication and perpetuation of a living dramatic literature, support of writers by making known what they write—led Theatre Communications Group to begin the ambitious, unprecedented project that includes *Plays in Process*, the script distribution service, and the *New Plays USA* anthology series. The concerns are still with us today—no single enterprise could or should answer them totally.

Many horses have been ridden into battle as writers—Michael Feingold, Richard Gilman and myself—have introduced the previous three volumes of this collection. Banners have been unfurled, proclamations made. Our main themes have been that no single theatre or street of theatres can be called our National Theatre, but instead the designation is truly nationwide, including hundreds of institutions in every region; that the best dramatic writing is produced and the most significant playwrights work in this National Theatre; that what those writers create is astonishing, not only in amount, but also in range—in form from traditional to experimental, in content from personal sketch to public canvas.

In his introduction to *New Plays USA 4*, Ross Wetzsteon puts some of the battle chargers out to permanent pasture and, once and for all, claims for the plays, playwrights and theatres that make a book like this one possible the primacy they deserve as essential articulators of both our private and our national selves. It's high time too! They're not off-off anything. If some of them are "regional," it's because they're rooted, like any significant art must be. If you are one of those who insists that American drama lacks social, political and spiritual scope, you haven't encountered them. Here's your chance! You might take a look at the other volumes also.

What distinguishes the *New Plays USA* series is not only the plays it contains but also the method by which they were chosen. Like no other system, this process makes use of the creative energies of the entire National Theatre alluded to above. The plays in this volume were selected from the 24 issued as manuscripts during the 1985–86 and 1986–87 seasons of *Plays in Process* and from the plays published during that period in TCG's *American Theatre* magazine. Both *Plays in Process* and *American Theatre* depend for their material on the national network of nonprofit professional theatres, which now produce and sustain all of those who write for the stage in this country.

The plays in this volume have come a long way. First, a theatre selected each of them from the literally thousands submitted for consideration every year. Each became part of a theatre's season of fully produced works. Probably that theatre, and others as well, had been focusing creative and material resources on the writer and the play for some time, developing a relationship in the course of developing the work. Once the play was scheduled for production, the theatre's artistic director or literary manager sent it on to TCG for consideration.

More than 250 plays came to TCG in this way during the past two years. Last season alone, 155 were received, 50 percent more than in any other year, and a very persuasive gauge of the American theatre's health and productivity. *New Plays USA 4* is thus the tip of a very large iceberg. It does not contain all of the good plays staged in this country during the two-year period, but it does contain an excellent and, for the future of the art, heartening representation of them.

Also hopeful is the fact that the writers in this volume are being helped financially by receiving Playwrights USA Awards, substantial grants which were started in 1984 with *New Plays USA 2*. They are made possible by a grant to TCG from Home Box Office, Inc.—an enlightened corporate investment, no strings attached, in what will be written in this country in the future.

As director of TCG's Literary Services programs, I oversee the selection for *Plays in Process* and *New Plays USA*. My thanks to those busy and generous souls who spent so many weekends, holidays and not-so-holidays serving on the *Plays in Process* Selection Committee, which is the first stage of choosing the plays for these volumes. Just the few accomplishments listed by their names below show how vital they are to our theatre's operation: Colette Brooks, who has worked extensively as a dramaturg and artistic associate in the Off-Off Broadway theatre;

Clinton Turner Davis, director, production manager, and founder and co-chairman of the board of the Non-Traditional Casting Project; George Ferencz, director and founder of CEMENT; Jack Gelber, award-winning director and writer, whose plays include *The Connection* and *The Cuban Thing*; Mary B. Robinson, director and former associate artistic director of Hartford Stage Company; playwright Sheldon Rosen, whose work has been widely produced in Canada and the U.S.; Don Shewey, journalist, theatre critic and author of *Sam Shepard* and, with Susan Schacter, *Caught in the Act: New York Actors Face to Face*; Catherine Slade, actor, teacher, director, and artistic director of Manhattan Bridge Company; Kathleen Tolan, actor, director and author of *A Weekend Near Madison*; Ross Wetzsteon, senior editor of *The Village Voice*. Brooks, Davis, Shewey and Wetzsteon also served on the selection committee for this volume.

The person who really organizes the great shifting of scripts that the process entails, and who, once they are selected, patiently and with great sensitivity coaxes them from the stage to the page, is my colleague Gillian Richards. Additional editing for plays in this volume was provided by M. Elizabeth Osborn and Ray Sweatman, with assistance from Roger Durling. Thanks to them all!

JAMES LEVERETT
January 1988

Introduction

Ross Wetzsteon

"Woe, in the aesthetic line," said Henry James, "to any example that requires the escort of a precept. It is like a guest arriving to dine accompanied by constables." The hosts of the previous three volumes in this series have all made tentative gestures at providing their guests with escorts, at discerning thematic connections or patterns of concern, but have all declined to call in the constables, a tradition I am delighted to follow. I will note—in the spirit of Vladimir Nabokov, who warned his students that the word "cosmic" is always in danger of losing its "s"—that two of the playwrights you're about to meet are named Jon, a trend that hasn't quite reached the proportion of the English fondness for David. I'll even risk adding that four of the five plays confront matters of race, but this is already flirting with what is always called, in introductions of this sort, "a spurious unity." For finally— and this is perhaps the only generalization one can make with any assurance about any group of gifted artists—whatever they have in common is the least interesting thing about them.

This wasn't true of all the playwrights considered for inclusion in this volume, alas—the more than 250 nominated by the artistic directors of the constituents of Theatre Communications Group for its *Plays in Process* project—and if I focus first on the negative, it's only to establish the context within which every artistic achievement almost miraculously survives. One of the many privileges of sitting on the *PIP* reading committee turned out to be getting a glimpse of what was on the minds of those young and not so young playwrights who, not yet having found their own voices, spoke instead in the echoes of trends. Now if trends tell us nothing about the aesthetics of playwriting, they reveal a great deal about the precepts of society, and by definition are *only* interesting for what they have in common. During my year on the committee, the most frequent generic thread was plays about the elderly, and I'm told by those who served the following year that the recurrent motif was plays about Vietnam. Nobody, as far as I know, wrote about elderly Vietnamese—on the principle of Lincoln's Doctor's Dog—but a number of playwrights, in their academic experimentalism, seemed to be signalling through their grants, and a handful, in their small aspirations to the big screen, must already be pricing beach houses in Malibu.

But only an ungracious host makes fun of the uninvited. My excuse, I hope, is that I'm trying to encourage young playwrights to add their visions to the zeitgeist, not vandalize it for their ideas. On a more serious level—almost anything is more serious than the zeitgeist—for every playwright who merely borrowed sentiments from the lending library of commonplace assumptions, who merely recycled political prejudices in the guise of socially conscious engagement, who merely mimicked the mannerisms of exemplary success (David Mamet seems to have become the most conspicuous model in the late '80s), there were dozens who revealed the tone and texture of idiosyncratic obsession, of inimitable individuality, of personal vision; and it's difficult to remain demoralized by the much mooted malaise of the '80s when confronted by this outpouring of irrepressible creativity.

It should be clear by now that my own bias as a script-reader—once past suspicion of "professional" craftsmanship, annoyance with ingratiating "quirkiness," and abhorrence of "surefire" manipulation—was for the energy of originality, for the pulse of the utterly unexpected, for a glimpse of blood on the knuckles or mania in the eyes. Playwrights worth nurturing—to continue the biological metaphor—have the genes of drama not just in their blood but in their teeth. A somewhat simpler way of putting it would be to say that I felt we should select playwrights whose next scripts we also wanted to see. Of course this is usually little more than a perfunctory nod of condescending encouragement, but in the case of the playwrights in this volume it's both acknowledgment of their achievement and proof that they were not so much born as doomed to a life in the theatre.

The Film Society takes place far from the centers of power, and the victims of the social system it depicts—initially the white students of a private school in South Africa and ultimately the blacks of the country they are being trained to rule— never appear onstage, but Jon Robin Baitz does more than encapsulate the rot of a society in the rot of one of its institutions, he realizes that crucial, precipitating events are often small moral failures that accumulate with overwhelmingly tragic consequences. How little of South Africa we see, how much about South Africa we learn. For in focusing on the psychological bonds of the family, on the emotional ties of an enclosed community of friends and colleagues, Baitz reveals the ways in which they simultaneously define the self and deny its expression—and by extension the ways in which tentative gestures of social rebellion become immobilized by rigid cultural traditions. Baitz's title isn't nearly as oblique as it initially appears, for when the teacher orders *Touch of Mink* to show his students he receives *Touch of Evil* instead—so easily do decent, troubled people (much like you and I) slide from fantasies of the good life into the banality of evil.

The expressive center of any play, as everyone in the theatre learns soon enough, isn't always in its dialogue, and while the absent victims of *The Film Society* are the focus of its moral vision, the virtually speechless protagonist of *Kind Ness* provides its emotional resonance. Indeed, Buzz is one of the most touchingly human characters in contemporary drama—though he happens to be a gorilla. It's important to remind readers of Ping Chong's delightfully heartbreaking and genially chilly script to visualize Buzz's presence onstage throughout most of its apparently aimless and inconsequential scenes. Buzz may have little to say, but the dramatic encounters aren't so much between the speakers as between Buzz's silence and the casual cruelties he overhears—cruelties based on nothing more, and nothing less, than the distinctions in "kind" which should make us value our uniqueness instead. Buzz's very lack of expressiveness, either verbal or facial, forces us to respond on his behalf, and thus leads us into his pained but forgiving spirit, his heart of lightness. Differences between people, as the space in the title hints, as the opening slide show suggests, and as the subsequent scenes just as subtly demonstrate, make kindness not just possible but imperative, for differences between people are the source not only of our loneliness but our love.

The baby—another loud though speechless character, another forceful though absent presence—gives *Tent Meeting* its aura of tragi-farcical mystery, and keeps the adventures of a self-ordained preacher, his two eccentric children and his "Holy Infant" grandchild suspended in some immeasurable space above the simplistic dimensions within which the subject of revivalism is invariably confined. Larry Larson, Levi Lee and Rebecca Wackler slyly invoke and just as slyly distance themselves from the Holy Family theme, but while the play can't be elevated to the realm of the supernatural, neither can it be reduced to the landscape of the psyche (the mere lunacy of religious fanatics) or the wasteland of the contemporary (the mere satirizing of mercenary apostles). The authors, in discovering spiritual possibility even in the midst of spiritual deception, insist on the kind of forthright ambiguity that provokes rather than pronounces—we leave the theatre knowing considerably less than when we entered, and aware of considerably more.

It might seem anomalous to describe Jon Klein's *T Bone N Weasel* as a comedy of the dispossessed—your tired, your poor, your huddled masses yearning to breathe free aren't usually considered a locus of laughter—until we recall the comically paired drifters from Don Quixote and Sancho Panza to Vladimir and Estragon, and in particular the long American tradition of the resilient outcast, the resourceful vagabond, the cracker-barrel, cornpone humorists of the frontier. Klein's lineage, in fact, extends directly back to Mark Twain, for T-Bone and Weasel are nothing less than Huck and Jim brought into the 1980s, their raft a stolen Buick, their King and Duke the wackily sinister characters they meet on their meandering journey. Like their prototypes, T-Bone and Weasel encounter representatives of state, church, business and what passes for high society. And in the most intriguing parallel—for beneath its ebulliently comedic surface this play is no more a slapstick odyssey than was Twain's masterpiece—when the white man suffers an attack of conscience it becomes, for his black partner, an act of betrayal. Huck refused to return to civilization—he'd been there before. T-Bone and Weasel make the same decision—how little that civilization has changed in a century.

George C. Wolfe's comedy of the dispossessed also has a long lineage—like Jewish humor, black humor has traditionally been self-mocking—but since the distinction between laughing at and laughing with has as much to do with social power as emotional sensitivity, this voice has rarely been heard in our theatre. In daring to satirize the enslaving myths of black culture, *The Colored Museum* is simultaneously an integral part of America's black heritage and an audaciously original extension of public discourse—a hilariously serious challenge, to both whites and blacks, to discard the iconography of race and replace it with a vision of our common humanity. Among other things, Wolfe is asserting that blacks should demand psychological as well as political rights, in particular the privilege of self-parody—one of the few encouraging signs in a decade of resurgent racism. But even in his revue-skit format—which makes palatable what otherwise might seem inflammatory—he recognizes that rage and compassion, far from being incompatible, must mutually motivate the battle against bigotry. For Wolfe's paradoxical point is that to move beyond our history we must never forget our past.

"A poem," Robert Penn Warren once said, "starts from an observed fact of life and only then does the search begin for the issue—the ethical or dramatic issue—in that fact." Warren could just as well have been speaking of a play—or, for that matter, an introduction. So if the fact is these five plays, what is the issue?

Off Broadway, the nonprofit movement, regional theatre—all began in opposition, indeed all have a denial rather than an affirmation in the very names they've chosen for themselves. But one of the points these plays prove is that it's long past time for the American theatre to stop defining itself by what it's not. This tropism is so ingrained, in fact, that it's tempting to lift a mental forefinger and launch into yet another art vs. commerce diatribe contrasting the aesthetic achievement of these playwrights with the meretricious marketplace of Broadway, Hollywood and television—precisely the kind of mind-jerk thinking it's become increasingly necessary to combat.

Certainly there was a time when it had to be asserted that success should be measured on the stage rather than at the box office, but that argument has long been won—thanks in no small measure to the organization and project responsible for this anthology. Yet while none of us believe that the activities taking place Tuesday through Sunday evenings in a 20-block area in mid-Manhattan continue to set the standards to which we must place ourselves in opposition, habits of thought often linger long after the conditions they describe have ceased to exist, and too many of us still tend to define our stance as adversarial. "We are not involved in commodity theatre," artistic directors from Bangor to Boise declaim, "we are not interested in electronic pabulum." Obviously this attitude is inarguable—except that it finds our value less in what we accomplish than in what we reject, and thus regards our theatre less as an offering to our culture than as our alternative to its decadence. But the only standards we have to measure ourselves against are our own—does Lutèce defend itself by arguing that it's an improvement on Wendy's?—so let's take the "not" out of our thinking as these playwrights have taken it out of our theatre.

For one thing, the aesthetic of opposition encourages the simultaneously snobbish and self-pitying solipsism that characterized the intellectual climate of the 1950s—the decade, of course, in which Off Broadway was born—the sense of lonely artists surrounded by an uncomprehending culture, regarding their subordinate status as the proof of their superior sensibility, and thus confining themselves within a coterie community. This infatuation with the myth of the misunderstood artist is another habit of mind that dies hard—which wouldn't particularly matter except that no vital theatre has ever set itself apart from its culture, let alone taken pride in its isolation.

But more important, the aesthetic of opposition helps perpetuate the Two Theatres syndrome of which we were so proud in the 1960s, but which, for all its contributions, also exacerbated the cultural schizophrenia theatre could do so much to ameliorate. Those who feel nostalgia for the lofts and storefronts and church basements of the counterculture—another movement that defined itself by what it was not—shouldn't overlook the fact that far from reaffirming the traditional role of theatre they were participating, however necessarily and however hopefully, in an unprecedented violation of its unifying spirit. For in the most common definitions of the Two Theatres—Broadway vs. Off Broadway, commercial vs. artistic, mainstream vs. avant-garde—there remained an unfortunate implication, indeed in most cases an insistence, that the split was not only immutable but salutary. But characterize the split in other language—entertainment vs. provocation, say—and its artificiality, even its unhealthiness, becomes immediately apparent. Was there an Off Epidaurus? A non-Globe? Did Greek or Elizabethan theatregoers ask themselves, "What'll it be tonight, mindless spectacle or stimulating experiment?" The Two Theatres reflected a divided culture and resulted from a particular set of historical circumstances—but historical necessity shouldn't be confused with articles of faith and a divided culture shouldn't be cause for congratulation. To accept, to insist on, to glorify the Two Theatres is not only to concede the irrelevance of theatre but to submit to the very fragmentation of sensibility theatre could play a prominent role in overcoming.

There's yet another way of characterizing the split between the Two Theatres—the one celebrates while the other criticizes the dominant values of the society—and since I've used the word "opposition" so pejoratively I hasten to add that I'm writing on the fairly safe assumption that the people and institutions with power in any society almost always betray rather than embody its *essential* values. When we say things like "Broadway plays merely confirm our culture's values while we call them into question," we are, in effect, conceding that the dominant is equivalent to the essential. Since it's obvious that the greatest threat to the Constitution in our lifetime has come from the Oval Office itself, why is it any more difficult to understand that the greatest violators of our cultural traditions are those who sit in even larger offices in mid-Manhattan or suburban Los Angeles? To marginalize oneself in this context, to think of one's position as adversarial, is to hand over our culture to the barbarians by default. The point is not to refrain from opposing them but to refuse to acknowledge that they are the repository of our heritage in the first place, to understand that they have merely appropriated our traditions in the guise of the status quo, to insist that they are not celebrating our society's values but their corruption.

Now this may seem like a semantic quibble, but it's more than a matter of morale for us to learn to take as much pride in our achievements as in our defiance. For the culture is ours, if not the power, and once we recognize this fact, our theatre could begin to take on its healing role—ironically, a function it fulfills even when, especially when, it confronts the perversions of power. In this regard, it's instructive to remember that writers for the theatre, unlike poets or novelists, have never gone unrecognized in their own lifetimes (Büchner merely proves the rule). While an Emily Dickinson or a Herman Melville may be discovered decades after their deaths, playwrights are as instantaneous as dancers, and who ever heard of a Martha Graham or a Merce Cunningham only appreciated by later generations? This immediacy, this present-tense connection to its community, means that of all the arts theatre has the greatest potential to stand at the center of its culture. It's not necessary to foresee a Golden Age in order to strive for this potential, but at the very least it is necessary to stop regarding ourselves as off-, as non-, as outside. Off Broadway, nonprofit, regional? Why not call Broadway Off Theatre, commercial venues nonart, New York unrooted? The "not" belongs to *them*.

I don't imagine that any of the playwrights gathered in this book gave a moment's thought to defining their work in relation to Broadway, movies, or TV, to say nothing of seeking the escort of precept. On the contrary, one of the reasons they're in this collection is precisely because they're self-defining. They may have chosen avant-garde or conventional forms, they may have chosen traditional or adversarial themes, but these choices are secondary to their commitment both to individual expression and a unified theatre. These plays, whatever they have to say in whatever form, do not speak from one community to another, but assume creative participation in a common culture. Listening to the voices in this volume reaffirms the fact that the state of the theatre can only be discovered in the state of its art.

Ross Wetzsteon has been a theatre critic at *The Village Voice* for 20 years, and has served as chairman of the Obie Committee (which gives annual awards for creative achievement in the Off-Broadway theatre) for the past 15 years. He has written extensively on theatre for such publications as *Partisan Review, American Theatre, Plays and Players, New York, Horizon, Saturday Review* and *Rolling Stone.*

NEW PLAYS USA

USA

4

The Film Society
Jon Robin Baitz

About Jon Robin Baitz

Jon Robin Baitz was born in Los Angeles in 1961. He grew up in the U.S. and Brazil, and in South Africa, where he was educated from the age of 10-16. He apprenticed in playwriting at the Padua Hills Playwrights' Workshop and Festival. His play *Mizlansky/Zilinsky*, produced by L.A. Theatre Works in 1985, won an L.A. *Weekly* Award for outstanding writing. He adapted and directed Delmore Schwartz's *In Dreams Begin Responsibilities* for the Mark Taper Forum's literary cabaret in 1986. During 1986-87 he was Playwright-in-Residence with the New York Stage and Film Company and spent the summers of 1986 and 1987 in residence with the company at Vassar College. He is currently working on a play *Dutch Landscape*, commissioned by the Mark Taper Forum, which was given a workshop production there in the summer of 1987 and is tentatively scheduled for full production in 1988. Baitz was the recipient of a 1987 Charles H. Revson Fellowship from Playwrights Horizons and a 1987 Berman-Bloch Fellowship from Los Angeles Theatre Center.

About the Play

The premiere production of *The Film Society*, under the direction of Robert Egan, was presented as part of the 8th Los Angeles Theatre Center Festival. It played at the Theatre Center from January 9 through February 22, 1987. A British production of the play, directed by David Attenborough, opened at the Hampstead Theatre Club in London in January 1988. Extracts from *The Film Society* were published in *The Best Plays of 1986-87*, edited by Otis Guernsey. The play was circulated as a *Plays in Process* script early in 1988.

The playwright wishes to thank Robert Egan for the time and thought he has put into the life of this play, and Ulu Grosbard for an ongoing education in the theatre.

Characters

JONATHON BALTON, in his 40s.
NAN SINCLAIR, in her 40s.
TERRY SINCLAIR, in his 40s.
MRS. BALTON (SYLVIA), in her 60s.
NEVILLE SUTTER, close to 70.
HAMISH FOX, in his 70s.

Time

1970.

Place

Durban, Natal Province, South Africa.

The Play

The Film Society

The consciences of the English are unnaturally agitated by Africa.

> —Evelyn Waugh
> *A Tourist in Africa*, 1959

ACT ONE

Scene 1

September, 1970. A dark, rain-sodden afternoon. A decrepit classroom, redolent of moldy books, and the pencil shavings of generations of boys being ground into the hardwood floor. Little clues as to the nature of this place: on the walls are three scattered maps—England, Africa, the world; above the chalkboard sits a mounted seabird, missing most of its plumage; a virtually expired palm in a cracked Zulu pot sits in the corner, along with a rather lovely scale model of a tramp steamer.

Sitting in the darkness is JONATHON BALTON, *watching the final scene of Orson Welles's* Touch of Evil. *The film, save for the flickering play of light and shadow on* JONATHON'S *face, is unseen by the audience.*

Suddenly there is the dull roll of tropical thunder, drowning out the sound of the film, followed by a brilliant flash of lightning which illuminates the stage for an instant as the film abruptly halts. JONATHON *sits utterly still, not at all sure of what to do other than listen to the rain beating down on the corrugated-iron roof.* HE *lights a cigar and, using his match for illumination, makes his way to the French doors and looks out. There, in the rain, a banner is being hastily pulled down. It reads "BLENHEIM SCHOOL FOR BOYS—CENTENARY 1870–1970. ONE HUNDRED YEARS OF PRIDE, RIGOR & REASON." As the banner disappears,* JONATHON'S *film starts up again with a lurch and* HE *quickly sits down to watch the conclusion.*

MAN'S VOICE (*On film*): Well. Hank was a great detective all right.
WOMAN'S VOICE (*On film*): And a lousy cop.
MAN'S VOICE: Is that all you have to say for him?

Pianola theme on soundtrack.

WOMAN'S VOICE: He was some kind of man. What does it matter what you say about people?
MAN'S VOICE: Goodbye, Tanya.
WOMAN'S VOICE: Adios.

The music swells up and JONATHON *sways along with it. The spinning of the take-up reel eventually catches his attention.* HE *sighs, switches off the projector, and pours himself a teacup full of Scotch from a bottle on his desk.* NAN *and* TERRY SINCLAIR *enter, stand in the doorway unnoticed by* JONATHON.

NAN: Jonathon . . . ?
JONATHON: Uhm?
TERRY: Hello? Jonathon? May we turn on a light?
JONATHON (*Suddenly shaken out of his reverie*): Oh, Christ, Nan . . . Terry! I'm—I'm in a fog. These films. (HE *shields his eyes as* TERRY *turns on the light*) Ooh. Bright.
TERRY: Were you taking a nap?
JONATHON: No, I just had film society.
NAN: Didn't get much of a crowd, then, did you?
JONATHON: No, no—we actually had a good turnout; it's just that I had ordered *That Touch of Mink*, which I quite like, but it got buggered up and somehow they sent me something called *Touch of Evil* instead. With Mexicans and corruption in it.
TERRY: We've been looking for you. We wanted to talk to you after what happened yesterday, and you were gone . . .
JONATHON (*Ignoring* TERRY, *cutting him off*): Not the usual sort of film-society fare—it was an utter mystery to the boys, I think. I had to watch it again.
TERRY: Jonathon, I do want to explain—I didn't intend to tear the place up quite to this extent.
NAN: Why didn't you call us last night? We saw you running out of here. . . . We tried to find you.
JONATHON (*A beat;* HE *nods slightly, looks out the window*): They just took down the banner. Did you see?
NAN: Yes. Jonathon, I wouldn't mind a drink just now . . .
TERRY: Yes.
JONATHON (*Points to desk drawer*): You know where. Scotch, teacups. (*Still looking outside*) The boys made that banner in here. One hundred years of pride, rigor and reason. I told them—they musn't use water paint.
TERRY (*Taking Scotch from* NAN, *holds his cup up in a toast*): Or perhaps, more ap-

propriately, a century of narcolepsy, food poisoning and sadism? Eh? Jonathon—are you angry . . . or something?

JONATHON: Food poisoning and sadism. That's quite funny, quite droll. So, right. You've come to tell me you've both been given the sack, right? Is that it?

TERRY: Actually, nothing has happened.

NAN: Sutter and Fox haven't called us in. They've been in some sort of meeting with some parents or something.

JONATHON: Oh. They've left you alone. . . . Well. Maybe it's all going to blow over.

TERRY: I've been trying to get in to see Neville since this morning. They're shut in, in his office . . .

JONATHON: Are you totally mad? Do you want to provoke him further? Keep away from them! Let them cool down. Do you realize—do you realize that half the school failed to show up today?

NAN: They're probably all busy signing up at Durban Boys High.

JONATHON: Well can you blame them? When I saw you marching that native up to the podium, I said to myself, "Terrific. That's it—he's finally gone and done it for good this time." Nan—I can't believe you'd involve yourself in this. Terry, sure, one comes to expect the worst. But not you . . .

NAN: What makes you think I had anything to do with it? I was in the dark, love, actually. Just like you.

TERRY: This was my own event. I mean, look—I didn't imagine that the bloody police were going to be called, did I? I—I didn't set out to have some poor man arrested and thrown into Durban Jail, Jonathon. God.

JONATHON: But the fact is, all it was meant to be, Ter, was a Centenary Day gala. I mean, it's a lovely day, albeit somewhat dull; but still, with tea and meringues and a couple of harmless speeches about tradition and all that, it makes a nice break from the rest of the drudgery around here, doesn't it? We all know how you feel about everything, but this is hardly the place to bring on a bearded native revolutionary. Screaming about equality.

NAN: Well. In point of fact, there was no screaming, Jonathon.

JONATHON: There was shouting. Who was he, anyway?

TERRY: A friend. Bazewo. Reverend Bazewo. Has a school in Kwamashu township. I went to the police, they won't give me any information at all. If anyone should've been arrested, it should've been me.

JONATHON: Why not go on a bit of a holiday or something, instead of attempting to destroy your life? It'll get harder for everyone, if you keep this up. Buy some new clothes, or a stereo or something.

TERRY: You don't think I should go see the old man, try and sort the whole business out, right now? It's this waiting—I mean, what's the worst that could happen?

JONATHON: It's a very bad idea to go looking for him. Let them come to you. He'll probably shout a bit. I mean, Fox is the one to worry about.

TERRY: I can handle him.

JONATHON: Please, Ter. Nan, tell him—it's all very well to sit about on Sunday afternoon, in some pub at the beachfront, making fun of the government and all, or have some Africans over for tea, quietly, now and then. But this business is asking for trouble.

NAN: But there is an undeniable air of stagnation here. This is meant to be some sort of progressive school.

JONATHON: It is! You're the first woman to teach here.

NAN: You've been pointing that out to me for a year and a half, as if I were some sort of lab animal.

JONATHON: Look. For the most part—the atmosphere is improving here.

NAN: In what way, Jonathon?

JONATHON: My film society, for one.

TERRY: Oh, God. Please.

JONATHON: No. It's true. You are so impatient, you give nothing a chance. It used to be all forced marches and military training and navigating by the stars and rugger all over the place. No cultural life whatsoever. Nan, you know the last time the dramatics society put something on was a Christmas pageant when Ter and I were boys here. You know that! This is the first time anything's been allowed to flourish—

TERRY: But it's the most obvious kind of superficial—

JONATHON (Cuts him off, waving his arms): I mean, you've merely to look at Gilerakis and his pen-pal society. One boy. Ended up sending postcards to his niece in Hong Kong or Bolivia or someplace. Not to mention Viltonian and his snake club or reptile society or lizard boys or whatever the hell they called themselves. He had three boys, one was bitten, and the entire thing packed up.

NAN: True.

JONATHON: Not to mention seashell club. Boys lollying about the bloody beachfront all day. Headmaster Sutter went mad. I remember—I was one of them. 1945.

NAN: Jonathon. How can you say things are getting better when, two days ago, I was called in to Sutter's office—to review my teaching methods. You could be the next one, you know!

JONATHON: But I haven't got any.

TERRY: It's not funny. They'll start dragging some of us in for ideological debriefings soon, probably.

JONATHON: If you stopped annoying them, they'd leave you alone. What happened?

NAN: What happened was they went into a panic about history. We sat there, eating those horrible sugary biscuits made by mad Mrs. Sutter, and discussing how I was to approach the Boer War. And just as I was descending into the most merciful diabetic coma, Fox launches into me—with his version of the Zulu wars.

JONATHON: How dare they!

NAN: Which, from the way he described them, were fought at the foot of Mount Sinai, with him loading rifles. And Neville sipping gin.

TERRY: And the point is—no—listen. Do you know why this happened?

JONATHON: You must have been doing something odd, I don't know.

NAN: It was that little bugger, Mowatt.

JONATHON: Who?

NAN: Head shaped like a quail egg, mongoose-brown hair, bored, listless eyes.

JONATHON: My dear girl, you describe half the boys here.

NAN: He told them that I'd been lecturing on the permanent slave class we've made of the Zulus.

JONATHON: Have you been? Really?

NAN: Well I mean, I'm not as stupid as Terry.

TERRY: After all, that's *my* favorite speech, Jonathon.

JONATHON: Well then you were *thinking* it, Nan. Listen, we'd better keep out of everyone's way for a bit. Including the boys'.

NAN: I'd love to, but I'd never get away with it.

JONATHON: Oh, you'd be amazed at how much you can get away with. I have yet to open a textbook once this term.

TERRY: How do you teach?

JONATHON: Oh believe me, things get done. I mean, when you were on vacation in Malaga and I had to take both of your ghastly history classes, all I did was show them the Micahel Caine film where ten men wipe out the entire Zulu army. Everyone gets a Victoria Cross at the end and hardly suffers so much as a scratch. Then you take 'em down to see the native dancers and give 'em a bloody great quiz and there you have it—South African history in a nutshell. *(Pause)* Look—couldn't you go in there and simply apologize? . . . It'd be the smart thing to do, wouldn't it? Sure! That's it!

TERRY: Is it as simple as all that, Jonathon? The boys need something else. Another story. The ones we learnt here twenty years ago won't serve them today. They screwed us up too.

JONATHON: Politics, Terry. (HE *shakes his head, puts on his coat*) I'm the last person to talk to about politics: I can't even manage to get a print of *That Touch of Mink.*

TERRY: It's not funny anymore, Jon. I mean, it's 1970: look at the world now. Not exactly quiet, is it? It's children, detention, marches, riots and imprisonment. You know? So what if, around here, it's still lawn bowls and the orchid show. The rest of the world is not quiet.

JONATHON *(Thinks for a moment)*: No. It's not. Is it?

NAN: Listen, I have an idea. We're all a bit rattled . . . and all. Let's go downtown and have some dinner. The three of us. Jonathon—we haven't in ages.

JONATHON *(Pause)*: I—I can't. I'd love to, but they're showing a very interesting film at the cinema on the beachfront, and I keep missing it. It's the last night. (HE *begins to exit*)

NAN: Right. Sure.

JONATHON *(Stops)*: It's all about an unconventional lady in America and her boy. And all the troubles. (HE *is halfway out and stops again*) Look. Just let it all die down, both of you. Okay?

HE *stands for a moment.* TERRY *nods and* JONATHON *exits.*

NAN: Perhaps that's not such a bad idea. I mean, there'll come a point when . . . you know?

TERRY: Oh, God, let's not worry about it so much, eh? I mean, they're not likely to fire me, love. It's much more fun if I'm here, so they can slowly turn me about, and drive us mad, eh? Cheers.

TERRY *raises his glass, drinks as lights fade.*

Scene 2

The living room of MRS. BALTON's *beachfront flat: a vaguely Edwardian room but with an air of tropical decay.* SYLVIA BALTON *wears a flamboyant African kaftan.* JONATHON *is sitting in a comfortable chair in a corner of the room.*

JONATHON: The point is, they substituted films without telling anyone. I mean, I thought I was going to get *Auntie Mame*. The marquee still said *Pajama Game*. Instead, there was a grotesque Italian film. Loud music and angry women everywhere.

MRS. BALTON (*Not listening*): How dreadful.

JONATHON: About a film director. Incomprehensible.

MRS. BALTON: Ghastly.

JONATHON: Fell asleep somewhere towards the middle.

MRS. BALTON: So you'll never know who had the basket?

JONATHON: That was another film, Mother.

MRS. BALTON: Ring for a whisky, love.

JONATHON (*Reaches over to side table, rings a small bell*): Wonder to me that nanny can still hear this thingie.

MRS. BALTON: Ming was at the veterinarian today.

JONATHON: The point is, I seem to be having bad luck with my choice of cinema, lately, what with corrupt Mexican policemen and mad Italian directors. Course we *did* have *That Touch of Mink* recently, which *was* exceptional.

MRS. BALTON: Ring a bit more, love. Light me another.

JONATHON (*Lights two cigarettes, hands both to* MRS. BALTON): And the woman who plays organ for bingo at the cinema has either died or is terribly ill, so that was a washout as well.

MRS. BALTON: I just want one! I do want that drink . . .

JONATHON (*Ringing the bell*): Her ears are getting impossible.

MRS. BALTON: Well, she is getting on. Ming, it seems, has worms.

JONATHON: Poor thing.

MRS. BALTON: I saw them in her waste. Gray squirming tubes with a foul stench.

JONATHON: She's a very nasty cat, that's for sure.

MRS. BALTON: But killed scores of birds when she was young, at the farm. Always bringing them into the lounge with their wings hanging off . . .

JONATHON: Is there something you wish to discuss, Mother?

MRS. BALTON: Keep ringing, dear. I do want that drink rather badly.

JONATHON (Ringing): Well it seems to be useless.

MRS. BALTON: Her hearing is fading right out, poor kitten. She was running the vacuum this morning, right next to the telephone, which was ringing and ringing, and she didn't hear it at all. I stood and watched the whole thing.

JONATHON (Ringing quietly): Well, a bell's a bell, isn't it? I mean—exactly.

MRS. BALTON: Jonathon. You've been very odd for the past few days.

JONATHON: Have not.

MRS. BALTON: Did you know that the accountants have been in every day this week?

JONATHON: Oh, what do they want?

MRS. BALTON: Well. It seems that we have accounts in Cape Town, and some in London, and now, they tell me, they've found a bit in Zurich, which your father never bothered telling anyone about.

JONATHON: Nice to have an international flavor.

MRS. BALTON: No. The point is, you are totally ignorant of our monies, dear. You've not the first clue. I've let you avoid it for far too long.

JONATHON: What a bore you're becoming.

MRS. BALTON: Well I don't mind being boring.

JONATHON: Look, darling, do be realistic. I haven't the slightest idea of currencies and exchanges, and the stock market might as well be in Balinese. I'd only make a balls of it.

MRS. BALTON: You are capable of being extraordinarily practical when it suits you!

JONATHON: Do you expect—do you expect me to spend my few hours of freedom each day slaving over your ridiculous pigeon-scrawls in a ledger book? Now do you or do you not want to hear the rest of my film? Because I'm getting very, very tired! Why the hell can't that bloody, bloody woman give us a drink? What's the point of having servants if they're not going to get you a drink? (HE rings madly)

MRS. BALTON: No, I do not want to talk about your hellish film, I want to talk about the accountants!

Pause.

JONATHON: It was not hellish. I didn't like it, but it wasn't hellish. Oh all right. God. What about 'em?

MRS. BALTON: The same story. They're Jews, they have some sense of the fiduciary, eh? Mr. Schorr came out onto the veranda at the end of the day and said, "Going well enough for now, but we'll have to see about it in the spring."

JONATHON: Darling, their idea of drama. Can hardly expect them to put themselves out of work, can you?

MRS. BALTON: Exactly. They take it for granted that nothing ever goes wrong. That's where their assumptions betray their ignorance. The accountants are totally naive.

JONATHON: Oh, God. The sound of your voice is driving me mad.

MRS. BALTON: But it is vital that one grasps the horrid realities of it all. Survival is not automatic in this life. The presumption of having been blessed by good fortune is absurd. Was not the farm a tangled bush of savagery before your father planted sugarcane? And did we not have to burn it back constantly?

JONATHON: Quite a business.

MRS. BALTON: A business. Exactly.

JONATHON: Well, I'd say it's useless to talk to me about business at this late date. I'm a schoolteacher, which is trying enough—especially at the moment, Mother. We haven't owned the farm since I was a boy, and yet it's your entire frame of reference. It's so unworldly, Mother. "The farm this, the farm that," it's enough! Besides, you should've twenty years ago told me to take business classes. Break into a sweat at long division. (HE *rings the bell contemplatively*)

Pause.

MRS. BALTON: Took nanny to the vet today with Ming, you know.

JONATHON: Really. . . . Why'd you do that?

MRS. BALTON: Welts. Big round welts. On her legs.

JONATHON: Fitzhugh doesn't see natives.

MRS. BALTON: Doesn't normally. Didn't care to. Came in dragging that vile cat and nanny, both of 'em terrified out of their wits.

JONATHON: Mother—Fitzhugh is the bloody vet! (HE *rings the bell uncertainly*)

MRS. BALTON: That's right. Gave me the most unpleasant look, and I said, "Listen Hughie, I paid for your veterinary college after your parents lost everything on raising the slowest race horses in all of Africa! See this woman? She can't work!" Had no choice in the matter.

JONATHON: Well, my God. What did he do?

MRS. BALTON: Gave her a giant injection.

JONATHON: Are you telling me—are you telling me—the bloody veterinarian gave our nanny a giant injection?

MRS. BALTON: Yes. And he said it would make her very, very drowsy.

JONATHON (*Ringing uncertainly*): Ooh. Poor thing.

Pause while MRS. BALTON *watches her son.*

MRS. BALTON: Jonathon. You can stop ringing now. Can't you?

Pause. JONATHON *puts down the bell.*

JONATHON: I expect that's why she's not answering, eh? Well, I wouldn't go on about business and survival, if I were you, when you can't even remember putting the maid under heavy sedation with horse tranquilizers.

MRS. BALTON: I'm as clear-headed as I've ever been. Understand? Best bring me a whisky, love.

JONATHON (*Rises, crosses to the drinks tray*): Do you mean . . . you've had me ringing all night, knowing nanny is passed out in her room? You're a bit cruel, don't you think?

MRS. BALTON: Perhaps cruelty is necessary in order to cut through your incredible fog, eh? And please, please, please, not floating about in great heaps of *ice*.

JONATHON (*Deliberately fills her glass with ice and hands her her drink*): What do you suppose is in nanny's injections?

MRS. BALTON: Special vitamins. Keep you going for ages.

JONATHON: Maybe I'll go see the damn vet myself. You've been ghastly all week.

Pause.

MRS. BALTON: Saw Neville Sutter at the beachfront today. Tea. Said Nan Sinclair's involved in all the troubles. Talk of slave classes and all that rubbish.

JONATHON: Yes, tell me—do you think nanny back there, knocked out by you and bloody Fitzhugh, considers herself a slave? Part of a slave class?

MRS. BALTON: Did Nan Sinclair call our Nanny Mabote a slave?

JONATHON: We do pay her? She could go on some sort of excursion if she liked?

MRS. BALTON: Well, she is very old. She does like to stay in her room.

JONATHON: We do *pay* her?

MRS. BALTON: Of course we do! Not to worry.

JONATHON (*Rings the bell gently*): I wonder what nanny would make of all this. This bell, ringing away, year after year. And the fact is, whenever it rings, why, you'd best answer it. All of this ringing of bells. When I was a little boy, they rang as an accurate clock, a treble reminding one of one's duties. And the Blenheim bells as well—I used to be terrified of them, just ringing in another hour of horror they were, but now, they just tell one how far along in the day one's gone. They even begin to sound somewhat encouraging—as the day gradually falls. And coming home, I always loved the drinks bell. Used to ring it when I was alone in the house. Whatever happens to the day? Tring! Drinks! Trang! Supper! —And so on, and so forth . . . the bells. (*Pause*) Still the same bells. Same commands, same results. I've heard these bells ringing for forty years. Forty years of sameness. I never thought, at Blenheim, trudging up the stairs to that bleak treble, that one day I'd be setting them off. Now I'm the one ringing them. All these bells all over the place. Interesting about bells, isn't it? Mother . . . nanny.

MRS. BALTON *is asleep.* JONATHON *rings and the lights dim.*

Scene 3

JONATHON's *classroom.* HE *is at his desk, wading unhappily through a pile of essays.*

JONATHON (*Reading incredulously*): "The Panama Canal links . . . Africa and America . . . "? God. How do they get into this school? (HE *reaches into his desk, takes out a cigar, unwraps and cuts but does not light it, puts it in his mouth. Writing as* HE *speaks*) "Cleasby. Don't you know that . . . uh, survival is not automatic in this life?" Failed again, Cleasby.

JONATHON *stares out, daydreaming, and does not notice* NEVILLE SUTTER *entering.*

SUTTER: Jonathon?

JONATHON: Neville!

SUTTER: Here late, aren't you?

JONATHON: So're you!

SUTTER: Yes. But I live here, don't I?

JONATHON: Well there you are.

SUTTER: Terribly cold for September.

JONATHON: But warm in here, isn't it?

SUTTER: Better in than out.

JONATHON: They say there's something going on with the polar icecaps.

SUTTER: Yes. They're melting. Be underwater any day now. Icecaps and penguins.

JONATHON: Was just thinking. Don't like the school uniform.

SUTTER: Perfectly fine uniform.

JONATHON: No. In fact, when I was a boy, I asked you why we didn't have long trousers. "This is Africa, gotta be tough."

SUTTER: Excuse me?

JONATHON: Your reply. I said, "Well it's cold here, long trousers'd be much better." And that was your answer. "Africa, gotta be tough." And when I'm asked the same question, know what I say?

SUTTER: Africa, gotta be tough?

JONATHON: No, I say, "Headmaster Sutter feels, this being Africa and all that, you boys best toughen yourselves up!" And they laugh like hell, you know, 'cause they're pretty fucking tough already, these little shits.

SUTTER: Oh please. Let's not be gutter. I'm not in the mood.

JONATHON: It's just that when one is with children all day and then an adult happens to wander in, it makes one a bit giddy.

SUTTER: Your cigar? One of your dad's?

JONATHON: Yes. Exactly.

SUTTER: That would be a . . . Punch? Double Corona? Pre-Castro?

JONATHON: That's the cigar.

SUTTER: For Christ's sake, why isn't it lit?

JONATHON: Oh, I seldom actually *smoke* 'em. Why're you asking . . .? Oh! Would you like it?

SUTTER *(Pause)*: Oh. Thank you. *(JONATHON hands him cigar and matches. HE lights it, smokes)* We used to smoke at the Yacht Club together. Won once. So. . . . Did you have your film society today?

JONATHON *(Instantly suspicious)*: Why're you asking?

SUTTER: What do you mean "why?" I'm headmaster—take an interest in the various projects going on.

JONATHON *(Scornful)*: Yes. Like reptile society and seashell club.

SUTTER: Oh, don't remind me. Did you?

JONATHON: Actually, no. And I'm quite upset. McNally just marched in and took them all off on some sort of forced march or hike or arsonists training decathlon. I mean, came right in—stole my boys. This has never happened before, Nev.

SUTTER: Well. Have you shown any travel films?

JONATHON: *Travel* films?

SUTTER: Exactly. Say Malaysia, Australia, Ohio and Greece.

JONATHON: Ohio and *Greece*?

SUTTER: Or even better still—closer to home: say Cape Town and Kimberly?

JONATHON: Who the hell wants to see bloody Kimberly? Not even if you live there! I'd have a room full of empty boys—of empty desks, I mean.

SUTTER: But I've got a marvelous collection of eight-millimeters shot by Mrs. S. on her trips around the country.

JONATHON: Why not call it "little-slide-show society"? You said I could have free rein with film society.

SUTTER: I know I did. I know what I *said*.

Pause.

JONATHON: You let McNally take my boys.

SUTTER: We've had, thanks to Terry, four boys so far—pulling out, as of next week. All going to Durban High.

JONATHON: Good! Let 'em go, what's it to do with film society?

SUTTER: Plenty. They give us money. We need money. Jonathon, Terry's guest of honor here has died of a heart attack in his cell, I mean, haven't you seen the bloody newspapers today?

JONATHON: Good God, no. I—I had exams to mark. . . . Oh, that's . . .

SUTTER: Well think of this as one of many shock waves resulting from Centenary Day, and you'll have some idea of what I'm saying . . . regarding film society.

JONATHON: I'm utterly lost . . . I . . . *(HE sits down)*

SUTTER: And of course the parents are now very suspicious and frightened. They're forming a parents' committee, and when that happens, it's hell. Putsches, coups d'état, purges. You see: moods change. Parents have been fairly passive until bloody Terry had to turn Centenary Day into a commie fest. Now they think this is some sort of terribly bohemian institution.

JONATHON: Blenheim? Are they mad?

SUTTER: You don't understand. There's to be a New Blenheim. They want—total discipline.

JONATHON: How dare they!

SUTTER: And even you, my dear boy, are going to feel the pinch.

JONATHON: Go on.

SUTTER: Parents are wondering what's going on in the dark here—in the middle of the day, middle of the week. What're these boys watching? What're they doing?

JONATHON: Tell them to take their boys! They can all go to Durban High or hell for that matter! We don't care, do we? Tell them to fuck off! Fuck 'em! Just tell them really to go and fuck themselves!

SUTTER: I would never be so socially unattractive. We do care, is the point. Can't have classrooms without boys.

JONATHON: Bloody marvelous idea. Look, Nev. You admitted, didn't you, that there had to be something besides cricket, rugger, and all the drudgery that tends to build up. *(Beat)* An alternative?

SUTTER: Yes. No. Look. Crucial match coming up against Durban High, and I drove by there yesterday. They're quite on the ball, marching about the fields in their short-back-and-sides, all amazingly regimented working-class-salt-of-the-earth-raw-Afrikaner earnestness right out of the Great bloody Trek, and they're going to beat the bloody stuffing out of us again. The parents feel we're behind, and the New Blenheim should be more in the way of a trial.

JONATHON: Yes, I can see that they would. But to my mind, the thing that separates Blenheim from Durban High is that our boys come out of here with imagination! Yes, we've always encouraged boys to . . . look out at the world and feel, uh, yes, well, a certain . . . something.

SUTTER: I really wish you wouldn't argue with me. I'm the headmaster. I know what I'm doing. I do own the school, remember? Sometimes it seems everyone forgets.

JONATHON: Leave my film society out of your New Blenheim, Neville, please! I beg of you.

SUTTER: But, my dear boy, you mustn't take survival for granted. This is one of those gruesome periods of readjustment, and no compromise, no discipline, means no parent support, no Blenheim and no film society.

Pause. JONATHON *nods.*

JONATHON: It's Terry's fault—I've warned him a thousand times. (HE *manages a slight, bitter laugh*)

SUTTER *(Looks at him for a moment)*: Well, actually, that was my next bit of news, Jonathon.

JONATHON: Oh God, Neville.

SUTTER: Have you glasses?

JONATHON (Points to desk): Teacups. Top left.

SUTTER (Pours himself a drink): Yes. One's spirits tend to flag at about half past three . . .

JONATHON: It's the blood sugar dropping. Well, what is it, Neville?

SUTTER: We're thinking we might have to let them go, you see.

JONATHON: That would be a stupid, stupid mistake.

SUTTER: Haven't you heard a word I've told you? Hasn't he brought it upon himself? How many times has he skirted this? The colored folk singers up at bloody assembly? What about that? The attacks on the government in senior history class?

JONATHON: I know . . . I know all about that. But look. Look. Shout at him a bit or something, I don't know. And Nan? Why must you drag her in—she had nothing to do with any of it, you know. Yes. It's true.

SUTTER: How could she not, damn it? They live together.

JONATHON: You've known Terry for thirty-some years. Is he not a very sly man, when he wants to be? (Pause) Look. He's the only one here with any brains.

SUTTER: Do you think I like having to consider these kinds of steps?

JONATHON: I don't know. Do you? God, everyone is so dull and nervous. Look, if you must do something, suspend him for a few weeks or something. He could use a holiday, believe me. (Pause) As for Nan, well, you know as well as I that she's the best here.

SUTTER: The parents' committee is a bit suspicious of her.

JONATHON: She has no interest in Terry's political thingie, if you ask me. She's indulging him. It's like when he bought that motorcycle and tore around town with her clinging to the back like a marmoset. He grew tired of it, and it's gone. Same with the political thingie. Besides, it's rather amusing.

SUTTER (Pause): I do hate to let the parents' committee push us about quite so much.

JONATHON: There you are, eh? Exactly.

SUTTER (Pause): Well, we shall have to see.

JONATHON: And besides. She's the only one who can teach Latin. I can't. You couldn't conjugate a verb in a millenium.

SUTTER (Pause): That's not true. God damn him, anyway. Suspension . . . well. Look. There's something else.

JONATHON: Oh dear, I thought there might be.

SUTTER (Drinks before speaking): Yes. How'd you feel about being assistant?

JONATHON: Assistant what? Hey?

SUTTER: Headmaster. Assistant headmaster!

JONATHON: Good God, Neville! Hamish Fox is assistant head!

SUTTER: Yes. Well he's got spinal cancer. And my eyes continue to go out on me. Sting constantly.

JONATHON: There's eyes for you.

SUTTER: If you were to pass it up, I'd have to go to McNally.

JONATHON: Good Christ!

SUTTER: That's my point, exactly.

JONATHON: This place is turning into hell suddenly. What's going on?

SUTTER: Look. You've had a quiet time of it until now. It's all lurched forward unremarkably, but when you become assistant head, you lose a certain invisibility, and I know you enjoy your invisibility. But you'll find yourself more of the representative. Follow? And you've got to acknowledge what it is you're representing. Fox, McNally, parents' committees—the whole bang-shoot. Understand?

Pause. JONATHON *closes his eyes and thinks.*

JONATHON: Time for a change, eh?

SUTTER: That's the point.

JONATHON: Assistant head, eh? Well, I hope it all quiets down. How'd it be if I showed a travel short once a week?

SUTTER: A nice exposure to culture that the parents will appreciate.

JONATHON: Keep McNally away from my boys and leave Nan alone for a bit.

SUTTER: Agreed. Good. Thank God, now how 'bout a little toast?

JONATHON: Smashing.

SUTTER: Er. Let's see. A toast . . . ?

BOTH MEN *stand still for a moment,* JONATHON *watching* SUTTER *attentively. Finally,* SUTTER *merely shrugs and downs his drink.* JONATHON *follows suit as lights fade.*

Scene 4

NAN *and* TERRY'S *beachfront flat. It has a sort of neglected Bauhaus air to it.* TERRY *is sitting in an old armchair, looking out at the water.* NAN *enters, carrying cartons of Chinese food.*

NAN (*As* SHE *opens the door*): Hello, love. I tried to phone. No answer. I've brought supper.

TERRY (*Just sits, does not look up*): Rather late, isn't it.

NAN: I'm sorry . . .

TERRY: No. I suppose I must get used to being alone in this flat. (HE *gets up, kisses* NAN) Chinese. They're honorary whites. I wonder if all six billion of 'em, or just the ones living here.

Pause. TERRY *picks a newspaper up off the floor.*

NAN: I saw, love.

TERRY: People stopped believing "heart attack in his cell" years ago. Honestly. They won't allow a public funeral either. Of course. *(Pause)* I said to him, "Bazewo. These people are broad-minded enough . . ." (HE *gestures helplessly)*

NAN: Love. I honestly think the best thing for me to do is just quit.

TERRY: We've discussed it already and—

NAN: I keep expecting you to meet up with me after assembly. I'm not going to be able to make it there alone.

Pause.

TERRY: Well what? Go to Durban Girls High with all the lumpy-ankled matrons and coach field hockey and geography? *(Beat)* No. Durban. God. Look at that beachfront. Little amusement park. All rust and booze. (HE *looks out the window)* . . . Sunken garden filled with perverts and cops. Right out of bad Graham Greene. *(Pause)* Not even suspension. Just the sack. Like that. Twenty years. Look. A drink, eh?

NAN *(Pouring two glasses of Scotch):* It seems dishonorable for me to stay on now, Terry. I mean, I've had a day of it now. They're watching me like a hawk, and the teachers' lounge emptied when I came in.

TERRY: Nan. You remember those overwrought paintings in Munich I took you to see?

NAN: Max Beckmann. Sure.

TERRY: Well I was looking back, you see, at the catalogue. All the arms, just bloodied stumps. (HE *smiles at* NAN *and picks a book off the floor)* Look. The man with the corpse tied to his back. And Beckmann's note. "You carry along with you the corpse of your memories, defeats. Of the murder everyone commits once in his life."

NAN: Listen, I was thinking—we could take a break, get away for a little while, eh?

TERRY: The title of the Beckmann, actually, love, is "Departure."

NAN: . . . I see. And . . . ?

TERRY: There was Hitler on the radio, opening the Degenerate Art Exhibit. A few years later. And Beckmann starts to pack—having eight pieces in that show. Just left, for good. Next morning.

NAN: I'm not sure I follow.

TERRY: Come on! Don't play thick! I mean, I think our telephone is bugged, Nan! Okay? There's some little fuck with a Sony down at police headquarters, taping you . . . why do you think I didn't answer? I heard his heavy Afrikaner breathing! I should recognize it; I'm half Boer.

NAN: You must . . . I'm sorry. I'm not sure what you're saying.

Pause.

TERRY: I think we should emigrate.

NAN: Oh, God. I didn't want to hate myself for being a shrew. I never ever said "Listen, be careful." Did I? Or "I told you so"?

TERRY: Well go ahead. It's not too late.

NAN: Because, all of a sudden, it's—it's all banned books and French Marxists running around the place.

TERRY: I should like, I think, to leave, before being placed under some sort of house arrest. I would go mad, here. After one day . . .

NAN: Of course last year, when it suddenly became about "meetings in the townships" and all. . . . You didn't consider this?

TERRY: Nan.

NAN: I have family here. You might hate this beachfront, but I grew up on it! Well I hope you don't think I'm just going to say "sure, let's pack," just like that, do you?

TERRY: Of course not.

NAN: If we left, where would we go? What would you do?

TERRY: London. Paris. I don't know that I could teach ever again. I should like to work in a pub. Write.

NAN: We've very little money.

TERRY: I thought I might take a drive up to my parents' farm.

NAN: You don't even speak to them.

TERRY: Well, I think they'd be relieved to give me something, to see me off for good. I mean, I could try and get a temporary position somewhere, save a bit.

NAN: And if I didn't want to leave? If I decided I couldn't? (Pause) You suddenly turn forty and political, Terry, and everyone else must as well.

TERRY: But there's been no reason not to. (Pause) At Blenheim, I learnt how to present a case for that which I felt to be right.

NAN (Laughs and sighs, drinks): Well, they didn't mean it. Did they, eh?

TERRY: It would seem not. Well, men like Sutter and Fox are the type of fungus that only grows at a place like Blenheim. I'm better off.

NAN: They've made Jonathon assistant head.

TERRY: What?

NAN: There was a staff meeting. Hamish Fox is retiring. Didn't mention why.

TERRY: He's been ill. This is impossible.

NAN: Nevertheless. Sylvia Balton was there. There was sherry. Jonathon looking baffled. And the rest of the staff had expressions on their faces like yours. As if Neville were supposed to say "just joking" any minute. But it's not a joke.

TERRY: They will eviscerate him.

NAN: Who?

TERRY: The boys, the parents. Well. Sylvia Balton. Waiting in the wings. The way she knocks back the Pall Malls and Glen Livet, she must realize she's not about to beat any Georgians in the longevity race. This is called plotting for your son.

NAN: Well, it's good for him—he'll be a step up.

Pause.

TERRY: No! I could've changed the place! And he wouldn't have a clue! All alone, on a bus. Cross town—can't you see him? Off to see some tinny little romance? Just this gap, this hole in him. Filled with celluloid.

NAN: Terry, God. This is Jonathon you're going on against.

TERRY: I bet he knew all along they were gonna sack me!

NAN: It's so unattractive, this paranoid bullshit. Jonathon? Jonathon?

Pause.

TERRY (*Smiles, cold*): Yes. It is, isn't it? One becomes suspicious. Everything about the place starts becoming hateful. I sound like one of those toothless Trotskyites from University of Natal.

Pause.

NAN: Let's have a bit to eat.

TERRY (*Looks at the food, shakes his head*): I can't.

NAN: Did you stay cooped up in this flat all day? Terry? You haven't been out, or eaten?

TERRY: There was no money for lunch, so I shared Jackson's rice and beans. We sat out on the veranda.

NAN: I should've left cash.

TERRY: They had a shark attack. Did you hear about it on the radio? We saw it. Right out there, at the colored beach. Some garden boy or something just swallowed up. Spot of red in the water, which became a line of red. Fading out eastward. Gradually.

NAN: Oh Christ, Ter.

TERRY: Problems with the shark nets. Lucky they closed the beach, as I was thinking of a swim.

NAN: Ter—I am frightened for you—for both of us. I am. Everything. You brought that man up, you didn't even tell me what you were up to. These past six months have built up . . .

TERRY: Oh, there's nothing to be frighened of, love, I mean, we must be the only people in Durban to have in their employment a homosexual Zulu. It's mad, not frightening—any of it. I suggested to Jackson that the beans might be a bit softer, and he started to cry. I mean, one might very well ask him what there is to be frightened of. Quite a turn from your spear-chucking, assegai-toting, barefoot-thorn-treading warrior is Jackson, standing about, watching some boy dragged out to sea, and weeping over his *beans*! It's funny. Margaret Mead-wise-anthropologically speaking! Laugh! Don't be afraid! I'm not, and if I'm not, you sure as hell have no reason to be!

NAN: But I understand what you have been through and what you must be accusing yourself of! And I want to help you, Terry!

TERRY: I am not afraid! They pulled Bazewo off the podium and dragged him off to Durban Jail to kill him! I can't even get bloody arrested! I feel utterly defeated and paunchy! *(Beat)* I should tell Jonathon what they're going to do to him. He'll end up in a hospital. *(Lights fade down)* My passport's expired.

TERRY *looks at* NAN *as lights dim.*

Scene 5

MRS. BALTON's *flat.* JONATHON *is surrounded by a number of summer suits.* MRS. BALTON *has on an absurd African kaftan and is clutching a whisky and a cigarette.*

MRS. BALTON: Aren't they marvelous?

JONATHON: Quite a world! The world of clothes, eh?

MRS. BALTON: But to succeed in your field? A marvel!

JONATHON: And then one has one's suits, eh.

MRS. BALTON: Why not try on the yellow?

JONATHON: If you like. (HE *begins undressing)* Very odd, all of it. After we moved to the city from the farm and I went off to Blenheim, I was quite worried about managing—as you know. But you know what? It doesn't seem to make the slightest bit of difference at all! I've done fine, it seems, without the least bit of managing—one worries and frets, and then they go and make you assistant bloody headmaster.

MRS. BALTON: What you mean is, you're realizing you have natural leadership tendencies.

JONATHON: But that's my point! I don't, you see! None whatsoever!

MRS. BALTON: Perhaps you would if you wore better undies. There's a bloody great hole the size of a Krugerrand in your backside.

JONATHON: Nobody ever sees the damn things, Mother. Quite a world, the world of . . . the suit. (HE *puts on the yellow linen jacket)* How do I look?

MRS. BALTON: Like your father! He was a whippet, an aristocrat in his linen suits! I'll never forget the first time I saw him, at the club, his head tilted to one side, his mouth slightly open, his face as red as a lobster from that yacht of his—his eyes so hazel. You look just like him! Turn around.

JONATHON *(Turns)*: Suppose we've made a success of it then, haven't we?

MRS. BALTON: Without a doubt.

TERRY *enters tentatively.*

TERRY: There's a problem with the bell. I rang and rang.

MRS. BALTON: It's been broken for ages, you know that. You look ghastly, Terry! Are you all right?

TERRY: I'm fine, Sylvia, love. Jonathon, I just heard—I . . . wanted to talk to you . . .

JONATHON: I was—I was going to telephone you. Do you like the suit?

TERRY: The touch of yellow's very nice.

JONATHON: Yes. Ter, it's been so ghastly, with all the—hasn't it? (Pause) You were convinced that they'd leave you alone. I mean, always. It was the same when we were boys, wasn't it? You never got in trouble.

TERRY: No, but that doesn't matter now.

JONATHON: You'd have been assistant head.

TERRY: What're you going to do?

JONATHON: Oh, there's a lot. The New Blenheim: I'm to get estimates on fixing the changing rooms in the junior school, right away, as well as new maps for all the rooms . . . stupid business, things like that. Stray cats living in the storeroom . . .

MRS. BALTON: Ming has cat leukemia. Been coughing blood for days.

JONATHON: Mother.

TERRY: She's a very old cat, isn't she, Sylvia? Missing her teeth?

MRS. BALTON: Not so gone. In cat years younger than nanny, who's also ill.

TERRY: Yes, but both are younger than yourself, eh?

MRS. BALTON (Smiling appreciatively): A bit, love.

JONATHON: Go do something with the cottage pie, would you, Mother? It's taking forever.

MRS. BALTON sits.

TERRY: Jonathon. May we discuss your appointment? Some advice, if I may?

JONATHON (Beat; HE also sits, sighs, shakes his head): Advice? It's 'cause of you that I have to show slides of Hottentots in film society. Little tape machine that goes "bing" and tells you to advance to the next slide. (Pause) Advice.

TERRY: I should imagine you'd be a hell of a lot better off if you stopped going on about movies for a bit, and started talking about discipline.

JONATHON: Yes, well I'm not going to be that kind of assistant head. What—you think I'm going to scream about haircuts and wave a cane about like Fox? Honestly. What else?

TERRY: Look, face it—they're going to have you caning boys for missing sports practice. Lists of—do you want this job? With the figure of Fox judging. Being compared to him?

JONATHON: Terry, I just want everything to calm down! I want you back! I was going to ask.

TERRY: No, no, no. Are you mad? Listen, I wouldn't come back to Blenheim— that's over now. I just want you to be careful.

JONATHON: Oh. Well, I am. I mean, nothing if not careful.

TERRY: Did you know they were going to let me go?

JONATHON: I had no idea. Honestly. Look—I mean, it could've been McNally.

Pause.

TERRY: We were boys here together—you hated it!

JONATHON: I was a boy! It didn't cater to my particular . . .

TERRY: It catered to nothing! Pride, rigor, reason? Apparitions. Look—look at what's happening to your film society!

MRS. BALTON: Terry, what has happened to you? The man who was so capable, dry? Good with a laugh?

TERRY: He is on holiday at the moment. Well, Jon?

JONATHON: It's just a film society! Don't bring it into this! It's hardly political. God. Everyone has this totally idiotic idea!

TERRY: Not political? Jonathon. You bring boys into a room, and you show them films. They see. They imagine. And they think. That, I believe, is highly political. You laugh at politics—as you are being swept away by them. You laughed at me all year, as I tried to change things—but Jonathon, there are three generations brainwashed by Fox and company. All the lies of an outdated colonialism washing over them; and they won't know what hit them. It'll seem bitterly unfair to them as their throats are slit, won't it? Well, I have come here to tell you: you have this small bit of power now, and I think you need to use it. I'm not sure how, except to try and get them to think differently. The alternative is to continue with Fox's brainwashing. You do have a choice, Jonathon. And it is a political one. (Pause) And a favor—don't cut Nan out like the others.

JONATHON: I would never, Terry! Damn it!

TERRY: It's that one discovers a bit too late exactly how humorless Blenheim is at heart.

JONATHON: I know that much better than you ever did! You were busy being cricket captain and head prefect!

TERRY: And now we're older and it's not like cinema, fading out in the dark. It's very real.

JONATHON: I could get you back!

TERRY: Well let me tell you, we're thinking of buggering off. Abroad.

JONATHON: Abroad. Oh God. I've heard you go on about "buggering off" since we were sixteen. You're not going.

MRS. BALTON: It's just like the farm. Isn't it, Terry?

TERRY: How, Sylvia? No. This is the opposite. The farm was alive. I mean—Africa. Wet with its very life. Still. Red sun and bush.

MRS. BALTON: But really, it's exactly like the farm. I remember—the Baltons and the Sinclairs—struggling with half of Zululand—fighting—and sugarcane, as far as the eye could see. And you were very quick with a whip, weren't you? You'd whip the natives into a raw pulp if you didn't have fresh cream in the morning. They buckled down under you, Ter. There was always blood being shed by you. Exactly like the farm.

TERRY: Times change, I think, don't they, love?

MRS. BALTON: Not so sure. Still blood being shed, eh? Pity.

Pause.

JONATHON: I should check on the cottage pie, I expect. Probably it's burnt by now. What with nanny ill, everything seems to have become ballsed-up. (HE *begins to exit, stops*) You—you both think: "Oh, well, Jonathon is going to be able to exercise some kind of power or something, or make some sort of mark." I became a schoolmaster 'cause it was quiet and there was no work as a radio actor in Natal, to speak of. (*Beat*) There's nothing to do. Of course, I'd do anything for Nan, and anything for you if you asked. And—and I resent being told to talk less of film society. My only safe harbor, it seems, from everyone—and nobody leaves it alone! (*Beat*) I'm sure dinner's destroyed . . . (HE *exits*)

MRS. BALTON: Are you eating with us, love? (SHE *crosses to the drinks tray and pours herself a Scotch*) It's just like when you were a boy. You were always coming round, causing all sorts of trouble, driving everyone mad. Do you remember the time you were sick in the swimming pool?

Pause.

TERRY: No.

Lights fade down.

Scene 6

JONATHON's *classroom.* HAMISH FOX, *a small man, is addressing* SUTTER *and* JONATHON, *both of whom look rather unhappy.*

FOX: And why do I see Terry Sinclair's name here? On this agenda?
JONATHON: Well, if you'll let me explain: what it finally—it was more a matter of the senior matriculation tutorial thingies—not a staff position at all, just something . . . where he might come by once a week for the seniors—well, I've certainly not broached the subject with him, but the thing of it is, we used to have a ninety-six-percent pass rate, and thanks—I'd say mostly due to—uhm . . . Terry.
SUTTER: Yes. Quite. There is that.
FOX: It would not be appropriate, would it, headmaster? (*Pause.* HE *smiles*) I didn't think it would.
SUTTER: Steady on, Hamish, you've only just right this second come from chemotherapy.
FOX: Perhaps, Jonathon, you might inquire as to Mr. Fidel Castro's availability, next?
JONATHON: Fidel. . . . Ah! Hah! Yes, no, no. No.

FOX: I did recommend you. I wonder if I have doubts now.

JONATHON (*After a beat*): Well, it's just. . . . It takes a bit of getting one's feet wet and all. Right?

SUTTER: Nobody has any doubts, Jonathon. Hamish, honestly, you mustn't get excited. But, Jonathon. What Hamish is trying to say is—I think it's not dissimilar to when we were in the foreign service; one often wanted to accommodate friends. Not unlike any position of choice, eh, Hammy?

FOX (*After a pause*): In Kenya, they found my sister-in-law—with a Mau Mau's spear inserted through the anus, up the rectum, and into the intestines.

SUTTER: Perhaps we might talk about Jonathon's duties?

FOX: Of course, but it's all in the interests of clarity. One becomes concerned that there might be a shift; we might become like one of those cafes of bizarre ideology that have sprung up. The battles of two hundred years ago have not been concluded, have they? No. Who's to win? The easily-persuadable-by-Stalinists Africans, with the Terry Sinclairs urging them on?

SUTTER: Exactly the point. First on the agenda is sports practice.

FOX: Did you know, when I saw the gentleman with the priest's collar up on the podium, I had to smile? There it was, the genesis of decay and rot of Africa, having spread down the continent, like, dare I say it, the cancer in my own spine.

Pause.

SUTTER: Indeed, yes. Very interesting, Hamish. Be up to you to make sure the field's kept trimmed for cricket practice. They're losing balls in the grass, it seems.

FOX: There's also the small matter of caning.

SUTTER: But mostly just making sure the algae doesn't get too thick in the pool, my boy . . .

FOX: The African staff has a tendency to go through the boys' pockets while they're playing sports. Thousands of rands gone missing over the years.

SUTTER: . . . notices to parents-day tea, smiles, phone calls about little Evan and Timothy, the usual . . . oh. Yes, and actually, a job I rather enjoyed: the retaining walls are swarming with lizards, and I like to fill up the holes with dry ice, and take the pellet gun and get 'em. Nothing like seeing a gecko dashing about in one's sights.

FOX: And Neville and I feel quite strongly that as part of the New Blenheim, it would be a very clever gesture to revive yachting club.

JONATHON: Yachting club?

FOX: We have a perfectly fine dinghy in the shed that hasn't seen water in quarter of a century.

JONATHON: I see.

FOX: Your responsibility.

JONATHON: Me?

SUTTER: Lovely on the bay, in December.

FOX: Which won't leave much time for your cinema society, will it?

JONATHON: My film society?

FOX: Exactly! Film society. New conditions. Neville and I agree . . .

SUTTER (*Cutting him off*): Yes, well. That's quite enough for today, actually, Hamish. You must be exhausted. We'll continue tomorrow at lunch, perhaps?

JONATHON (*Gets up*): I—I . . . have some boys waiting. If I may? (HE *exits rapidly*)

SUTTER: Honestly, Hamish.

FOX: I've just got two things to say.

SUTTER (*Sighing*): Go ahead.

FOX: Not at all like his father. Or mother.

SUTTER: Yes. A blessing, as I see it. And the other?

FOX (*Pause*): Name the new hall the Christopher and Sylvia Balton Hall, put up a plaque and proceed forth, eh?

SUTTER (*An exhausted whisper*): Yes. That's my point. Isn't it?

Lights fade down.

Scene 7

JONATHON's *classroom.*

JONATHON (*Addressing his class*): Well, the fact of it is, instead of meeting thrice weekly as anticipated, we'll be having these screenings more or less on Thursday afternoons at half past three. And it seems you'd best bring with you an excuse from field activities such as cadets or sports. Also, detention boys are no longer permitted to come to film society in order to work off detention time. Mind you, detention boys, if you decide to get caned instead of detention, then you could have time to come to film society, unless the reason for the punishment was not going to field activity, in which case, perhaps we'll see you next term if you have a more agreeable schedule. (*Pause*)

Yes. I know, it's all a bit complicated, but what's one to do? It has always been, at Blenheim. When I was a boy, it was much more difficult than it is now. So there's no reason not to be optimistic, eh? I mean, look—if you blokes think Mr. Fox a strict man, you should've seen old McFarquhar! With his steel plate in his skull from World War One. (*Pause*) There were teachers here who . . . boys could not manage. They simply did not survive. (*Pause*)

For those of you happily joining us for the first time, what happens here is that I show films. No tests, no . . . demands. Occasionally, the odd bit of post-film discussion, and say—if some famous film star happened to be in Durban, well, one of the benefits of the film society is that you might get to meet him. You know, I used to be a radio actor—which is quite different, I suppose, from films. (*Pause*)

We used to sit in the studio: Mr. Sinclair, Mrs. Sinclair, and I. The old Radio Natal studios, and one would just lose oneself, really. It was all that one had. The rest of the world of no consequence. And one might find that coming out . . . coming out into the street from the studio, you might be dazed—in the sunlight . . . it would all seem translucent, shimmering. And my thought was . . . that coming out after film society . . . might be just a bit like that. *(Pause)* One finds that after Blenheim, the world . . . the world. *(Pause)*

We have a wonderful film about reptiles today.

JONATHON *stands quite still, looking out; then* HE *slowly moves his hand to the projector and switches it on. Lights down.*

END OF ACT ONE

ACT TWO

Scene 1

Two months later, November. JONATHON, *wearing one of his new suits, angrily slams into his classroom, goes straight to his desk, stops and looks out for a moment before pulling a bottle of Scotch from his drawer.* HE *pours a little into a glass and waits.* NAN *rushes in.*

NAN: Jonathon!

JONATHON: I don't bloody want to discuss it!

NAN: Yes, but I just wanted to thank you for putting an end to that ghastly meeting.

JONATHON: Oh no, no. I totally humiliated myself, didn't I?

NAN: Not at all! For decades, people have been dying to tell McNally to shut up.

JONATHON: It's madness! They sit there, laughing at me! You make suggestions on how to help 'em, and countless plans—I mean, entire nights spent at a desk—and they sit about roaring! I am the assistant headmaster! And McNally, this dreadful, spongy, red-faced madman, is snickering at me? The man's IQ is lower than the temperature in this room! I mean, when he starts going on about his regiment and Angola, and rifles, I nearly have to stop myself from vomiting.

NAN: You did make rather a dramatic exit. That was a hell of a speech you gave.

JONATHON: Don't flatter me. You liked it? It was totally off the top of my head.

NAN: Of course I did. I think all those things you said about pulling together, and the push forward, and, and . . . cleaning the floors were very true.

JONATHON: But they laugh at me! Your hear them!

NAN: But Jonathon, love, you did speak for half an hour about . . . plasterwork.

JONATHON: If they think they can get me to storm out of every meeting, they've another think coming. Oh yes, I know it's dull, my dear, but nobody does anything about it, except to blame me.

NAN: I know it's discouraging, love, but you are having an effect.

JONATHON: I've done it all! Did you know there are bats—a herd of bats—living in the mango trees, attacking boys from the junior school? The eucalyptus grove has termites the size of Land Rovers scurrying about. Any day now we'll have a tree come crashing down, wiping out the entire third form. A pickpocket in the changing room stealing lunch money, and in the lunchroom, rotten pork pies. Two-and-a-half boys sick!

NAN: But, Jonathon, love. You cannot possibly do all of it.

JONATHON: Exactly! The bloody swimming pool looks like a science experiment— boys go in, have to send a team to find 'em. . . . We had a monkey come out of the mangrove at cricket practice last week and swipe a ball. The only one we had. Who do you think got blamed?

NAN (*Laughing*): You?

JONATHON: Exac-exactly! Fox—God knows why *he* was here, he's meant to be in bed, but the man keeps patrolling like some sort of military zombie—Fox told the story of why the British lost the battle of Islan-Dwana, because they didn't have hammers or something. I don't know—couldn't open the ammo boxes, nails rusting in the humidity—and they all died. I have no idea what it had to do with monkeys swiping cricket balls, but still . . .

NAN: It's mad! It's getting worse! I tell you, it is! They're all mad . . . *(Laughing)*

JONATHON *(Trying to remain poker-faced)*: Don't laugh! Please! You have no sympathy.

NAN: Of course I do! But it's funny!

JONATHON *(Begins to laugh)*: I got a note, first thing this morning, from Neville— oh, Jesus, I've got to sit down. (HE *launches into a brilliant imitation of* SUTTER) "Jonathon, in happening to walk past the junior school toilets . . . in strolling past the junior school toilets, I was assailed by the most unimaginable stench . . ." *(Pause)* "Please investigate. Best, Neville."

THEY BOTH *explode.*

NAN: Get out your scuba gear, darling. I need a drink, fast!

JONATHON *(Pouring her a Scotch)*: So, I go down there, right? And it's like a trip to the seventh circle of hell, I swear. The man is absolutely bloody on target! Water, everywhere, sort of, well . . . brown, unfortunately, with little bits of offal floating towards the showers, all of which are sending out huge great primeval mists of steam—the windows have this gruel-like film over them— and instead of toilet paper, there's little bits of shredded newspaper in the stalls, like a hamster's cage. I swear, the bowel movements of the very young are a total mystery to me. I mean, they've utterly destroyed their own toilet! Well, it turns out, neither Malcolm or Montgomery have set foot in there to clean . . . for months. *(Pause.* HE *picks up a cane and swings it rather sadly)* Had to fire 'em both. Not the great pleasure it's cracked up to be, but sort of . . . not the horror, either. You know—my father, horrid as he was, was easily able to delegate authority. They're all going to find themselves very, very, very, very busy—and then we'll have far less time for staff meetings about maintenance and community, and plaster. "Yes, McNally, if you wish to retain command of your junior-commando marching band next term, I suggest you take responsibility for keeping the field cut, eh? Otherwise, mate, you might just find yourself in charge of the fucking reptile society, and Viltonian'll get rugger! Then we'll see, eh?"

NAN *(After a pause)*: Getting into the spirit of the New Blenheim, are we?

JONATHON: I just want to put a stop to all of it. I never dreamt this job was just one huge campaign.

NAN: And should one be more like Fox?

JONATHON: He was effective, Nan. One of the great vulgarians of Africa, but useful. *(Swings the cane ruefully)* And so much better at caning than I.

NAN: Right.

JONATHON: Well, don't look at me like that, please! It seems that if one is to get anywhere around here these days, you'd better learn how to cane. You too!

"How could you idiotic little buggers miss three out of ten on a history quiz?" Whack! "What? Skipped rugger—again, Crawford? Don't you know what'll happen to you? You'll grow up just like JONATHON BALTON!" (HE *swings wildly*) That's what works here.

NAN: Perhaps you might have McNally attend to the caning? Or get rid of it altogether?

JONATHON: Well, I'd love to. In one fell swoop, just—gone. But this insane parents' committee—they actually seem to be encouraging us to beat their boys harder! Besides, give bloody McNally a cane and he'd be slicing boys in half. (*Pause.* HE *looks at her and shrugs*) How does one think, Nan, when thinking . . . has not been necessary?

NAN: And you can tell me when it has not been necessary, love?

Pause.

JONATHON: Well, they're watching me. Look. The way I see it is, first, get rid of the bats and the termites and the mildew, and then let's think about doing away with the parents' committees, and then, my dear, let's rid ourselves of the McNallys. Let's drink up, shall we?

NAN: Yes. You know—I saw you shooting lizards this morning.

JONATHON: Just trying to scare them, really. But I've had to postpone film society three times in a row. So typical. A film society that no longer meets. I said to Nev, at lunch, I said, "Nobody has any imagination anymore." Which he considered, and pronounced a blessing. (*Pause*) Nobody, that is, except you. Remember when we used to go sailing?

NAN: Yes, you hated sailing.

JONATHON: Did not.

NAN: Yes! It was Terry who did all the work. You were too busy being ill, or whining constantly about the waves and capsizing.

JONATHON: But *you* enjoyed sailing, didn't you?

NAN: Actually, yes. Jonathon. Why are we talking about sailing?

JONATHON: Well, in addition to everything else, they've been going on and on for the past two months about wanting me to take on sailing.

NAN: What sailing?

JONATHON (*Sighs, not happy*): I'm to help with the Durban Yacht Club Junior Races—Sutter feels that a team from Blenheim should enter.

NAN: But what for?

JONATHON: Neville believes that if we win, we'd attract a new sort—nautical boys. You know . . .

NAN: But it's absurd!

JONATHON: Makes sense from a PR standpoint. Could be prestigious.

NAN: By why you?

JONATHON: Neville recalled that the three of us had that dinghy—thingie. I was hoping you might take it on as I haven't a clue.

NAN: Quite impossible, and you know it. I'm teaching all of Terry's classes and half of Fox's. It's hard enough as it is.

JONATHON: We all have a load to bear these days.

NAN: Why not—surely you can ask Viltonian?

JONATHON: Oh, let's leave the poor wretch alone for once, shall we? He's in mourning—all his snakes died.

NAN: McNally, then?

JONATHON: Right, you try and get the man away from cadets, then. Only you, I'm afraid.

NAN: I see. Oh. Well, Jesus, Jonathon.

JONATHON: Look, love, you'd look awfully good to the parents' committee if you took on the damn yachting. They're not very keen on you, you know.

NAN: Do you think I care about them? Listen, I need to spend more time with Terry as it is. I mean, not that you call him anymore. (Pause) I may as well bring this up now, Jonathon. We are having a very bad time.

JONATHON: He doesn't want to talk to me, Nan. I've tried.

NAN: I'm talking about money.

JONATHON: Oh.

NAN: There's none left. Look, Ter and I were like some sort of bargain here—a cheapo package deal; like two for one, I think. Ter was the one, I was some extra little bonus. Well on my wages alone, the two of us are sinking.

JONATHON: I had absolutely no idea.

NAN: I mean, they want to evict us from the flat. We haven't paid the rent. And all our accounts at the shops are shut down. Last week he charged three hundred rands at the bookshop—gave dictionaries out at the school where Bazewo taught—sat there, weeping, passing out books. I mean, honestly? Yachting? Yachting? Fuck it.

JONATHON: You should've—you should've said something! Come to me sooner. This is—this is the one area where I can help with no problem at all. (HE takes out his checkbook)

NAN: He went out to Zululand, right? He went out to see his parents, and they wouldn't even talk to him, Jonathon. I mean—the more I know of parents, it's all about committees and protecting lifestyle, fashion, finally. And—and if the children dissent—they—they abandon them.

JONATHON: Five thousand rands. Just take it.

NAN: No. I don't want to take your money. I mean, I know you mean well. And I appreciate it, but I don't want a loan.

JONATHON: What is it then? I don't understand?

NAN: I want a raise.

JONATHON: Don't be absurd. There's no money for plastering, let alone raises. Just take the check, for Christ's sake. I have this money, my father left it sitting about in *boxes*.

NAN: I won't take it, Jonathon, for one reason: we're honestly going to leave.

JONATHON: I've heard that, you know. I have. But you're not. Are you?

NAN: Terry has nothing here. We've decided . . .

JONATHON: Look. Just take the check, will you?

NAN: I can't do it, Jonathon. When we leave, we're not coming back. And taking your money would be simply taking advantage. But listen, if I'm paid what I deserve, I'll be able to put some away. We could be out of here in six months. That's it.

JONATHON: I tried it! You remember? When I went to London, I took our stupid, idiotic little Lux Radio Theatre tapes: this stupid idea, we'd all get jobs in radio drama at the BBC? Insane! Simply insane. And I ended up, you know where? In the bloody isolation ward of some hospital in South Kensington with spinal meningitis! Tapes just lay next to me on the bed!

NAN: Jonathon—I don't even want to go! I'm—

JONATHON: It's ancient ghastly Paki doctors with shaking hands! That's leaving! It's spinal taps, missing the spine—that's leaving! It's a hospital room with wood soap and a clock!

NAN: My husband is—

JONATHON: Overseas is vastly overrated! I was dying there. Do you think they like South Africans? Well let me tell you, they hate us. They laugh at us, and corner us!

NAN: But my husband is asphyxiating here and nobody is helping him and I don't know what else to do!

JONATHON (Savage): Well, just be sure, if you're at some pub in Swiss fucking Cottage, you tell them, when they ask, that you're Australian! (Pause) I'll be alone. I'll be nothing.

NAN: Jonathon, but we must all—all of us—try and build something as best we can.

JONATHON: Isn't there anything else? I mean—must it be . . . like that? (HE looks away from her)

NAN: Oh, God. There—there might have been other ways, once. But now . . .

JONATHON (Turns to her; low, unemotional): I shall get you an extra two fifty a week starting today.

NAN (Somewhat shocked): Two hundred and fifty . . . ? Jonathon? Can you. . . . I don't know what to say—that's . . .

JONATHON: . . . Providing, of course, you take on the yachting, starting tomorrow.

NAN: Pardon me? What . . . what is this, Jonathon?

JONATHON (Pause): It's a condition, Nan. A condition. Well. I still have Faber pencils and blotting paper to order. Lots of work still. (Smiles at a stunned NAN, looks out window) There goes the cricket team. Aren't they . . . super . . . super . . . ?

JONATHON looks at NAN, smiling, as lights fade down.

Scene 2

NAN and TERRY's flat. TERRY is sitting, quite still, in his corner chair as NAN is heard letting herself in. SHE enters, holding a small bag of groceries.

TERRY: Well. Good. See me, sitting here? Like an odd and patient breed of dog, eh?

NAN *(Braces herself, smiles)*: A long and bad, stupid day, Terry. So we'll give it a rest, for tonight, right?

TERRY *(Pause; HE looks at the bag)*: They actually let you take merchandise out of there? I mean, I have to shout for a lamb chop.

NAN: He's not so bad.

TERRY: He is a little Indian racist, and I don't think we should be giving him our business.

NAN *(As calm as TERRY)*: . . . . And why now, suddenly?

TERRY *(Shrugs, smiling)*: He wouldn't sell me my smokes.

NAN: As long as there's a social context—for your boycott . . . *(Pause. SHE sighs, crosses to him)* Terry.

TERRY: There's no such thing as social context. It's all just chemical, you know? I've been wrong all along. It's all about mommy, daddy, genes, and neurons or something. So. What? Why so late? Watching a flick with old Jonathon? A musical?

NAN *(Pause)*: Ah. I see.

TERRY *(Laughs a bit)*: Ah? You see?

NAN: The "ah" of recognition. As in "Ah, he's just spent the day in some sort of rage."

Pause. TERRY nods.

TERRY *(Looks at the bag of groceries, picks out a tin of tea)*: Please, must you buy this cheap kaffir tea? I mean, I don't expect, like, Fortnum's Russian Caravan exactly, but something other than Twin Roses. Something that gives one the illusion that there's something mysterious to look forward to.

NAN: What I should do—is stop myself, rather soon, if I were you, love. Don't you think?

TERRY: The bug is off the phone.

NAN: . . . Really? How—how can you tell?

TERRY: 'Cause they shut the phone off. We never paid them. I actually like this kind of little ironic victory.

NAN: I'll have it on tomorrow.

TERRY: Needn't bother. It's only you, or Jonathon—stuttering.

NAN: *What is wrong?*

TERRY *(Pause)*: Jackson's been arrested.

NAN: What for?

TERRY: What for? What do you think? You couldn't possibly imagine him out agitating, could you? He was violating the pass laws.

NAN: You . . . you got him out, Ter?

TERRY (*Calm, but utterly exhausted*): That was interesting. My family name still carries. I think of myself as some sort of pariah, an outcast? But do the Bantu Affairs police know me? They're busy with their own usual array of murky, oblique affairs. So. I got dressed, very carefully, and I went down to their little corner of hell with its stench of burning-rubber reality, and I said to the warrant officer, "Listen mate, that is my bloody servant you've got there, and my servant has windows to wash, and toilets to clean, and a lot to learn, so just hand him over to me, and I'll smack him." (*Pause*) And there was this hesitation. The suspicion of my Afrikaner brethren is boundless. So. I stood there, and looked him in the eye, rather contemptuously, and addressed him in Afrikaans: "Hey, bloke. My grandfather *ran* your lousy outfit. I deserve a bit of respect and a lot of leeway." And he nods. (*Pause*) This man has never heard of Blenheim. (*Pause*) And he hands me Jackson.

NAN: So—he's all right?

TERRY: Oh, fine.

NAN: Jesus, it's endless.

TERRY: Isn't it? Of course, you've just come from a "long, bad and stupid day" yourself.

NAN: Actually, I have come from a pretty shoddy bit of manipulation and humiliation, and it has left me feeling pretty stupid, so, Christ knows, I don't need to walk in here and be insulted by you.

TERRY (*Picks up a letter from the table beside his chair*): Please don't tell me about your lousy day at Blenheim and your humiliations. Please. Not now. (*Pause*) Because . . . I have just received a letter from Victor Frame offering a job at the Escola Americana in Rio de Janeiro, and I can't take it because we don't have enough money to get out!

NAN: Victor Frame? Let me see . . .

TERRY: Blenheim. Class of '47. Was on the cricket team when I was captain. Worshipped me. There was a time, you see, when I was a very interesting man.

NAN: Well—well, I got a raise, Terry, so . . . we could go. In about six months . . .

TERRY: A raise? That's impossible—they're on the verge of shutting down, and I did it to them!

NAN: No. Jonathon got me a raise.

TERRY (*Roaring with laughter*): Jonathon? Show you a double feature, perhaps, but give you a raise? Never.

NAN: He's growing into the job. He made me take on yachting for the raise.

TERRY: Yachting? You? Don't be absurd. These boys would kill you out there—you'd be floating face down in Durban Harbor, Mowatt dancing on the prow. You misunderstood, a raise is quite impossible.

Pause.

NAN: Listen to me. I can get us out of here. I know it's been hard, I know you've not been able to get work . . . so I'll not let this . . .

TERRY (*Cuts her off*): Well, darling. Seeing as you got a raise, why don't you get Jackson back?

NAN: What do you mean?

TERRY: Spending our last cent to have Jackson sprung? I let him go. I sent him packing.

NAN: Wait a second—are you telling me you fired Jackson? Jesus, what the hell is wrong with you? Where the hell do you think the man is going to go? He has nowhere!

TERRY: And we have no money! It is enough of this crap! It's a miasma, and I'm sick and tired of it! Weakness, silence, servants. You should've seen him. Waiting for the dusty, green kaffir bus. I watched him from the window. He stood at the bus stop, weeping, Nan. Watching his buses arrive, watching them depart, and he could not move! No. The man just stood there, frozen, terrified. This stick figure, convulsed down the road, looking up here? Banished? I couldn't watch it any longer. (*Pause*) Goodbye, Jackson.

NAN: I see.

TERRY: I mean, God, please—don't, please—don't start coming in here talking about a raise! It's like some sort of ghastly quiz show for morons; nobody can get it right!

Pause. NAN *looks at him, nods.*

NAN: No. No. this is—this is remarkably clear to me, really.

TERRY: What're you talking about?

NAN: It's all right. You can say it. It's quite okay. You don't want to leave, do you?

TERRY: Pardon?

NAN: I'll repeat it. You have no intention of leaving, that's it, isn't it. Jackson, frozen . . . and terrified? Or Terry? You couldn't watch it any longer.

TERRY: That kind of patronizing, indulgent tone may work with your home-economics class but not with me.

NAN (*Calm*): It would be fine, if you would just stop the pretense, then.

TERRY: Playing at Freud? Amateur Ladies-Charity-Tea Psychiatric Contest, runner-up, eh?

Pause.

NAN (*Quiet*): Don't speak to me like that, please, anymore, Terry. I have watched you clothe yourself in your stances. A middle-aged man rushing out to smoke dope and buy the Beatles—hipper than your students, always. I have watched you—yearning for Blenheim—something you consider "diseased." Can't you just admit that you never really wanted to go? Tied as you are, at heart, to old boys, this beachfront, this small world here? I mean, it's just a matter of this fading of honesty—because it's fine not to be able to go. It's the posing that's so mortifying. You're so much better than that, sometimes. Don't you understand? Because I do want you to understand that this whole wretched business is breaking my heart.

Long pause.

TERRY (*Sits down*): Some days, I walk past Blenheim—when I can leave this flat. Past the white brick wall, you know? I'll just stand there for a moment, right? Recalling. Just . . . a specific day, when I was a boy, standing in the same bloody spot. You know, with the fucking mosquitos buzzing, and the heat rushing down, the salt air and humidity . . . I see myself, holding my cricket kit, in the same spot, twenty-five years ago . . . so happy. So amazed that a boyhood could be so perfect. I'll just stand there. As if I should be reduced to memory, already.

NAN: What is it that you remember that is so . . . paralyzing?

TERRY: . . . The terible bafflement of belonging here. All these gestures towards belonging. You tell yourself, "Well, my parents were gentleman farmers, this is my class." But I didn't belong. Too much Afrikaner in me, as a boy. So, I said, "Right—I belong to the academics," who—it turns out—I've detested, really. Perhaps I belong to the disenfranchised? And a man ends up dead—because of a gesture. There's no end to it, needing. Belonging. I finally, I think, only belong at Blenheim, oddly enough, teaching, somehow. And in—in this marriage. And the irony is, I have let Blenheim destroy me—you don't know how frustrating it is to feel yourself being wasted and not knowing how—and I, Nan, have destroyed our marriage.

NAN: No. That's not true.

Pause.

TERRY (*Takes a deep breath*): . . . No.

NAN (*Looks at letter*): Brazil . . . God. Brazil.

Pause.

TERRY: . . . Another world. Would have liked to have shown you the . . . Amazon. They say it'll be gone soon. Mining.

Lights fade down. NAN *puts down the letter and hugs* TERRY.

Scene 3

MRS. BALTON'S *flat.* SUTTER *and* MRS. BALTON.

MRS. BALTON: You see, if you look out over the veranda—that little red thingie in the water?

SUTTER: I can't possibly see that far anymore, Sylvia.

MRS. BALTON: Shark-net buoy. Swim past there and they'll eat you up like they did that girl a few months ago.

SUTTER: Never cared for the water myself.

MRS. BALTON: Christopher and I used to swim out for miles.

SUTTER: Extraordinary.

MRS. BALTON: How's the farm?

SUTTER: Haven't been for ages. Joyce has shingles again.

MRS. BALTON: You did the right thing, holding on to it.

SUTTER: It's just the house and some acres—had to sell some more this term, in fact.

MRS. BALTON: City is becoming harder to bear, daily. Like Bombay and Cairo.

SUTTER: I knew we'd end up there one day. Still have the same herd boy. Ninety-one. Isn't doing much now—lives in the same shack. Bring him his tea and biscuit myself when I'm there. Brings a tear every time. You'll come for Christmas, as usual, of course.

MRS. BALTON: Very upsetting seeing my old farm just across from yours. In the country, one can still smell old Africa. Clean, English sort of Africa, hint of something else out of range.

SUTTER: Well, that's all gone now. Here in the city as well.

MRS. BALTON: But one doesn't want to end one's days in the city. Remember what this town used to be like? Banquets at the Oyster Box Hotel?

SUTTER: The old beachfront? Three Monkeys Coffeehouse? Remember?

MRS. BALTON: The old Durban, the old style. Indian waiters with sashes about their waists and bright red thingies?

SUTTER: Jonathon is doing a remarkable job, Sylvia.

MRS. BALTON: And you're surprised?

SUTTER: A bit, yes. So soon.

MRS. BALTON: It shouldn't surprise you; he's Christopher's and my son.

SUTTER: True, but at Blenheim one sees many sons. Even Hamish Fox is happy.

MRS. BALTON: Hamish Fox's happiness could not be of less consequence.

SUTTER: Yes, well it is to me. My heavy, eh? Syl, love. We need that rather large push we've all been talking about, right now . . . and of course, we're asking certain families to help.

MRS. BALTON: Nev, love. The point is this—Blenheim needs more than a mere push. You are on the verge of bankruptcy, are you not.

SUTTER: Exactly where we are, yes.

MRS. BALTON: You've continued to lose old support, have you not?

SUTTER: That's true, yes.

MRS. BALTON: And the new families have formed some sort of parents' committee, have they not?

SUTTER: Sylvia, must we negotiate like Jews? Tell me your terms, I'll tell you if they can be met.

MRS. BALTON: I am prepared to make a permanent endowment.

SUTTER: Please go on.

MRS. BALTON: You must retire within twelve months and Jonathon must be made headmaster.

SUTTER: I thought it might be something like that, dear.

MRS. BALTON: Or I could take my money and go off and buy some little farm somewhere, which would leave very little for endowments. I'd need to ask the accountant, Mr. Schorr.

SUTTER: Jonathon . . . as headmaster. May I remind you, when I bought Blenheim, your husband loaned me the money?

MRS. BALTON: A lot. With no qualms, and no interest.

SUTTER: Exactly. And I thought I could build a gentleman's sort of place, with a rigorous approach to education, and yet at the same time be rather humane. Wasn't that the oddest youthful presumption?

MRS. BALTON: I used to find sugarcane farming romantic. One learns perspective, Neville. Jonathon is the only way.

SUTTER: And when I purchased Blenheim from McFarquhar, it really was rather nightmarish. 1936. So primitive. Floggings day and night, forced marches into the bush—barefoot, smell of rotten wood everywhere, rising up to one's nostrils at every turn. Boys with infections and bleeding welts from beatings, and fully one third of them with broken limbs from rugby against the Afrikaner school. Which they never lost. And the staff, Sylvia? You and Christopher never really knew them, you never mingled with the hoi polloi, did you?

MRS. BALTON: I'm sure they were most remarkable men, Neville.

SUTTER: The original Blenheim staff? They came with the place when I bought it. Religious hysterics exiled from England by their families—fat rejects with quivering, bluish lips, breathing heavily after the little boys; shell-shocked Great War fodder, reliving the trenches in the classroom . . . the flotsam and jetsam of the empire. But you know, the truly mind-boggling thing—is that Blenheim has never been as popular as it was then! And I gradually replaced that clutch of barnyard animals with a more reasonable lot. And I was so proud when Jonathon and Terry came on. It seemed the final dissolution of the old Blenheim. And look where it's got me.

MRS. BALTON: I shouldn't punish myself quite so hard, Nev. Could always pack it in, close the doors. Turn it into a nursing home. I'm told those do well.

SUTTER: Ah, yes. There you are. Built something, got to defend it. Jonathon'll be head, of course, Sylvia. But don't ask me for a date; he's not ready yet.

MRS. BALTON: I do think next term is sufficient, actually. And I should like, if I may, to have something in writing.

SUTTER (Pause): Sylvia, would you care to repeat that?

MRS. BALTON: A simple contract, Neville. It's business, Neville. Business.

SUTTER (Pause): Look, Sylvia, at who we are. And look, Sylvia, at what we are, and tell me when a handshake has not been utterly sufficient.

MRS. BALTON *(Beat)*: But, Neville, it is precisely because of who and what we are that I *do* want a contract.

SUTTER *(Pause)*: I see. Oh.

MRS. BALTON *offers him her pen as the lights fade down.*

Scene 4

Early morning. A bench on the Blenheim grounds, behind which is the wall surrounding the school—very old, crumbled, and quite possibly only being held upright by the tangle of bougainvillea vines that ensnares it. NAN *and* JONATHON *sit quietly for a moment.*

JONATHON: Dead quiet, this time of day. (HE *takes a flask from his coat, drinks, offers it to* NAN)

NAN: Bit early, don't you think?

JONATHON *(Lighting a cigar)*: Coffee. With a drop of brandy.

NAN: Breakfast?

JONATHON: I try, as a sort of experiment, to see how little I can get by on, these days. (HE *points off*) They begin construction on the new building next week.

NAN: Ah. The push. The Great Leap Forward?

JONATHON: The New Blenheim. Rather a brilliant aggressive move on Neville's part. Sort of a cross between Versailles and Walter Gropius. Daring.

NAN: But not too daring, of course?

JONATHON: I am told that we are looking at a marvelous future. A new generation. Who will be the alternative to Durban High with its Bible studies, rifle ranges, and Afrikaner surnames?

NAN: The New Blenheim, I expect? Don't you think there's just a bit of irony, Jon? In the Push Forward? I mean, it's more like the Great Leap Backwards.

JONATHON: It does somehow seem overly something-or-other, sometimes.

NAN: You had your film society before? Is there room for that in the New Blenheim? Anymore than there was in the old?

JONATHON: It's hardly forever.

NAN: No, it is, I think. Forever. This perpetual line of Jonathon Baltons, Terry Sinclairs and Ian McNallys. Like a factory—

JONATHON: Look. That's fine, yes. I came from Blenheim and all, but you're leaving, Nan. You're buggering off to god-knows-where. I'm left here, trying to make sense—trying to make adjustments, trying to learn this new business, and I don't know what's going on . . . *(Pause)* I mean, you're going off to have some sort of *life.*

NAN: Do you know, he was—he was very persuasive about not wanting to ever have children. I would—I would say yes to anything that he said. Wanted.

But it's like—it's like some sort of amnesia—emotional amnesia; we look very different to one another now. Look. We're staying, we're not leaving.

JONATHON: I see.

NAN: And honestly, it started off because my husband started to like to go to a couple of rallies, meetings in basements. We've aged badly. And I realize . . . I have missed something. That these boys were hardly enough for us. That our children might have made us so much better, finally. And as I walk up the hill here in the morning, my stomach tightens. The assumption that we've been born into this unchangeable, nonmalleable life down here, even as we're proven wrong—by the very way we fight, struggle, behave. I think a choice must be made. I see my husband, and realize that.

JONATHON: I know of no choices, Nan. I have looked for them. They are a luxury.

NAN: But then we are failing in every respect. Jonathon—you were rather happy—doing something valuable, such as it was. Your film society, with those awful films we all made fun of and laughed at you about—it was a start, wasn't it? Love? And now—at this point—for you to say, "I shall go on with this business, as instructed . . ."—that's a bitter defeat. We are a school for morticians, learning to inter ourselves as we graduate.

JONATHON: Well, what—what the hell would you have me do, eh? Nan? What?

NAN: You could get Terry back. For an education that we might have given our children. I don't know . . . I see all the years of exhausted, acerbic witty stagnation that was dished out here piling up. You and Terry wasted fifteen years here, or perhaps it need not have been wasted—just an education. But I don't want to be party to allowing another generation to grow up smiling blithely, sipping gin, making biological and historical arguments for their supremacy, and playing at cricket, only to meet Fox's assegai-up-the-bum death.

Pause.

JONATHON: I love it—one of the things I love, in the cinema, is—heroism in unexpected places.

NAN: Oh, Jonathon. Have you heard a word of this?

JONATHON: Terry, Nan, and Jonathon. Yes. The three of us, eh?

NAN: This is not some sort of little film!

JONATHON: No. You know, they're putting my parents' name up on the new building? Balton Hall, eh? Can you imagine? Isn't it bloody amazing? *(Pause)* I used to think the drama in our own lives, Nan, could never match the drama of the cinema.

JONATHON *smiles as lights fade down.*

Scene 5

NAN (*Addressing her class*): When I asked for essays on the Zulus, I wasn't looking for detailed accounts of native laziness in your father's factory, Cleasby. Nor am I interested in your examination of native killing techniques. It's tired, and I'm tired of it. It's as if your Africa were some kind of Atlantis, with drums and spears. It's not the one we're in. (*Pause*).

I thought we might, then, try these essays again? Somehow demythologized, okay? I was thinking—as I was reading them—I was thinking back, remembering, because . . . my family had a number of maids as I was growing up. And there was a blur—a period of faces, names I can't connect—but there was Edna. And she had been with us for some years—this good-natured, virtually invisible friend. Whose life was actually far more complicated than ours. My father did nothing, really. There was a vastness of leisure time, a morass. (*Pause*)

And Edna had this husband who worked in the mines, whom she saw with less and less frequency over the years. My mother found his presence—his dusty, coarse skin—upsetting, even if he was only to spend the night in the little room behind the garage. He was never actually forbidden; it was a kind of subtle discouragement. And—it was the same with her children—who had been cast out to the grandmother's little squash patch and mud hut in Zululand . . . somewhere. So everyone might be reunited at Christmas for a couple of days or so. Eventually, the circumstances of this thwarted, enslaved life, all the wretchedness, made functioning as a human being harder and harder. (*Pause*)

And of course, as it becomes harder to function as a human being, it makes being a good servant pretty much an impossibility. (*Pause*)

She became moody. Forgetting to bathe, becoming, finally, something of a darkness in our home. And as Edna's personality became that of a toast-burning hag, I started to develop an intense dislike for her. There was a point where my family's main source of bored, wintry . . . amusement—the height of morbidity, finally—was to, over dinner, discuss the decline of Edna, discuss it, in fact, as she served. (*Pause*)

And of course, she began to sour. Her humanness became overwhelming, like meat left out far too long. And when the dimension of her life overtook our own, she was, finally, simply sent away. (*Pause*)

And the next week, it began again—with a new servant. So really, I mean, this kind of Atlantis you describe, it hardly does credit to the real one, which has its own violence, its own terrors, quite independent of Fox's Africa of guns and sweat and war. That Africa—denies what we are. Our own brand of monstrousness. Surely there have been lives that have meant something to you? And I would very much like to know about that. Do you understand this?

HAMISH FOX *has entered, has stood in the doorway a few moments.*

FOX: Ergh.

NAN: Oh! Hello . . .? Class, please stand up.

FOX: Sit. I just came to fetch some items, if you don't mind, Mrs. Sinclair. I'd like to have my goodbyes with the boys, please.

NAN *(Starting to exit)*: Yes, of course. Please. Go ahead.

FOX: Many years of rubbish collected in here. You'll be amazed, Mrs. Sinclair, when you come and fetch it all.

NAN: Yes. I expect I will. (SHE *exits*)

FOX *(To the class)*: When writing an essay, every thought must be crystal clear. Picture the sentence before you. Does it look correct? The comma in the right place? Spelling accurate? And the thought itself. How is that? Your penmanship must not waver, because when it does, it weakens the idea. And of equal importance is that you do not let an inkblot foul the paper. Nothing is so damaging as an inkblot, like some vile black stain, occluding the light, breaking clarity. Make certain that the ink is running smoothly through the body of the pen, to the nib, which must never be bent. The nib must be as clean as the surgeon's scalpel—as vital an instrument. Imprint of the manufacturer must always be visible on the nib, or blots will occur. Do not put red ink into a pen which has had blue or black. Rather, keep three pens. If you cannot afford three pens, then you must wash the one thoroughly before putting in the new color of ink. From the blue book, learn three new words a day. You must be able to convey the clarity of your intent, under fire, in the office, on the field; clarity of expression equals success. Your privilege is this education, which separates you from the savage; and in the years ahead, this will be—a most formidable weapon. *(Pause)*

I would also say, if I may be a bit more personal for a moment, that I would prefer it if nobody visited me in hospital—a strain on all parties that is best avoided. So, without further rigamarole, I shall see you, I'm certain, after Boxing Day, when I shall tell you about the idiocy of the Maginot Line. And Douglas Bader, the war hero with no legs.

FOX *exits slowly as lights fade down.*

Scene 6

JONATHON'S *classroom.* JONATHON *and* SUTTER.

SUTTER: You must understand, this is very upsetting.

JONATHON: Oh dear.

SUTTER: What the hell's the matter with her?

JONATHON: Well now, we don't know exactly what went on, do we?

SUTTER: Hamish Fox—Hamish Fox comes in and tells me of some sort of mad-woman speech in social bloody history class?

JONATHON: Yes. This from a man who's less evolved than the creature for which he's named.

SUTTER: Don't be clever, Jonathon. The Mowatts. The Ashburnhams and the Halliwells have all decided to withdraw their boys at end of term if nothing is done.

JONATHON: Look, if Blenheim is to move forward, don't you think we should be permitted to do it without the constant terrorization of our staff by hysterics? Don't you agree, Nev?

SUTTER: Of course I fucking agree! But the point is, that Mowatt woman is the most fertile female in Natal. I was looking forward to another four boys at least! I mean, the whole business has gone way, way too far!

JONATHON: Sometimes boys come back, don't they?

SUTTER (Scornful): Oh, thank you. (HE stumbles over a chair) Christ—I can't see! She must've known that with things the way they are this would cost her her damn job!

JONATHON: I was expecting something like that. Are you serious?

SUTTER: Deadly serious. I'm too tired for this. Why the hell should we be destroyed over this? We've all seen fine boys come out of here—I'm not going to just sit here and watch it being chipped away at! The parents' committee is repulsive, though utterly correct; we need a purge—a bloodletting—their words exactly!

JONATHON: Well, then, I have the right idea—fire McNally, hell I'll do it! Let's be bloody aggressive about it—bring back Terry! And if—if you stand there, telling me that he's a fucking communist, I'll be out the door myself, old man, I swear it!

SUTTER (Pause; HE raises his eyebrow, regards JONATHON): I know he's not a com-munist. But that's not the point. He could be a cross between Mao Tse-tung and Medusa, for all I care. He's not coming back. I've got to have surgery on my eyes, or I shall end up being led about by a water spaniel. I'm going to Cape Town for surgery, and I'm leaving you in charge, believe it or not; and I have decided, Jonathon, that it is to be your responsibility to end this business. She's to have her last day on Friday. And be gone after lunch.

JONATHON: It is just giving in to those dull horrors who drop their kids off here every morning. Why? Why, Neville?

SUTTER: It is not for further discussion. I'm exhausted. It has been decided.

JONATHON: But why must I do it, then?

SUTTER (Icy): Because, I, Jonathon, am going blind.

JONATHON: But I cannot even—I can't do it—

SUTTER (Thundering): No discussion! I am dead from discussion! And diplomacy! It . . . is . . . ended! And I want new septic tanks, please, Jonathon, by the

time I return. The smell of offal around here is overwhelming. Mrs. S. can't
entertain the parents' committee.

JONATHON (*After a pause*): I ask you this. One question, Neville. What is left?

SUTTER (*Pause*): What is left, Jonathon, is Blenheim.

Lights fade down.

Scene 7

Early evening. The bench by the wall on the school grounds. TERRY *is sitting alone.*
HE *is cleanshaven, calm, and well-dressed in khaki twills, a striped shirt and a*
sweater.

TERRY: It's very lovely, isn't it, when it's this quiet?

JONATHON (*Entering, his jacket carried over his shoulder, a cigar in his teeth*): My favorite
times: early morning, and in the evening, after they've left. When it's empty.
Good to see you, Ter.

TERRY: Yes. You look well. This is all agreeing with you, eh?

Pause.

JONATHON (*Quietly*): Yes, it is. I showed myself a film just now. Mr. *Blandings Builds*
His . . . Dream House. Very sad, funny. Sort of. Hmn.

TERRY (*Leaning over, picks up a stone*): You know, once when I was a boy, I found
a spearhead here?

JONATHON: I remember. But I think, in fact, it was planted by Fox. (*Pause*) Are
you well? You look better.

TERRY (*Shrugs, embarrassed*): I think. Yes. Been a hell of a time . . . I . . . (*Pause*)
They're building Balton Hall?

JONATHON (*Points off, nods*): Neville's gone off. Left me in charge. They're doing
something to his corneas.

TERRY: Yes. And left you to do as you will?

JONATHON: . . . I suppose. . . . Yes. He has.

TERRY: Jon—I had an interview, ah, at the University of Natal. But the poor old
head of English, and Speech and Drama, just a tired, fucked old bloke—
they've got half his faculty gone—whispered in my ear, "Love to take you
on, Ter. But it's just not on, old boy." (*Pause*) "Can't . . . take any chances
now," he said.

JONATHON: Ah.

TERRY: Yes. They have their own troubles. A Jesuit in the law school arrested.

JONATHON: Yes. I read it. Look up there, up the hill—they're burning sugarcane . . .
smell it?

TERRY (*Looking off left*): I know—I was thinking before you came, watching it. That wall of fire. It's like the huge, roaring wall of flame between us and the rest of the world. How do you ever get through it? The fiery wall of mythology? McNally's stories of Negroes descending en masse from Harlem; Fox's Pakis and Arabs taking over London. . . . Look at that fire. It's growing and growing. The hatred for the rest of the world. And how do you find passage through it?

JONATHON: I wonder. You were trying, weren't you? Somehow. To connect. . . . At the centenary? (*Pause*) Look. Give this to Nan, will you? I missed her this afternoon, meeting Sutter. Her raise—first check. (HE *reaches into his pocket and hands* TERRY *a check*)

TERRY: They've got you signing checks now, eh?

JONATHON: Yes. A heady feeling indeed.

TERRY: Not much more to give you, then, is there?

JONATHON: It all seems to be working out, somehow, for once, I think.

TERRY: Jonathon. That fire. Blenheim—for me, is the only place to fight that fire. I am—a schoolmaster . . . I should like to come back. I am asking. I grew up here, I am a product of "Pride, Rigor and Reason." And I realize, lately, that that motto was a luxury; that Blenheim, finally, only pretends to reason. The presumption that our class is above the sweat and viciousness that surrounds us has been—stripped away. (*Pause*) But we came from here. And perhaps it's not impossible that some sort of reason, and pride—I don't know about rigor—they might begin to make themselves felt. (*Pause*) I am in my forties. I should like to return.

Long pause.

JONATHON (*Takes a deep breath*): Yes. Nan told me. (*Pause*) That would be very good.

Lights fade down.

Scene 8

A cemetery by the Indian Ocean. It stretches off, a pastoral green, under an intense sun. In the distance, there is the crashing sound of waves hitting rocks. JONATHON *and* SUTTER *enter, the latter with a patch over one eye.*

JONATHON: Neville. Do you think you should rest? You've only just gotten off an airplane.

SUTTER: No. I shall rest tomorrow, at the farm. (HE *pulls a flask out of his blazer pocket*) Drink?

JONATHON: Yes. Thank you.

SUTTER: Huge cemetery, isn't it?

JONATHON: Never been in here.

SUTTER (*Pointing off*): The old Durban faces—all out. Seems the only time we see one another is when one of us dies. Was a time when, instead of a grave, we met at the cricket finals. I do wish more of the old boys had shown. To say goodbye to Hamish. This saddens.

JONATHON: You didn't see them! The Mowatts, the Cleasbys.

SUTTER: Must be my eyes.

JONATHON: How was the airplane?

SUTTER: Mrs. S. was bilious and broke out in shingles. A spell of bad luck, eh? Her shingles. My eyes—spending money madly.

JONATHON: But it should turn about in the spring.

SUTTER: Wish I had a biscuit with my whisky. This eye treatment? They use a laser, burns a hole, you can hear the eye sizzling like bacon. They insist it's painless, but really, it's hell.

JONATHON: But useful, eh?

SUTTER: You did a remarkable job, making Hamish's funeral arrangements and all.

JONATHON: Yes. And I've put a nice Christmas tree in assembly hall.

SUTTER: You know, I looked at my body in the mirror before the funeral. I'm all white, all soft. Little veins, like a tea doily, under the white. Like a map. An old and tattered map. Up my left leg is a vein that looks remarkably like the Blue Nile. Been up 'em both.

JONATHON: Ah.

SUTTER: Quite interesting, seeing the old crowd here, out to bury Hamish. Because I looked at them, and they're white and veiny too. Cumberland told me that he had little capillaries exploding all over his left side. Showed me. Looked like Ghana, from years and years, his doctor told him, of drinking cane spirits. Gotta stop drinking, they tell him, and we had a bit of a laugh over that. I mean—what's the point, at this stage, eh? (*Pause*) What a pathetic bunch of old men and their stray wives, standing about in a cemetery. A clutch of rheumy-eyed, sodden, yellow-toothed old gentleman farmers and their distorted wives, all of us with nowhere to go. And yet, look out there—the sulfuric, red-streaked, mad sea. Pounding on the rocks. A dead end for me. (*Pause*) Not only have you not fired her, but you've given her a raise. I looked at the ledger before I came. Why?

JONATHON (*Sighing*): I'm sorry. Well then, here we are. Should I pack up my things?

SUTTER: Let's discuss it.

JONATHON: Oh, let's not, Nev. Let's not be clever, shall we? Just fire me, if you're going to.

SUTTER: Jonathon. You needn't stand there like a fifth former about to get a hiding.

JONATHON: But, Neville, you see, I've always been terrified of those who judge—always wanted to please authority. First Father, then Mother, Terry . . . and now, you.

SUTTER: I know.

JONATHON (*Pauses, takes a deep breath*): Neville. Do you honestly believe that I do not know why I was made assistant head? All it took was the tiny bit of intuition I've got. Mother. It's shameful, Nev, to think I'd be so dull-witted as to not understand. And so . . . at the point of realization—the epiphany—one feels pretty dreadful, pretty damn ugly. Incapable, swindled. And for you to assume utter unquestioning on my part, the absolute certainty of my taking orders, makes me feel utterly pathetic.

SUTTER: Not my intent, Jonathon.

JONATHON: So why not help my only friends? Two people who have had the best intentions—the most fair-minded. . . . You know why I am friends with Terry? Because since we were boys—he could always be good enough for the both of us. And Nan—they're not like us. Why not help two such friends?

Pause.

SUTTER: And what about politics, Jonathon?

JONATHON: Politics?

SUTTER: Exactly.

JONATHON (*Looks at* SUTTER *for a long moment*): And after forty years, why is it . . . that *now* . . . I should suddenly find myself involved in, of all things, *your* . . . politics?

SUTTER: An education, isn't it?

JONATHON: Because, if we're all to end up white, corroded bodies at the edge of the sea, I'd rather have the memory of my own cowardice, my own shriveling-up. Anything, something other than this exhaustion, this—depletion—this ceaseless, repulsive dignity.

SUTTER: I agree completely.

JONATHON: And that is why I did not fire her.

SUTTER: Jonathon, lad. Listen, please.

JONATHON: But you see, I think—I think . . . it's gone far enough. Let's stop, shall we? I've had quite enough.

SUTTER: No cinematic histrionics, if you will.

JONATHON: Neville, you don't understand.

SUTTER: It is you, again, who do not understand. Though it is refreshing to hear you make so much sense for once. Look. Your mother does help us. True. But your mother's money did not make you assistant headmaster. Though it is convenient for her to think that she protects you.

JONATHON: Oh, yes it was.

SUTTER: No. It is you that I have thought of. Your well-being, and Blenheim's. I have built and defended that place, and it's virtually killed me. It's more, ultimately, than just the dry bones of mere ritual. I could've found another way, if I thought you were wrong. You're far more interesting than either of your parents. Your mother is a viper, and your father was like a killer whale, gulping in air. So do me this favor. This thing. Fire Nan, and then you're headmaster of Blenheim.

JONATHON: I won't do it to Nan.

SUTTER: It is your only chance, your only hope. There are, you must realize, very definite, very cogent reasons for this business. Do you remember what I told you when you took assistant head? "You find yourself becoming more the representative. And you've got to acknowledge what it is you're representing." I need to know, now, what, and who, it is you are representing. You must let her go—then I'll know you're ready.

MRS. BALTON (Entering): That's very good, Neville. I think you're right.

JONATHON: Oh, Mother. I'm not interested in discussing it with you. Both of you. Look. Let me put it clearly: just fire me.

MRS. BALTON: It's the coldest of worlds out there. I've told you many times. but you've not listened. If you left Blenheim, how would you spend your days? (Pause) You know, don't you? You'd end up serving me tea on a tray, just like nanny, wasting away in her room. You think you are lonely now, but without Blenheim, the days will just stretch ahead of you, agonizingly, Jonathon. And you will find yourself an old man, with frail hands, outrageous scarves, in an ocean-front flat, eating pudding on a white plate. Absolutely—irredeemably isolated.

JONATHON: That's not true!

MRS. BALTON: As if in a hole. And your pleasure? You will go to the cinema, alone, purchase your ticket, sit in the dark; and you'll walk out, a little closer to death.

JONATHON: No.

MRS. BALTON: No. You can't do that anymore, can you, Jonathon? You have begun to enjoy this new experience. This power. Have you not? Your new suits? You are more careful in your bathing, in combing your hair. You have been admired, effective. And it would end.

JONATHON: Listen to yourself, Mother.

MRS. BALTON: And I have lived for you. I cannot allow this to happen. Because I won't be here to protect you. Be realistic.

JONATHON: Like you? It doesn't interest me.

MRS. BALTON: You are destined to be lonely, Jonathon. It is only a matter of degree. The choice is yours. Life is such a trifle, such a small thing. And one is left with what little one has built.

JONATHON: What have we built, Mother?

MRS. BALTON: A relatively quiet, somewhat safe, permanently endowed home for my boy. Blenheim School for Boys.

JONATHON: A home? With no friends. Like our home, Mother.

SUTTER: As you climb the hill of fortune, may you never meet a friend.

MRS. BALTON: Do you know what would happen if Nan stayed on and you brought back Terry? Could you build the Blenheim you want? Nobody else wants it. And you didn't even have the stamina to sustain your film society. You would destroy yourself for two people who will live without you, and whom you can never have.

Long pause.

JONATHON: You are a brutal and savage woman, which you know. But what nobody has ever told you is that, actually, you are an extraordinarily shallow one as well. (HE *begins to exit*)

SUTTER: Jonathon! (JONATHON *stops*) Whatever you decide now—you are going to have to live with. Forever. There is no going back. Do you understand?

JONATHON *looks at them both, then walks off.*

(*Pointing off*) Look over the wall, Sylvia. The Hindus are burying their dead. Let's go and have a look, shall we?

Light fade down.

Scene 9

JONATHON's *classroom. A small Christmas tree stands in one corner.* JONATHON *is at his desk. On the blackboard is a note: "Classes dismissed in order to attend the funeral of Mr. Fox."*

JONATHON (*Looking at the map of Africa*): Zululand. . . . Never ever should've left the farm . . . never let her convince you. Father. Never come here at all.

Pause. NAN *and* TERRY *enter.*

Ah, there you are. Nice funeral, wasn't it?

NAN: No. There was hardly anyone there for him. I mean—not to sentimentalize him, but . . .

TERRY: He had nobody, really.

JONATHON: Frightening, isn't it? And sad. Did you know that he shrunk to the size of a pygmy before he finally died?

NAN: Are you all right? You look pale.

JONATHON: This was only my second funeral. My father's the only other. You were very fond of my father, weren't you, Terry? Horses, and all that. But you didn't really know him. Did you?

TERRY: . . . No. I mean, the public version only. Right? You look like you could use a drink, Jonathon . . .

JONATHON: No. Just tired out. I was thinking of the farm. Every Saturday night, father'd give one of the cows to the natives. A treat. Few farms did that. But actually, it was no sacrifice, just a small feeble animal. And yet . . . cane-cutters, herd boys, all of them . . . would look forward to Saturday night. The compound would come alive. That mad Zulu pop music on the Bantu radio. I'd sit in nanny's lap, watching. It was all very festive. (*Beat*)
   I was mostly interested in the killing of the cow. Used to be they used

a knife, and that was vivid, very much a thing of the bush. To see the creature's dull eyes flashing, hooves scraping at the dirt as the knife was led across the throat—and the blood running into a gourd on the ground. But the part that fascinated me the most was when it was dead. Its evisceration. The skin drawn slowly back, and the veins exposed, black blood clotting into the reddish dust of the compound, which would be dead quiet, somber. Little ivory-colored and purple-hued sacks filled with bile and acid and urine. Balloons of undigested grass, bones cracked, and muscles pulsing gently, as a fire was readied. And the tongue, the great curled muscle, unraveled, cut out, and the teeth and jaw laid bare. *(Pause)*

But it is one Saturday in particular that I remember. It was my birthday, and I was given the honor of killing the cow. I was eleven. The knife was dispensed with, and my father gave me a pistol with tiny silver-tipped bullets. I was to blow out the brains from a little spot between the eyes, and this death had none of the ritual of the knife. It was an assassination, and I believe the natives knew this. Unbearable to have this cow led to me, docile, and uncomplaining. She was tied to a post, with a little strand of rope, and I tried to do the thing very quickly. But you see, I did not do a proper job of it. And the bullet ricocheted off her skull and down into the jaw—this shattered pulp of bone and blood, through which she screamed, you see, as I recall it. And tore loose from her feebly tied rope. And there she was, with saliva and plasma all about, bolting into the cane fields, everyone stunned. She was gone. And I stood there. Frozen. *(Pause)*

And I looked up, and saw my father standing on the veranda of the main house with my mother—and he said something to her and went inside, and nanny came to me. And of course, by this time, I was crying. The natives staring at their feet—mortified. No laughter—which might have been preferable. *(Pause)*

And then my father came out of the house with his shotgun, got on his horse, and rode into the field, and there was a single muffled blast, and nanny put me to bed. A quiet supper that night, no singing or dancing, and of course, not long after, we moved into the city—my mother's idea. So I was just thinking about my father, and all.

Pause.

TERRY: It's natural. Funerals. It's death . . . that makes us think. Not life, usually, unfortunately.

JONATHON: Nature. No, it has nothing to do with nature, Terry. And also, after all is said and done, after all our reasoning, and . . . grasping, searching . . . nobody really . . . cares.

TERRY: Well I used to think that.

JONATHON: No. You don't understand, Terry. It will not be possible for you to come back to Blenheim.

TERRY: It will not be possible for me to . . .? Jonathon? What has happened?

JONATHON: You see, the fact is . . . I have been made headmaster. And, Nan. You . . .
are fired.

NAN: I don't understand? Jonathon? You just gave me a raise . . . I'm not . . . we . . .
were . . .

TERRY: They have made you headmaster? And. . . . No, I understand, Nan.

JONATHON: Terry. No, you can't. Because you have always said, and I know this,
"There is something terribly odd about Jonathon." Yes. But what is it? I can
answer this now. The thing that is odd is that he fails to understand, to engage.
But you are wrong.

TERRY: Yes.

NAN: I have—there is nothing to say, here. To this.

TERRY: You . . . let this happen to yourself, you know, Jonathon. All these years
of retreat, of movies, of radio dramatics, of small concerns; you laid yourself
out: a weak and spongy man, finally, nurtured and encouraged—by a dying
society. I used to warn you. That the world was not as quiet as you wanted
to believe, not anymore. That wall of fire, Jonathon—it is finally—right outside your door. (Pause) Let's go, Nan.

NAN: Terry . . .

JONATHON: Wait. You see—that is it! Your presence here would always be a judgment. The echo of a whispered word on a veranda. (Pause) I will say "no"
to the complications of your language, your grammar. I will say "no" to the
demands of your conversation, and the rightness of your politics. You have
this idea. It is of change. And you hand me a gun. But where is it pointing?
It is at my head. I say "no," and I will survive. Hope? Expectations? Imagination? No. None. Never here. You see, in this room—with its shades open,
its projector gone, for good—a monster. That is what you don't understand.
You said you were a product of Blenheim, Terry? I am the true product of
Blenheim. Blenheim's monster, walking, skipping down the halls. As a boy.
And as a man.

Pause. TERRY looks at JONATHON, then begins to lead NAN out. NAN stops for a
moment.

NAN: Happy New Year, Jonathon.

NAN and TERRY exit.

JONATHON (A whisper): Yes. It is. (HE walks over to the desk, picks up a box of Christmas
tree decorations and goes to the tree. HE places a small star on the pinnacle. Then
HE takes from the box a tin of artificial snow, which HE begins to spray all over
the tree and, after a moment, slowly, straight up into the air, over his head. HE
lifts his hands to catch the white powder as it filters down upon him, swirling to
the floor)

END OF PLAY

Kind Ness
Ping Chong

in collaboration with Rober Babb, John Fleming, Brian Hallas, Jeannie Hutchins, Lenard Petit, Louise Smith and Louise Sunshine

About Ping Chong

Ping Chong, writer, director, choreographer and visual artist, was born in Toronto and raised in New York City. He is founder and artistic director of The Fiji Company. His work has been presented at major venues throughout the United States, including the Joyce Theatre and La Mama E.T.C. in New York; the Kennedy Center, Washington, D.C.; the Walker Arts Center, Minneapolis; the Museum of Contemporary Art, Chicago; and the Zellerbach Auditorium, San Francisco. Two of his works have been presented at the Brooklyn Academy of Music's Next Wave Festival: *The Games*, created in collaboration with Meredith Monk, in 1984, and *Angels of Swedenborg* in 1986. Abroad, his work has been seen at the Mickery Theatre in Amsterdam and at festivals including the Festival d'Automne in Paris, the Holland Festival and the Osaka World Festival. His most recent U.S. production was *Maraya—Acts of Nature in Geological Time*, performed at Apple Corps Theater, New York, in January 1988. Chong won a 1977 Obie award for *Humboldt's Current*. He has been the recipient of two National Endowment for the Arts fellowships in the New Genres category, a Guggenheim fellowship and a New York State Council on the Arts film fellowship.

About His Collaborators

Roger Babb has worked with Joseph Chaikin, Tim Buckley, Meredith Monk and The Talking Band. As a member of The Fiji Company, he wrote and created the roles of Rudy in *Kind Ness* and Jonathan Harker in *Nosferatu*, as well as performing in *Nuit Blanche* and *Angels of Swedenborg*. He is artistic director of Otrabanda Company, and has presented works at La Mama E.T.C. and St. Mark's Danspace in New York.

John Fleming is a "mover" with a background in mime, dance and the art of the mask. He creates the choreographic elements for which Ping Chong's work is noted. He created and performed the role of Buzz in *Kind Ness* and has worked with The Fiji Company in *Anna into Nightlight*, A.M./A.M.—*The Articulated Man* (on tour), *A Race, Astonishment and the Twins, Nosferatu* and *Maraya—Acts of Nature in Geological Time*. He was co-choreographer of *Angels of Swedenborg*. He also works with Otrabanda Company.

Brian Hallas played the Narrator in *Kind Ness* and collaborated on the play's soundtrack with Phil Lee. He appeared in and composed the music and soundtrack for *Astonishment and the Twins*, and created the soundtrack for *Nosferatu*. Hallas is a founding member of Bottom Doubt, a polymedia theatre based in Rhode Island, for which he performs and composes. He is also a member of Success Express, for whom he writes music and plays keyboard.

Jeannie Hutchins has worked with Ping Chong since 1977. She created the roles of Daphne in *Kind Ness*, Emma Humboldt in *Humboldt's Current* and Lucia Westenra in *Nosferatu*. She was in the original productions of Meredith Monk's *Quarry* and the Robert Wilson/Philip Glass opera *Einstein on the Beach*. Her own work has been produced regularly in New York since 1978. She received a 1986 Bessie Award for her performance work with The Fiji Company.

Lenard Petit is an actor, mime, dancer, director, choreographer and teacher. He has collaborated extensively with John Fleming in physical theatre. He created the role of Alvin in *Kind Ness* and appeared in *Angels of Swedenborg* and in *The Travelogue Series* by Meredith Monk and Ping Chong. He has also worked with Otrabanda Company, Richard Foreman and Matthew Maguire of Creation Production Company.

Louise Smith, a member of The Fiji Company since 1981, created the role of Lulu in *Kind Ness*. She appeared in *The Travelogue Series* by Meredith Monk and Ping Chong and collaborates with The Talking Band and Otrabanda Company. She has worked under directors Elizabeth Swados, Michael Kahn, Ralph Lee and Julie Taymor, appearing on stages throughout Europe, Japan and the United States. She played the lead role in Lizzie Borden's film *Working Girls*. She has written a work entitled *Small White House*.

Louise Sunshine has performed as a vocalist, dancer and actor in the work of Lenora Champagne, Juliet du Mont, Simone Forti and others. She has presented her own dance pieces in New York City since 1984. Her work on *Kind Ness*, in which she created the role of Dot, was her first collaboration with The Fiji Company.

About the Play

Kind Ness, conceived and directed by Ping Chong, was developed in workshop at Northeastern University, Boston. The university's Division of Fine Arts presented the premiere performances of the play April 10-12, 1986. In May of that year the play was presented at La Mama E.T.C. in New York. *Kind Ness* is to be circulated as a *Plays in Process* script in the spring of 1988.

The Fiji Company wishes to thank Sergei Tschernisch and Northeastern University for their support. Funding for the development and production of *Kind Ness* was provided, in part, by the Massachusetts Council on the Arts and Humanities, the National Endowment for the Arts and the Dalglish Foundation.

Playwright's Note

The play, which is performed without an intermission, consists of 12 scenes with the following titles:

1. A Slide Lecture
2. Daphne's Garden
3. First Day of School
4. Slapstick #1
5. Chez Buzz
6. Introductions
7. Slapstick #2
8. Questions and Answers
9. Bus Stop
10. Prom Nite
11. Testimonials
12. At the Zoo

The ages of the characters shift from scene to scene. For example, in *Bus Stop*, the six friends—Daphne, Alvin, Buzz, Lulu, Rudy and Dot—are eight or nine years old. In *Questions and Answers* they are college age. These shifts are indicated by simple means such as wig and costume changes.

When taped music is indicated at the start of a new scene, it plays throughout the scene unless otherwise specified.

Kind Ness is played on a bare stage. There is no curtain. The stage floor is painted white or has a white covering over it. There are six pairs of black wings with accompanying black teasers. On the back wall is a floor-to-ceiling white cyclorama. When lit, the cyclorama always has an even wash of color on it: It is lit only by the cyclorama strips and the stage lights never hit it. Downstage of the cyclorama, in front of the playing area, are two small white plaques, approximately 10 inches square, one stage left and one stage right. The plaques are lit by specials and change color with, or in counterpoint to, whatever color wash is on the cyclorama. The plaque lights are usually the first lights to come on in any scene. Since there is no set except for folding chairs which are carried on and off, and some styrofoam rocks in the last scene, the plaques help to give spatial definition to the stage. They also suggest that the audience is watching human specimens in a zoological environment.

Characters

NARRATOR, an offstage male voice, live on microphone. He is an all-purpose narrator. For example, he is the lecturer for the Scene 1 slide show, the translator for Buzz's gorilla talk, the voice of Mr. Conklin in Scene 3. His tone adjusts to the particular situation in hand.

DAPHNE, delicate, brunette; rich, vain and a little spoiled, but likeable; a WASP.

ALVIN, lithe and lanky with black horn-rimmed glasses and black hair which stands up like Alfalfa's in the *Our Gang* show. He's a lot like Jughead in the *Archie* comics. He's working-class, a French-Canadian from Maine; he speaks French fluently.

BUZZ, a good-natured and tolerant gorilla. His speech throughout the play is a series of vocalizations, carefully planned for rhythm, pitch, tone, etc.

LULU, a dumb blonde, but vulnerable; buxom and outgoing with a Barbie-doll quality, especially in the scenes where she's older; Irish Catholic.

RUDY, curly red hair, well-built; somewhat insensitive, a smart aleck, but likeable; well-to-do; Irish Catholic.

DOT, blind, awkward, heavy; olive skin; brainy, a little wacky in her own quick way; Jewish.

MR. CONKLIN, the stereotypical school principal; played in a mask by the actor who plays Rudy.

MRS. CONKLIN, his loud-mouthed, often drunk wife; played with mask and accessories by the actor who plays Lulu.

BWANA IN SLAPSTICK ROUTINES, played by the actor who plays Alvin.

APE IN SLAPSTICK ROUTINES, played by the actor who plays Buzz.

GORILLA IN ZOO, played by the actor who plays Rudy or Alvin.

STAGEHAND, relatively tall, dressed in black.

BARKER, played by the actor who plays the stagehand.

Time

Early 1950s-1960s.

Place

Suburbia, U.S.A.

The Play

Kind Ness

Scene 1
A Slide Lecture

As the audience enters the theatre, the stage is dark. A single folding chair sits downstage center. The plaques are lit in a primary color. Preset taped music is playing: someone like Dinah Washington singing '50s ballads, including "I Thought about You," which recurs later in the play in an abridged form. As the last song ends, the plaque lights fade out with the music. The tick-tock sound of a game-show clock is heard under the NARRATOR's voice. As his lecture proceeds, slides are projected on the cyclorama in the blackout. Except for the first, each slide is divided down the middle with an image on the right and an image on the left.

NARRATOR (Offstage; live voice on microphone): K-I-N-D-N-E-S-S. Kindness.

Slide 1: The word "Kind Ness."

Good evening, ladies and gentlemen. We're going to be showing you some images right now. While you're looking at them, we'd like you to think about what is alike and what is not alike. What is similar and what is dissimilar. What the images have in common and how they differ. Could we have the first slide, please. (Nothing happens) Could we have the first slide, please. (Slide appears) Thank you.

Slide 2: Red Rectangle. Blue Rectangle.

Now. For example, in these images what is alike is that both are vertical rectangles, they are both colors. What is dissimilar is that one is a hot color, the other is a cool color. Next.

Slide 3: A circle. A square.

These images are both centered in the frame, they are both geometric shapes, they both have iconographic significance in our daily lives. Next.

Slide 4: Triangle pointing up. Triangle pointing down.

Both images here are green, they both have sharp points. They are also geometric shapes. What is not alike is that one image is on the left, the other is on the right. Now, why don't you try one.

Slide 5: Addition sign. Subtraction sign.

Would you like to try another one?

Slide 6: Chinese ideogram. Chinese ideogram.

Good.

Slide 7: Chinese text. Arabic text.

(With an imperfect French accent) Ici sont deux images. L'image à gauche est un text chinois et l'image à droite est un text arabique. D'accord, quelle est la similarité? *(Pause)* Les textes sont une histoire de la sexualité des personnes outre. Continuez.

Slide 8: "100." Stick lines adding up to a hundred.

Ahhh! Bon!

Slide 9: "Binary." "Bifocal."

Binary, bifocal.

Slide 10: Computer terminal. Baby crying.
Slide 11: Bianca Jagger holding a knife. A set of knives.

Images of knives.

Slide 12: Plastic utensils. Keir Dullea as an astronaut.
Slide 13: Woman. Vacuum cleaner.

Both these images have to do with housework.

Slide 14: "Koran." "Torah."

Koran, Torah. (*Then more quickly*) Koran, Torah.

Slide 15: Red chair. Ann Blyth about to eat a red apple.
Slide 16: "Ante up." "Auntie Mame."

Ante up, Auntie Mame.

Slide 17: Woman from Este Lauder ad. Woman from Algeria.

The image on the right is of a woman who had to remove her veil in order for this photograph to be taken. The woman on the left did not have to remove her veil at all.

Slide 18: German designer chair. Masked terrorist.

Germany.

Slide 19: Tupperware. Elizabeth Taylor and Richard Burton in Cleopatra.

Images of nesting.

Slide 20: Tokyo Rose. Joan Collins.

The woman on the right is not Tokyo Rose.

Slide 21: "Flame." "Girlfriend."

Flame, girlfriend.

Slide 22: Man in glasses. Man in glasses.
Slide 23: Elsa Lanchester. And Boris Karloff in the Bride of Frankenstein.
Slide 24: Elsa Lanchester. Elsa Lanchester.

Could we go back, please.

Slide 25: Same as slide 23.

Thank you. These images are really one image. In fact, this image has been cleverly disguised to appear as two images by a superimposed black vertical line. This is one harmonious image rather than two dissonant ones.

Slide 26: Same as 24.

You'll have seen now three images of Elsa Lanchester. She was the wife of the late actor, Charles Laughton.

Slide 27: Algerian woman. Este Lauder woman.

The woman on the left has known invasion in her country. The woman on the right lives in a country that has never been invaded.

Slide 28: Anne Baxter. Janis Joplin.

Hair.

Slide 29: "Think tank." "Tank top."

Think tank, tank top.

Slide 30: Tiny Tim. Mae West.

Mmmm.

Slide 31: Marlene Dietrich looking into a mirror.

This is another cleverly disguised harmonious image, disguised to appear as two dissonant ones. The image is of Marlene Dietrich, a contemporary of Charles Laughton.

Slide 32: "Latent." "Talent."

Latent, talent.

Slide 33: "Diem." "Per Diem."

Diem, per diem.

Slide 34: Carmen Miranda. Carmen Miranda.

Carmen Miranda.

Slide 35: Couple from caveman film. Couple from On the Waterfront.
Slide 36: "Chimera." "Camera."

Chimera, camera. Chimera is Italian for camera.

Slide 37: Bald children. Concrete domes.

Images of roundness.

Slide 38: Juan Peron. Chou En-lai.

Juan Peron, Chou En-lai. Both these images are of men.

Slide 39: "George Raft." "George Sand."

George Raft, George Sand. Images having to do with beaches or water.

Slide 40: Worker. Follies girl.

The person on the left is a man.

Slide 41: "Late." "Et al."

Late, et al. *(Then faster)* Late, et al.

Slide 42: Kennedy. Refugees.

Images of rendezvous.

Slide 43: KKK. Woman holding cross.
Slide 44: Fidel Castro with Khrushchev. Disney with Mickey Mouse.

Images of Disneyland.

Slide 45: "W. Mandela." "W. Mozart."

W. Mandela is alive and is a native of Africa, W. Mozart is dead and was a citizen of Vienna. We hope this presentation has been helpful to you in being able to determine what is alike and what is not alike. What is similar and what is not similar. What the images have in common and how they differ. What is harmonious and what is dissonant. Thank you.

Scene 2
Daphne's Garden

Last slide has faded out with NARRATOR's *last line. Taped sound bumps up immediately: noise of buzzer flush with '60s folk-style werewolf song. As soon as song establishes itself—by the end of last line of lyric—plaque lights start to fade up in blood red, followed by cyclorama lights in blood red. When plaque lights are up to full,* DAPHNE *enters.* SHE *is seen silhouetted against the cyclorama, since no stage lights are up yet.* SHE *seats herself on the downstage folding chair, where* SHE *remains seated throughout the scene. As soon as* SHE *sits and opens her book, her taped voice is heard reading a passage from Jane Austen's* Pride and Prejudice. *In this scene,* DAPHNE *and* ALVIN *are 12 years old.*

DAPHNE *(Taped voice):* "My dear, dear Harriet, you will laugh when you know I am gone, and I cannot help laughing myself at your surprise tomorrow morning as soon as I am missed. For I am going to Gretna Green, and if you cannot guess with who, I shall think you a simpleton, for there is but one man in the world I love."

ALVIN *enters from upstage right, slinking across the back of the stage then zigzagging his way downstage from wing to wing, imitating a werewolf.* HE *is also seen in silhouette.*

"And he is an angel. I should never be happy without him, so think it no harm to be off. You need not send them word at Longbourn of my going if you do not like it, for it will make the surprise the greater when I write to them, and sign my name Lydia Wickham. What a good joke it will be! I can hardly write for laughing. *(Stage lights start to fade up as* ALVIN *gets closer to her)* Pray make my excuses to Pratt, for not keeping my engagement and dancing with him tonight. Tell him I hope he will excuse me when he knows all, and tell him I will dance with him at the next ball we meet—(ALVIN *is directly behind her.* SHE *is completely absorbed in her reading.* HE *mimes tearing out her brains and eating them, etc.)* and with great pleasure. I shall send for my clothes when I get to Longbourn; but I wish you would tell Sally to mend a great slit in my worked muslin gown before they're all packed up. Goodbye. Give my love to Colonel Forster. I hope you will drink to our good journey."

DAPHNE *screams, startled by* ALVIN's *stalking.* HE *laughs. The werewolf song is cut off and a tape of someone practicing on a nearby piano is played softly.*

(Live voice) Oh—you scared me half to death!
ALVIN: Hi Daphne. What are you reading?
DAPHNE: Something you'd neither appreciate nor understand.

ALVIN: Try me.

DAPHNE: I'd like to be alone right now.

ALVIN: I'd like to be alone too—with you.

DAPHNE: You have one trait—persistence. That could get you far.

ALVIN: Well try me.

DAPHNE: What do you want from me?

ALVIN: Everything.

DAPHNE: If I were to grant you even *this* much (*Holding up fingers to show a tiny amount*) of what you request, I'd be casting pearls before swine.

ALVIN: Daphne, take a walk with me.

DAPHNE: I will not take a walk with you—I take my walks forenoon and eve. In the afternoon I *try* to read.

ALVIN: Read my palm.

ALVIN *puts out his palm.* DAPHNE *pushes it away.*

DAPHNE: I can read your mind!

ALVIN: What am I thinking now?

DAPHNE: Must we spin fortune's wheel at this time?

ALVIN: No, but we could spin—

DAPHNE: Put a lid on it, Alvin!

ALVIN: Daphne, come with me to the woods. I'd like to show you something.

DAPHNE: I'd prefer a verbal description, thanks.

ALVIN: Verbal description, eh?

DAPHNE (*Nodding smugly*): Mmm-hmm. (ALVIN *gnaws her neck.* SHE *pushes him away in disgust*) Are you contemplating a rendezvous with maturity at any time in the near future?

ALVIN: Rendez-vous?

DAPHNE: That's French.

ALVIN: Yes, I know—my mother's French.

DAPHNE: And I suppose Papa is as well.

ALVIN: Oui. C'est exact. Absolument. Les deux et moi aussi—toute la famille est française.

DAPHNE: Are you making fun of me?

ALVIN: No!

DAPHNE: Then speak English, please.

ALVIN: You—me—woods come—now.

DAPHNE: Let me explicate the situation for you. . . . My mother is a Johnson.

ALVIN: My mother is a housewife!

DAPHNE: My family *is* coal in this country, Alvin.

ALVIN: My Uncle Emile, he died of black lung!

DAPHNE: I'm president of Honor Society.

ALVIN: I'm an altar boy.

DAPHNE: You're Catholic?!

ALVIN: Aren't you?

DAPHNE: Heavens, no!

ALVIN: Hey Daphne—let's go swimming!

DAPHNE: I don't swim, I sail.

ALVIN: I play stickball.

DAPHNE: I like polo.

ALVIN: My neighbor has polio.

DAPHNE: Daddy has gout.

ALVIN: Daph—could I play my Mel Tormé records for you?

DAPHNE: I'm afraid my taste runs more to *Die Zauberflöte* and *Cosí Fan Tutte!*

ALVIN: I go for spumoni myself!

DAPHNE *(Finally exasperated)*: Tennessee Williams.

ALVIN: Tennessee Ernie Ford.

DAPHNE: Cadillac.

ALVIN: Thunderbird.

DAPHNE: Aristotle.

ALVIN: St. Christopher.

DAPHNE: Magna cum laude.

ALVIN: Magnavox.

DAPHNE: Grace Kelly.

ALVIN: Gina Lollobrigida.

DAPHNE: Champagne.

ALVIN: Champale.

DAPHNE: Fool.

ALVIN: Asshole.

DAPHNE *(Pauses, a look of triumph on her face)*: Alvin.

ALVIN *(Sidles up to her, thinking HE's won her over)*: Daphne?

DAPHNE *(Speaks slowly, with emphasis)*: There are plenty more boys where you come from.

ALVIN *(Looks momentarily perplexed, but continues undaunted)*: What d'ya say, Daph—au bois? Oui ou non? *(DAPHNE turns away, pretending to read)* Je vous attends.

ALVIN *mimics a werewolf again, makes a mock slashing motion at* DAPHNE *and zigzags back upstage for his exit. As* HE *makes his slashing gesture, the werewolf song comes back on. Stage lights fade with his exit, leaving* DAPHNE *in silhouette again.* SHE *closes her book and gets up from chair, looking off after* ALVIN, *trying to decide whether to follow him.*

NARRATOR: Alike, or not alike? Harmonious, or dissonant?

DAPHNE *sits down again. As* SHE *sits, cyclorama lights and plaque lights bump out, as does werewolf song.*

Scene 3
First Day of School

A short cut from a scratchy old opera recording begins to play. At the same time a bell-buzzer sounds briefly. During the sounding of the bell-buzzer the plaque and cyclorama lights come up in an institutional green. When they are up to full, the NARRATOR's *voice is heard.*

NARRATOR (*As* MR. CONKLIN): All rise for the Pledge of Allegiance.

ALL (*Offstage; reciting raggedly, as children*): I pledge allegiance to the flag of the United States of America, and to the republic for which it stands, one nation, under God, indivisible, with liberty and justice for all.

One offstage CHILD *says "Amen."* CHILDREN *can be heard briefly fighting with one another.*

NARRATOR: Be seated. Good morning, everyone. This is Mr. Conklin, your principal. I want to welcome you all to the new school year. (*Stage lights start to fade up*) We hope you had a wonderful vacation. I have a few announcements: the B bus will be leaving on the A bus schedule for today only. I repeat. The B bus will be leaving on the A bus schedule for today only, that's in the north parking lot. Band and chorus tryouts will be held on Friday immediately after the final bell. There will be late buses for those of you who try out. I . . . what? . . . oh . . . I've just been handed another message. The ru-re-remedial reading course will be held on Tuesdays, and for after school, again, there will be late buses. Those of you who wish to sign up please do so. I want your undivided attention. We have a new student today, and I want you to make him feel at home. His name is Buzz.

BUZZ *enters from stage right center, walking briskly, and stands center stage, looking off into stage left wing. The offstage* CHILDREN *are laughing at him, calling him a monkey, etc. Then* ONE OR TWO OF THEM *hush the others.* BUZZ *turns downstage toward the audience, a little embarrassed.* HE *straightens up, folds his arms behind his back and begins to "speak." The* NARRATOR *translates, speaking alternately with* BUZZ.

(*Translating*) I love dinosaurs. Especially Tyrannosaurus rex. The Tyrannosaurus rex has six-inch teeth. His body is as long as a freight train. His jaws are about four feet long. His front legs are short and small, but they end in claws that are like iron. Tyrannosaurus rex is the most terrible animal that ever walked the earth. With his teeth and claws the killer attacks his prey, eats his fill, and slowly the great dinosaur walks into the jungle. There he stretches out beneath a palm tree. No other dinosaur would dare to bother him. Then

Tyrannosaurus rex wakes up hungry again. He goes forth to make another kill. That is his life: killing, eating and sleeping.

When BUZZ *finishes speaking,* HE *turns to face stage right and exits. All lights fade.*

Scene 4
Slapstick #1

At blackout, a tape of Jelly Roll Morton playing the piano comes up. Cyclorama, plaque and stage lights come up together with the music.

A traditional vaudevillian turn is performed. The actor who plays ALVIN *enters as a white* BWANA. HE *wears* ALVIN's *clothes, but has on a pith helmet and a Groucho Marx nose-and-glasses.* HE *carries a pair of binoculars and has a banana in his pocket.* HE *is followed, step by step, by an* APE, *played by the actor who plays* BUZZ, *wearing the same gorilla suit.*

As the BWANA *enters,* HE *is looking through his binoculars and doesn't notice the* APE, *who is always behind him. The* APE *steals the binoculars and looks through them, focusing on the banana in the* BWANA's *pocket. While the* BWANA *is looking about, the* APE *keeps grabbing at the banana but missing it. Then the* BWANA *stands still long enough for the* APE *to attempt to extricate the banana from the pocket. The* APE *pulls at the banana but it won't come out. All this time, the* BWANA's *attention is drawn to the imaginary flora and fauna and* HE *is unaware of the* APE's *attempts. Finally, the* APE *taps the* BWANA's *shoulder and the banana miraculously frees itself from the pocket. The* BWANA *takes back his binoculars and looks around with them again.* HE *sees the* APE *with the banana.* THEY BOTH *jump in fright. Then the* APE *makes signs with its hands and arms: first a wave, then a peace sign, then a fist. Each time, the* BWANA *responds in kind. Next, the* APE *makes the shape of a gun pointing at the* BWANA. *The* BWANA *looks at the "gun" curiously. The* APE *cocks the imaginary trigger. The* BWANA *looks closer. The* APE *pulls the trigger. The* BWANA *recoils holding his chest. The* APE *runs over and gestures that it's all a joke. The* APE *plays some more tricks at the* BWANA's *expense and* THEY *exit together.*

Scene 5
Chez Buzz

Jelly Roll Morton music crossfades with opera cut. All lights crossfade. A STAGEHAND *with a huge rock in his arms crosses from the upstage right wing to the upstage left wing. As* HE *exits,* BUZZ *enters from the downstage left wing carrying two folding chairs which* HE *sets next to each other, downstage right. Noticing dust on them,* HE *exits stage right and returns with a cloth to wipe them.* HE *goes off again and returns with a photo album.* HE *sits down and looks through it. The opera music* surges as LULU enters and stands just inside the centerstage left wing. SHE carries a record album. In this scene, LULU is visiting BUZZ. THEY are post-high-school age.

LULU stands looking lovingly at BUZZ, then crosses the stage toward him, walking to the rhythm of the music. SHE stands next to him, waiting until HE becomes aware of her.

LULU (Handing BUZZ the record): It's opera! I hope you like it!

BUZZ gestures with delight and looks at record. HE gestures and vocalizes that HE likes it.

Ooooo! Oh goody! Oh, I'm so glad.

BUZZ vocalizes and gestures to LULU to sit down as HE exits with the record. LULU looks around at the apartment and fluffs her bouffant hairdo. BUZZ reenters and sits down. LULU picks up the photo album from BUZZ's seat as HE sits.

Thank you. . . . Oh! What are these, Buzz? Pictures?! Oh, these are great! (SHE opens the album at random) I want to start at the beginning! Ooooo! My God! Look at you! Now, this was when you went to Santa Cruz, right?

BUZZ answers.

Boy, you're a regular California beach bum. (BUZZ mimes surfing) So tan! Hey Buzz, did you ever graduate from there?

BUZZ answers.

Ooooo! My God! You look so great in a cap and gown, so distinguished!

BUZZ gets up, asks LULU if SHE wants a drink.

I'd love one!

BUZZ speaks at the same time.

On the rocks, with a twist—ohhh! you always remember!

BUZZ exits stage right to get drinks. LULU continues looking at the pictures, shouting offstage to BUZZ.

Hey Buzz—whatever happened to that guy you were going to build a sailboat with?

BUZZ answers from offstage.

You're kidding! You know, I had a feeling he would go that way.

BUZZ *enters with a drink for* LULU.

These are great, Buzz. Ohhh! I love this one. (HE *hands her drink*) Oh thanks, cheers! (SHE *closes her eyes to savor drink*) Perfect! Perfect!

HE's *delighted* SHE *likes drink*.

Hey Buzz, isn't this you in front of La Scala? I didn't know you spent a year abroad? (BUZZ *holds up four fingers*) You're kidding! When?

BUZZ *goes into a brisk imitation of Italian gestures and vocalizations. At the same time, the opera music, which has been playing softly in the background, rises. Suddenly stopping in the middle of his happy Italian reminiscences,* BUZZ *gestures passionately to* LULU *to listen to the musical passage.*

Yes, it's beautiful! It's beautiful! (*Music subsides to previous level as* BUZZ *points to photo in album*) Oh Buzz, how old were you in this picture? (HE *indicates height of child*) Oh, look at your mother. She's so old world! She's really beautiful. I bet you still write to her. (BUZZ *draws hand across throat indicating that his mother was killed.* SHE *becomes momentarily embarrassed, then makes a rebound*) Oh God! I forgot—well, you look like you had a happy childhood. Ohhh! No! You have these pictures from Mardi Gras! When we all went as baseball players. Oh look—look at Alvin as Pee Wee Reese, Dot as Casey Stengel, Daphne as Joe Di Maggio. Oh no, look at Rudy as Satchel Page. Oh—and you were Yogi Berra, right? (BUZZ *mimes batting*) No—you were Babe Ruth. I was Yogi Berra.
NARRATOR: Lulu?
LULU (*Looking up behind audience*): Yes?
NARRATOR: When was the last time you saw Buzz?

As LULU *gets up, all lights crossfade with a special on her.* BUZZ *continues to look through album.*

LULU: I'd like to answer that question at a later time, if you don't mind.
NARRATOR: No, I don't mind.
LULU: Thank you.

LULU's *special fades to black as* SHE *walks out of it. At the same time, a Pepsi-Cola commercial from the '50s comes on. Cyclorama and plaque lights come up. At the end of commercial's first line,* ALVIN *enters in silhouette just as* HE *did in Scene 2, but this time from upstage left, zigzagging downstage and exiting as commercial ends and bell-buzzer rings.*

Scene 6
Introductions

In this scene, the GIRLS and BOYS are in the second grade. The scene is divided into five vignettes: (1) BUZZ meets DOT; (2) at THE CONKLINS'; (3) DAPHNE meets ALVIN; (4) BUZZ meets RUDY and LULU; (5) end of summer vacation. The dialogue and action counterpoint and complement the music which plays throughout the scene. The sound level is adjusted downwards during the dialogue. Each new section is set up choreographically, the PLAYERS for one section exiting as the PLAYERS for the next enter.

Taped synthesizer music with a driving beat to it comes up, then stage lights. DOT enters from downstage right and starts crossing diagonally to upstage left. SHE's blind. SHE wears dark glasses and carries a cane, which SHE taps. SHE proceeds about five feet then stops, facing diagonally upstage left. SHE stands tapping her cane in time to the music. SHE remains in place for most of the first vignette. MR. and MRS. CONKLIN enter from upstage left with BUZZ, coming downstage right on a diagonal toward DOT, moving slowly. MRS. CONKLIN is a little soused as usual.

MR. CONKLIN: Hello!

DOT: Hello!

MRS. CONKLIN: Hello!

DOT: Hello!

MR. CONKLIN: Hi Dot!

DOT: Hello!

MRS. CONKLIN: Hi Dot!

DOT: Hi!

MR. CONKLIN: Dot, we'd like you to meet Buzz.

DOT: Buzz!

MR. CONKLIN: Buzz, this is Dot.

DOT (Shyly): Dot.

MR. CONKLIN: Dot, this is Buzz.

DOT: Buzz.

MR. CONKLIN: You remember my wife Brenda, don't you Dot?

DOT: Brenda.

MRS. CONKLIN: You can call me Bunny.

DOT: Bunny.

MRS. CONKLIN: Hi, Dot!

DOT: Hi, Bunny.

MR. CONKLIN: Dot, Buzz has come all the way over here from Rwanda.

DOT: Rhode Island?

MRS. CONKLIN: In Africa, Dot.

DOT: Rhode Island in Africa?

MR. CONKLIN (Shouting): Rwanda in Africa, Dot!

MRS. CONKLIN (Disapproving): Daddy!

MR. CONKLIN: Buzz is over here to further his studies.

DOT: His studies, ohhh!

MRS. CONKLIN (*Stroking* BUZZ): He's one of Mr. Conklin's best students, aren't cha, Buzzy!

MR. CONKLIN (*Chuckling*): Why don't you two get together?

THE CONKLINS *shove* BUZZ *toward* DOT.

MRS. CONKLIN (*Nodding in approval*): Get acquainted!

MR. CONKLIN: Have a little tête-à-tête.

MRS. CONKLIN: Aren't they cute, Daddy?! Bye, Dot!

MR. CONKLIN: Goodbye, Buzz!

THE CONKLINS *exit backwards on their upstage diagonal.* DOT *and* BUZZ *join hands and run offstage on the downstage right diagonal. At the same time,* ALVIN *runs in backwards, diagonally, from the upstage left wing, followed by* DAPHNE. THEY *arc around toward the audience.* BUZZ *reenters from downstage right, also backwards, also on a diagonal.* HE *too arcs around to face the audience.* THE CONKLINS *reenter with an imaginary tray of snacks and candy.*

MR. CONKLIN: Hey, kids!

DAPHNE AND ALVIN: Hi!

MRS. CONKLIN: We have some refreshments for you!

MR. CONKLIN: Hello Daphne.

DAPHNE: Mr. Conklin.

MR. CONKLIN: Hello again there, Buzz.

MRS. CONKLIN: Hello Alvin, good to see you.

ALVIN: Hi, Bunny.

MR. CONKLIN: Hey kids, help yourselves. There's Ding-Dongs, there's little Yoo-Hoos, there's Hum-Hums.

MRS. CONKLIN: There's Yo-Yos, and Snick-Snacks, and Doo-Doos and Cheeses. (BUZZ *reaches for one, but* SHE *pulls tray away from him*) Your people don't eat cheese, do they?

BUZZ *shakes his head shyly.*

MR. CONKLIN: Put that in your mouth, Daphne!

MRS. CONKLIN: Eat 'em up, Alvin.

MR. CONKLIN: Alvin, your father find any work yet?

ALVIN *is horrified and hurt by this question and turns away.* MRS. CONKLIN *grabs* DAPHNE *and* BUZZ *by the shoulders.*

MRS. CONKLIN: Are you kids feeling relaxed?

DAPHNE: Totally relaxed.

MRS. CONKLIN: I'm so glad. I was saying to Daddy just the other day, Daddy—

MR. CONKLIN (*Interrupting*): Mother! Take your hands off the children!

MRS. CONKLIN: Good idea! (SHE *shoves them aside and joins* MR. CONKLIN)

MR. CONKLIN: Okay kids! You have a good time now.

MRS. CONKLIN: Enjoy yourselves, young people!

BUZZ *has one arm affectionately on* DAPHNE's *shoulder.* ALVIN, DAPHNE *and* BUZZ *wave.*

MR. CONKLIN: Keep your hands to yourselves.

BUZZ *drops his arm from* DAPHNE's *shoulder.*

MRS. CONKLIN: No hanky-panky!

THE CONKLINS *exit. At the same time* BUZZ *exits backwards and* ALVIN *hunches over downstage left, covering his face with his hands.* DAPHNE *touches* ALVIN's *shoulders and* HE *mimes being the werewolf again, growling at her. The next vignette is played on the diagonal from downstage left toward upstage right.*

DAPHNE (*Startled, but friendly*): Hello—you must be Alvin. I'm Daphne. (SHE *starts to head upstage very slowly as* SHE *speaks*)

ALVIN (*Shyly*): Hi Daphne!

DAPHNE: I'm very, very—rich. You're very, very poor.

ALVIN *turns away in shame for a second, then turns back toward her.*

ALVIN (*Following her upstage*): Can we still be friends?

DAPHNE: Acquaintances—oh, yes—acquaintances.

DAPHNE *quickly exits backwards, pursued by* ALVIN. LULU *enters from downstage right, heading diagonally toward upstage left.*

LULU (*Waving*): Hello, hi there, hello, hi there, hello, hi there, hello.

DOT *and* BUZZ *enter diagonally from upstage left.*

DOT: Lulu, I'd like you to meet Buzz. Buzz this is Lulu!

LULU: Hi, Buzz. You can call me Lu!

RUDY *comes running in from behind* LULU *on downstage right diagonal.*

RUDY: Hi there!

DOT: Rudy, Buzz. Buzz, Rudy.
RUDY: Hi Buzz, you can call me Ru!

RUDY and LULU pull BUZZ by his hands and HE falls forward onto the floor.

DOT: Buzz is a sparkling conversationalist.

LULU and RUDY sigh audibly at this revelation.

RUDY: Buzz, I'm already fascinated by you.
DOT: Why don't you go have a chat?
LULU: Come on, Buzz. (SHE and RUDY grab BUZZ, head back down diagonal toward downstage right) Let's go have some fun!

DOT has been skipping backwards back up her diagonal. SHE comes forward quickly to say her line.

DOT: Have a chitchat!

DOT exits backwards up her entrance diagonal. RUDY and LULU exit with BUZZ. ALL FOUR reenter choreographically, crisscrossing the stage in various configurations, sometimes backwards, sometimes forwards, heading on and off the stage. All this action is in counterpoint to the music.

ALVIN: Hi, Lulu!
LULU: Hi, Alvin!
RUDY: Hi, Dot!
DOT: Hi, Rudy!

More choreographic patterns before the next speech.

LULU: This summer I went to Rainbow Lake. Boy was it fun, tomato sauce and everything.

More choreographic patterns.

DAPHNE: My family took me to Africa to look at the wild animals. It was very boring.

Choreographic patterns are at their most complex.

ALVIN: I made five dollars . . . mowing the lawns. One time, I couldn't sleep all night . . . guess I'll never be a priest.

ALL join hands upstage center facing audience, swaying and singing their summer song.

ALL: In autumn time come quiet days
The mountain wears a golden haze
The vale is closer to the hill
The autumn brings a warning chill
Goodbye! Goodbye!
The summer days are gone
Goodbye! Goodbye!
The summer days are gone
The summer days are gone.
RUDY: Hey Buzz, let's go get some pop!
ALVIN: Did he say pop?! Oh, boy!

ALVIN runs off, followed by EVERYONE ELSE, except DOT. In their excitement, SHE's been left behind.

DOT: I'd love some pop! And some hot dogs, and some ice cream, and some candy, and some Juju-Bees, and some Hum-Hums, and some Tic-Tacs, and some Snoo-Snoos, and some Yo-Yos and some Bim-Bums . . .

Halfway through DOT's speech, DAPHNE enters running and takes her off. Blackout.

Scene 7
Slapstick #2

Jelly Roll Morton music comes on. Plaque lights, cyclorama lights and stage lights bump up as another traditional vaudevillian turn begins.

Like the first slapstick routine, this one is performed by the actor who plays BUZZ as an APE, and the actor who plays ALVIN as a white BWANA. The BWANA wears ALVIN's clothes but with a pith helmet and a Groucho Marx nose-and-glasses. The routine involves the BWANA bringing in folding chairs and carrying them to the opposite side of the stage. The APE keeps moving them back without the BWANA seeing him. At the end of the scene, which consists of variations on this gag, THEY exit.

Scene 8
Questions and Answers

Jelly Roll Morton music fades out as taped sound of someone practicing on an off-stage piano comes up. At the same time, the lights change and we hear RUDY's *voice offstage.*

In this scene the CHARACTERS *are young adults in their 20s. Since it's the mid '60s,* DOT *is now a hippie,* DAPHNE *wears a miniskirt, etc.*

RUDY: All right, now. (HE *enters wearing a white doctor's smock, a clipboard in his hand*) I'd like to get started now, ah. If you could just put your chairs in a line here, it's going to take about ten to fifteen minutes.

The OTHERS *start to enter from downstage right, all except* DOT, *who comes from upstage right, spatially disoriented.* ALVIN *enters last.* ALL *carry folding chairs.*

I'm going to ask some questions, that's all. Don't be afraid. It's okay. I want ahh . . . Daphne to be here. I want Buzz here.

DAPHNE (*Overlapping* RUDY's *last line*): There, Rudy?

RUDY: And I thought maybe Daphne, Alvin, Dot, and Lulu . . . (*Pointing to where* HE *wants them*) If that's okay with you.

LULU: Right over here, Rudy? Oooo! Dot, Dot, Dot! (SHE *helps* DOT *to her place*)

RUDY: Buzz, it's only going to take a couple of minutes. Let's get settled now, shall we. Just put your chairs in a line. Over there, Dot. Good!

DOT: Thanks, Lu.

RUDY: Everybody ready? Everybody comfortable? Okay.

LULU: Almost.

EVERYBODY *is sitting side by side facing the audience except* RUDY, *who is free to move around. During his question-and-answer session, the* OTHERS *ad-lib witty responses, raise their hands and/or shake their heads whenever appropriate.* RUDY *ad-libs interjections to the answers.*

RUDY: Hold your arms out to the side, close your eyes, touch your nose with your right index finger. (THEY *do this*) Very good. Okay, put your arms on top of your head. . . . Turn left, hold out your right leg. Now, anybody feel disassociated from their right foot?

DAPHNE: Absolutely.

LULU: Yeah.

DAPHNE: It's not bad at the moment.

RUDY: Good! Stand up . . . put your left leg out, put your left leg in, put your left leg out. Sit down. . . . Okay, put your right hand on your left wrist. Can you feel your pulse?

THEY *answer, ad-libbing something witty.*

Is it okay? Is it all right?

LULU *(Somewhat to herself):* It's a little slow.

RUDY: Okay, good! Platonic dualism, anybody know about that? (THEY *raise their hands)* Alvin.

ALVIN *(Getting up to answer):* Platonic dualism, that is that the world is separated into two objects: eternal objects and temporal objects. Eternal objects are the only objects we can have a true knowledge of. Temporal objects, those that assail the senses, we can only have an opinion about them.

RUDY: Very good, okay. *(Addressing audience)* Anybody feeling alienated from their body? Anybody ever feel alienated from their body? *(To the others)* All right, put your arms out in front, put your right leg out, stamp your left foot. Very good. I wanna ask you some questions now about how you're feeling at this particular moment, how you're feeling right now. Anybody feeling lonely? (HE *has his hand on* DAPHNE's *shoulder)*

DAPHNE: Not at the moment, Rudy.

RUDY *withdraws his hand quickly. The* OTHERS *ad-lib witty responses.*

RUDY: Anybody feeling, ahh, nervous?

DOT: Oh nervous, yeah nervous!

RUDY: What about angry?

DOT: Oh yeah, anger, yeah anger, yeah!

RUDY: Good. Okay, put your right hand on your chest. Take a deep breath in, and let it out. And in and out, and in and out, and in and out. Okay. Can you feel your heart beating?

LULU *(Laughing):* Are you kidding?

The OTHERS *respond in various ways.*

RUDY: Okay, do you ever feel afraid of dying?

ALL *respond in various ways.*

DAPHNE: Buzz, you're not afraid of dying?

RUDY: Brax Hixton. (ALL *raise their arms to the side, close their eyes, and try to bring the tips of their index fingers together in front of them)* Very good. Okay, an example of syllogistic or deductive inference, Lu.

LULU *(Standing):* That's when you go from the universal to the partiuclar. For example—all high-school students are human beings. Buzz was a high-school student, therefore Buzz is a human being.

RUDY: There you go.

DOT: That's good, Lu.

RUDY: Stand up, sit down, stand up, sit down, stand up, sit down, stand up, sit down, stand up, sit down. (BUZZ *is still standing*) Sit down, Buzz. All right, anybody feel like screaming? (THEY ALL *scream as loud as* THEY *can*) Good. (*To audience*) Anybody else feel like expressing themselves? (LULU *starts to respond,* HE *cuts her off*) Very good. All right now, did it ever occur to you that the person sitting beside you may, through a strange set of circumstances, become very important to you, could become a confidant, or an enemy, could become a lover. (DAPHNE *shakes her head since* SHE's *looking at* BUZZ) All right, very good. Stand up, will you. Put your left leg in, put your left leg out, put your left leg in, and shake it all about. (*Chuckles*) Very good! All right. (*To offstage*) Oh, Dr. Palm. Yeah—we're going to be done here in just a minute. That's a cute little suit you got there—where'd you get that, hmmm? All right—yes. I'll meet you downstairs—yeah—Hunan Palace, you got it. 4:30. (*Back to the others*) All right . . . have you ever felt any of the following—shame. (BUZZ *raises his hand*) Guilt. (BUZZ *and* LULU *raise their hands*) Remorse. (BUZZ, LULU *and* DOT *raise their hands*) Excellent. Let's say you're walking through the forest and you see a large black man carrying a pole . . .

DOT (*Angry*): I can't see.

RUDY: Let's say you're walking through the forest and you sense a large black man carrying a pole. He is (a) a fisherman—(ALVIN *raises his hand*) (b) a mugger—(DOT *raises her hand*) (c) God—(DAPHNE *raises her hand*) (d) a poacher. (BUZZ *raises his hand*) Very good. Okay. Neutral monism, Dot.

DOT (*Standing*): Neutral monism—that is that all is mind and the concept of nature itself is merely a construct of the mind.

RUDY: Very good, Dot. Chromosomes—how many you got, Lu?

LULU: Forty-six.

RUDY: Alvin, you got forty-six?

ALVIN: Forty-six.

RUDY *chooses a song, asks them if* THEY *know it.* THEY *say* THEY *do and start to sing it. After about two lines,* HE *cuts them off.*

RUDY: Very good. Lu, you're an American citizen?

LULU: Yes, I am.

RUDY: Could you tell us a little bit about your heritage, please.

LULU: Yes, I can. (*Standing*) My nationality is Irish Catholic. Occupations include proprietors, priests, politicians . . . and alcoholics. Family name: Hoolihan. Arleen, Coleen, Bernadine, Darlene, Eileen, Geraldine, Kathleen, Maureen, Noreen, Marlene . . .

RUDY: Thank you, Lu. Okay Dot—

DOT: Yeah.

RUDY: Are you an American citizen or not?

DOT: Yeah.

RUDY: Tell us about your heritage, Dot.

DOT (*Standing*): Glad to. My ancestors immigrated to this country in the late 1800s from the shtetls of Russia, Hungary and Poland. They settled on the Lower East Side of Manhattan and worked as tailors, moyels, teachers, rabbis, and glassmakers. Commonly used expressions include gatkes, oy gevalt, gottsedank, 'svet gornisht helfn, kinehore, and azoy geyt es in Amerike.

RUDY: Very good. Alvin, you're an American citizen aren't you?

ALVIN (*Standing*): Yeah, I'm an American.

RUDY: Tell us a little bit about your upbringing.

ALVIN: Well, I was born in this country, my parents were born in Canada, their parents were born in Brittany, France except for my grandmother on my father's side. She was an Algonquin Indian. Yeah. Trades include factory workers, paper-mill workers, lumberjacks, and mushroom gatherers.

RUDY: What about you, Daphne?

DAPHNE (*Standing*): I'm American . . . hundred percent . . . pure bred . . .

RUDY: Excellent. Buzz, you're an American citizen?

BUZZ *grunts.*

Oh, you're getting your papers. Well, tell us about your heritage, will you?

Tape of ominous music comes on, very low, to suggest distance between the events that BUZZ will recount and the present. When BUZZ gets up from his seat, all lights crossfade with a special on BUZZ. EVERYONE ELSE exits. BUZZ steps forward. HE makes sounds to tell his tale. The NARRATOR translates simultaneously.

NARRATOR (*Translating*): My family is from Rwanda, near the Congo. I was born on Mount Visoge, above the ten-thousand-foot level. My father was a silver-back, and my mother was the ranking female of our group. Mostly we ate Vernonia blossoms and, after the rains stopped, bamboo. I had a sister and two brothers, three half-sisters and two half-brothers. Both of my brothers got caught in poacher traps, contracted pneumonia and died. My mother was killed during a violent clash with another group. When I was seven years old, my father was decapitated, his hands and feet cut off and sold as souvenirs to a traveling European. They are now on display at Number 12 Barnestrasse, Frankfurt, West Germany, on a table in a parlor next to a nineteenth-century samovar from Kiev.

Special on BUZZ goes to black.

Scene 9
Bus Stop

Sound of gentle rain is heard. All stage lights fade up. The STAGEHAND *enters from upstage right wing with a boulder in his arms, crosses to upstage left wing and exits.* HE *reenters from centerstage left wing, pauses center stage to put the boulder down.*

NARRATOR: No. Not now.

STAGEHAND *crosses to centerstage right wing and exits.* LULU, *in a yellow slicker, comes running on from the centerstage right wing.*

    In the following scene the CHARACTERS *are second-graders who have just been let out of school.* THEY *ad-lib where appropriate.* THEY *play most of the scene facing the audience and the imaginary teachers who pass through the scene are always downstage of them.*

LULU *(Looking off left)*: Ohhh! Wait a minute, no wait a minute. Ohhh! Wait, wait, no wait, wait. *(Shouts)* Hold the bus! *(*SHE*'s missed the bus. Waiting for the next one,* SHE *fidgets, draws on a pad, etc.* SHE *speaks to an imaginary teacher)* Good afternoon, Mr. Psacheropolis.

After a moment or two with only the sound of the rain, RUDY *enters from centerstage right in a yellow slicker, hopping from one imaginary puddle to another.* HE *jumps into a puddle next to* LULU.

    Hey! *(*SHE *goes back to drawing on her pad)*
RUDY: Where's the bus?
LULU *(Nose in her pad)*: None of your B.I. business.

THEY *laugh and play a hand-slapping game.*

RUDY: Gimme some gum.
LULU *(Mimicking him)*: Gimme some gum.
RUDY: Come on, gimme some gum.
LULU *(Laughing at him)*: Oh come on, gimme some gum.
RUDY *(Shouts)*: Gimme some gum!

LULU *shrinks from him as if to say "Okay, okay, already!" and pulls a piece of gum out of her mouth.* SHE *hands it to him.* HE *puts it in his mouth, then sneaks a look at what* SHE*'s drawing.* SHE *hides it from his view.* THEY *whistle "Whistle While You Work."* DOT, *in a yellow slicker, enters alone from centerstage right.*

DAPHNE *(Offstage)*: Wait up, Dot . . . I'm coming . . . I'll be right there.

ALVIN *comes running in, followed by* DAPHNE. HE *grabs* DOT *by her cane and pulls her about, tormenting her.*

ALVIN: Hey Dot, this way, this way, this way.
DAPHNE *(Overlapping* ALVIN's *line)*: Alvin, stop bothering Dot—you're always bothering her—it's not fair.
DOT: Alvin, it's not funny.

ALVIN *laughs, lets go of* DOT. SHE *falters in front of* RUDY, *who grabs her.* HE *stands her between himself and* LULU. *Meanwhile* ALVIN *has seen a letter in* DAPHNE's *hand.* HE *swipes it and runs around the group with it,* DAPHNE *giving chase.*

RUDY: Seen any good movies lately, Dot?

DOT *hits* RUDY's *foot with her cane.* DAPHNE *runs after* ALVIN *around the group.* ALVIN *cackles maniacally.*

DAPHNE: Alvin, give it back. Alvin, Alvin come on, gimme the letter . . . I just got it today. Give it here, Alvin.

The OTHERS *join in the fun of the game and when* ALVIN *lands facing* DAPHNE, *laughing, holding the letter behind him with his back to* RUDY, RUDY *grabs it and passes it daisy-chain style down the line to* LULU.

Rudy . . . Dot . . . Lulu.

THEY *are interrupted by a teacher on his way out from school.*

ALL: Good afternoon, Mr. White.

Pause as THEY *turn their heads centerstage left, following the teacher off.* RUDY *and* ALVIN *converse inaudibly during the following exchange.*

DAPHNE: Lu, let me have it . . .
LULU *(Giving her the letter)*: Who's it from?
DAPHNE: It's from my brother, Arthur.
LULU: Oooh, the cute one?
DAPHNE: Yeah, he's overseas. . . . He writes me every couple of weeks. Look at the stamps for my collection! Let's look at it later—you can come over to my house.

DAPHNE *folds the letter up. Meanwhile* ALVIN *is inching toward* DOT, *up to no good again.* HE *lights a match and passes it in front of* DOT's *dark glasses.*

ALVIN: Hey Dot, see the light? (HE *turns* DOT *to face upstage*) This way, this way, the bus is coming this way, Dot.

DOT: Alvin, you're such a pain in the neck!

LULU (*With disgust*): Oh Alvin, cut it out.

DAPHNE: Grow up!

ALVIN's *got his hand on* DOT's *neck.*

DOT: What are you doing now?

ALVIN (*Lets go, laughing*): I'm being a pain in the neck.

LULU: Alvin, go stick your head in the toilet bowl.

ALVIN *turns his butt toward* LULU *and makes a farting noise.*

DAPHNE: It's so funny I forgot to laugh.

RUDY: Oh, go blow it out your ass, Daphne.

LULU: Oh yeah? Well, your ass looks like my face.

RUDY: Yeah, go put a bag over your face, ugly head.

DAPHNE: Thrills, chills and vibrations.

DOT (*With* DAPHNE *and* LULU *egging her on*): Well, when God gave out brains, you thought he said trains, he said make mine a choo-choo!

EVERYBODY's *silent, not getting* DOT's *point.*

LULU: I don't get it.

ALVIN (*Pulls an imaginary booger from his nose and hands it to* DAPHNE): Hey Daphne, booger salad. (HE *laughs*)

DAPHNE: Would you like a warm lunch, I'm ready to vomit.

ALVIN: Hey Rudy, you know what I smell, I smell three things, I smell farts, I smell halitosis, and I smell B.O.

LULU: Oh Alvin, your mother feeds you out of the toilet bowl.

RUDY: Oh yeah, I know what you are, but what am I?

LULU: Drop dead.

DAPHNE: Double likewise and no returns.

RUDY: Oh, fuck you!

THEY *all pretend to be shocked.*

LULU: I'm tellin'!

An imaginary teacher passes.

ALL: Good afternoon, Mrs. D'Amato.

THEY *follow her with their heads, imitate her and call her names after she's gone.*

DOT: Garlic breath!

LULU: Ohhh! You know what she did this morning? Listen to this. She came into class and she said, "Class, I want you to put your heads down right now." She said, "I want you to put your heads down and don't peek." Right? She said, "Class, I am very sorry, but I forgot to wear a slip to school today and I'm going to put it on right now."

THEY *laugh and ad-lib.*

DAPHNE: She didn't wear a slip to school? (SHE *bursts into giggles*)

LULU: She said, "I'm going to put it on right now, don't peek, okay?"

ALVIN: You were peeking, right?

LULU: Yeah, I was lookin', I was lookin'. So then, so then, she unbuttoned the first button of her blouse, right?

ALVIN: Ohh, ohh, ohh, did you see anything? Did you see anything?

LULU: Oh, wait a minute, wait a minute! She unbuttons the second button of her blouse and I saw the crack—(THEY *all laugh*) and then she unbuttoned the third button of her blouse and took off her entire shirt . . .

ALVIN (*Shouts*): Did you see her tits!?!

ALL (*Surprised by a teacher*): Good afternoon, Mr. Sikorsky.

THEY *slowly turn heads as teacher leaves stage left.*

LULU: Alvin—gazongas. (*Hands him sketch*) This is what she looks like.

ALVIN (*Laughing, passing it on*): Look at that, Rudy.

THEY *all laugh.*

RUDY (*Showing it to* DOT): Check it out, Dot.

DOT: Come on, Rudy. You know I can't see that.

LULU (*Looking at* DAPHNE's *letter*): Look at all the funny writing.

ALVIN *snatches letter from* DAPHNE.

ALVIN (*To* RUDY, *mimicking* LULU *in a falsetto*): Look at all the funny writing.

DAPHNE (*Grabbing letter back*): None of your beeswax Alvin, thank you very much.

ALVIN: Who's it from?

DAPHNE: It's from my brother Arthur—the one who got all the football trophies. He's overseas.

RUDY: Yeah, well what's he doing over there?

DAPHNE: Me to know and you to find out.

LULU: He's got his head in a toilet bowl—what do you think?

RUDY: Hey, c'mon. What's he doing there?

DAPHNE: He's in the service.

RUDY: Oh yeah? Is he a general or something?

DAPHNE: He's a lieutenant. Would you like to make a Federal case out of this?

RUDY: Oh yeah? What's he doing—dropping bombs on the gooks?

ALVIN *and* RUDY *start imitating war movies: fighter planes, machine guns, soldiers with bayonets yelling "Take that, you Yankee dog!" At the same time, the* GIRLS *are gossiping, looking at photos.*

DOT: They're so immature.

LULU: Oooh, you should see, Dot. What cute girlfriends.

DAPHNE: And you know what—he's still pinned to Mary Anne Jensen.

LULU: You're kidding?

DAPHNE: They got engaged right after graduation . . . . He's coming home in three weeks.

DOT: I remember Arthur.

DAPHNE: Yeah, you came to our house for dinner that time—

LULU (*Greeting a teacher*): Oh hi, Mr. Snow.

The BOYS *are stopped short in mid-mischief: "Die, you Yankee dog!"*

DAPHNE (*Folding her letter*): Hi Mr. Snow. I'll just put my letter away. (*Teacher says something to her*) Me, Mr. Snow? To the *office?* (SHE *turns to the others, perplexed, shrugs and waves*) See you guys. (SHE *exits centerstage right*)

ALVIN: Hey Daphne, see if you can buy me an "A" too, okay?

LULU (*Shouts*): Shut up, Alvin!

DOT: Where—where's Daphne going?

LULU: She's got to go to the office.

RUDY: Where's the bus?

LULU: None of your B.I.

THEY *whistle "Whistle While You Work."*

ALVIN (*Singing to melody*): Mussolini stepped on his weenie and now it doesn't work. Whistle while you work, Hitler is a jerk, Mussolini stepped on his weenie and—

DAPHNE (*Offstage; screams, sobs*): No! Make it not be true! Arthur, no! My favorite brother! Oh no!

DAPHNE *continues sobbing offstage.* BUZZ *runs in from centerstage right.*

LULU: Buzz, what happened?

BUZZ *answers, turns and looks offstage right toward* DAPHNE, *then runs off.* DOT, LULU, ALVIN *and* RUDY *say the following lines as* THEY *move in a line, backwards, toward offstage left.*

ALL: Yellow-belly commies, gooks, dirty Chinese bastards, pinko chinko, commie bastards, greaseball, Arab wog bastards, scumbag, honky, nigger, spear-chucker, Irish mackerel snapper, jungle bunny, faggot, jigaboo, redneck Jew bastard, Turk—

BUZZ *enters from centerstage right, steps in five feet or so as the last of the* KIDS *are going off.* THEY *continues their litany of abuse offstage until* THEY're *done.*

—colonial imperialist, Yankee go home, Arab dogs, Polack, goddam slant-eyes, wop, white-cracker assholes, Catholic, slopehead, spic, kike, nigger-lover, wetback.

At the words "colonial imperialist," taped sound of Schubert's String Quartet in C Major, op. 163 comes up. When the OTHERS *are all offstage,* BUZZ *stands center stage looking up, as if at the rain which can still be heard falling.* HE *turns in place slowly, clockwise, and as* HE *turns, cards with the word "RAIN" on them fly in. Interspersed with them are cards with names of countries currently in conflict on them—Sri Lanka, Israel, South Africa—one name to a card. The cards are all of uniform dimension. When* BUZZ *has completed his clockwise turn and is facing downstage again, the lights begin to fade. Schubert quartet and sound of rain fade out.* BUZZ *exits.*

Scene 10
Prom Nite

Music comes up. a tape loop of the '50s ballad "I Thought about You," which plays throughout the scene. A mirror ball descends and hangs above center stage. Cyclorama and plaque lights fade up, then stage lights.
    In this scene, EVERYONE *is dressed appropriately for prom night. All the movement is choreographed.* LULU *and* BUZZ *enter at the same time,* LULU *from downstage right,* BUZZ *from downstage left.* THEY *come toward each other and meet center stage.*

LULU: Oh Buzzie, you must be so excited. When do you have to register? Oh Buzz, you're gonna love California. Oh, it's so beautiful out there. Oh—and you have to go to this restaurant called House of Hunan. They have great noodles there . . . . My father always gets two orders . . .

During LULU's *speech,* DOT *comes running on from downstage right and* RUDY *from downstage left.* THEY *have their arms outstretched to meet center stage but* THEY *miss and go past one another. When* LULU *has spoken her last line,* SHE *dances up center stage with* BUZZ. *Then* THEY *dance upstage right and exit.* RUDY *grabs* DOT *and* THEY *stand center stage.*

RUDY (*Chuckling*): Hey Dot, you are outta sight, baby. Watch out, Dot!

RUDY *and* DOT *dance upstage.* DAPHNE *enters from downstage right and* ALVIN *from downstage left.* THEY *are walking to the music.*

DAPHNE: It's our last night, Alvin—let's bury the hatchet. Truce?
ALVIN: Agreed.

HE *grabs* DAPHNE *center stage and* THEY *dance upstage like the two previous couples.*

DOT: Rudy, you're such a jerk!

RUDY *and* DOT *dance off quickly.*

ALVIN: I'm so glad you said that, Daphne. Hey, you think I can put your father's name on my job application? I want to be a mailman.
DAPHNE: Oh sure, Alvin . . . whatever.
ALVIN: What are you doing this summer?
DAPHNE: I leave tomorrow for my archeological dig.
ALVIN: Where are you going?
DAPHNE: Morocco.

BUZZ *enters downstage right,* RUDY *downstage left,* BOTH *walking to the music.*

ALVIN: Morocco?

ALVIN *and* DAPHNE *spin off upstage right.* BUZZ *and* RUDY *land center stage.* DOT *enters downstage left.* LULU *enters downstage right.*

RUDY: Hey Buzz! Hey Buzz! Have you given any thought to Jesus? No? You know about Jesus, don'tcha Buzz? Oh Christ, he was a Jew.

DOT *and* LULU *stop downstage center.*

LULU: Dot!
DOT: Lu! I'm gonna miss you so much, Lu.
LULU: I'm gonna miss you too.
DOT: You have my number, right?
RUDY: His mother was a virgin.
LULU: Yeah, I have your number.

RUDY (*Exiting upstage left*): 566-6666.
DOT: Don't forget to call.
LULU: I won't forget, Dot.
DOT: Don't forget to write, Lu.
LULU: I won't forget to write.

LULU dances upstage right with BUZZ. DAPHNE enters from downstage right with her left shoulder strap pulled down, adjusting it as SHE enters. SHE crosses downstage in a hurry, followed by an apologetic but drunk ALVIN.

DAPHNE: Alvin, tonight was going to be different. We had an agreement!
LULU (*To DOT*): Keep in touch.

DAPHNE exits downstage left. ALVIN spins around and does a spastic, drunken, whirling dance, moving diagonally from downstage left toward upstage right. HE is followed by RUDY, who is shadowboxing, moving upstage on the same diagonal. LULU and BUZZ, who have been dancing, exit upstage right. DAPHNE reenters almost immediately from centerstage left, grabs DOT.

DAPHNE: Dot, I've got to talk to you. Alvin is worse than ever.

DAPHNE and DOT exit downstage left. ALVIN and RUDY exit on their upstage diagonal. Lights change. ALL run back on from upstage. THEY form three couples symmetrically distributed against the cyclorama: RUDY with DOT on the right, ALVIN and DAPHNE center stage, LULU and BUZZ on the left. The COUPLES dance downstage in three straight lines with a choreographed spin here and there. THEY stop.

RUDY: Memphis! What're you talking about there, Dot? Memphis?
LULU: Buzz!
DOT: I'm going down to be with my people, Rudy.
RUDY: What do you mean—your people?
DOT: I'm talking about Blind Lemon Jefferson, Blind Willie McTell, Blind Boy Fuller, Big Mama Thornton, Bessie Smith, Ma Rainey and John Lee Hooker.
ALVIN: Morocco, Daphne?
DAPHNE: That's right, Alvin.
RUDY: But those are black rhythm-and-blues singers, Dot.
ALVIN: With all those dark-skinned men!
DOT: That's right, bro'!
DAPHNE: I can't help it, I'm fascinated by Arab culture!
RUDY: Have you looked in the mirror lately, Dot?
ALVIN: But I love you, Daph!
DAPHNE: I'm sorry.
RUDY: You're a white Jewish girl from Scarsdale.
DOT: I'm a soul singer, brother!

DOT *sings "John Henry" as* SHE *and* RUDY *dance back upstage.* LULU, *who has been trying to make out with* BUZZ, *is rejected by him.* HE *runs upstage followed by* LULU. ALVIN *and* DAPHNE *are still downstage center but starting to move back upstage.*

RUDY: Forget it. It ain't gonna work, sweetheart.
LULU *(As* SHE *runs after* BUZZ*)*: Buzz! Buzz!
ALVIN: Here's a little something I got for you.

DAPHNE *ad-libs her protest.*

I hope you like it. I had it inscribed on the back . . . (SHE *protests some more.* HE *gets mad*) Fine! Go to Morocco! Cover up your face like some Arab princess, I don't care!

ALVIN *goes upstage.* LULU *dances with* RUDY, ALVIN *with* DOT, DAPHNE *with* BUZZ, *as if nothing has happened. Then* THEY ALL *exit.* BUZZ *runs in from downstage left.* LULU *runs in chasing after him.*

LULU: Oh Buzz! Oh Buzz! Let's do it, come on, let's do it tonight Buzz. I'm ready, I'm willing, I'm able. Buzz—I'm hot to trot!

BUZZ *and* LULU *exit as* RUDY *runs in laughing from downstage right and* DOT *from downstage left.* THEY BOTH *have their arms outstretched.* THEY *pass each other at center stage, then turn and come back toward center stage again.*

RUDY: Dot. Dance with me you crazy fool! Come on!

DOT *sings "John Henry."* SHE *and* RUDY *dance to upstage center.* DAPHNE *enters from downstage left followed by* ALVIN, *who is chasing after her like a dejected puppy dog.*

DAPHNE: Alvin, no. I won't have it.
ALVIN: Think of it, Daph—I could carry your bags for you. I'll get a passport when I go to the post office for my job interview.
DAPHNE: It's too humiliating.

DAPHNE *exits, leaving* ALVIN *on stage with his tail between his legs.* BUZZ *enters strolling jauntily from downstage right.* ALVIN *stops him.*

ALVIN (HE *has pulled out a pint of Jack Daniel's*): Hey Buzz, have a drink.

BUZZ *protests* HE *doesn't want one.*

Come on, buddy, drink with me. (BUZZ *shakes his head*) Come on Buzz. *(Shouts)* Hey you fucking monkey—drink!

LULU *and* DAPHNE *enter from downstage right.* THEY *watch* BUZZ *and* ALVIN, *who exit downstage right.*

DAPHNE: See what I mean? It's sickening—and I'm supposed to yield to that because of his desires?
LULU: Don't subject yourself to him, Daphne. He's a real turd.
DAPHNE: Thanks, Lulu.

As LULU *and* DAPHNE *exit downstage right,* BUZZ *and* ALVIN *stagger on drunk from upstage left.* ALVIN *beats his chest and makes* clichéd *gorilla sounds.*

ALVIN: Hey Buzz, is this how it goes?

BUZZ *and* ALVIN *laugh and stagger off.* LULU *runs on, followed by* DAPHNE.

LULU: Oh Daphne, do you think he'll ever change his mind?
DAPHNE: Of course he will. The animal urge will take over.

DAPHNE *and* LULU *exit.* EVERYBODY *runs back on except* ALVIN, *who staggers in drunk from downstage left heading toward* DAPHNE. DOT *suddenly stops dancing.*

DOT: I've had it! I'm sick and tired of the way you've been treating me all these years! You've made fun of me, played tricks on me . . . . You've treated me like I'm a freak! Well, what about Buzz?! He's a fucking monkey and you don't give him half the shit you give me!

DAPHNE *comes over to* DOT *and* DOT *yells at her.* DAPHNE *is totally shocked and angered.* THEY *fight.* RUDY *comes over and* DOT *slaps him aside.*

LULU *(Screaming):* This is terrible!

LULU *runs off.* RUDY *exits.* BUZZ *is flying drunk and starts to vomit. The prom falls apart.* MR. *and* MRS. CONKLIN *appear downstage right and* EVERYBODY *freezes.*

MR. CONKLIN *(*HE's *bombed):* Bunny, Bunny, Bunny.
MRS. CONKLIN *(Drunk as usual):* Oh Daddy, doesn't it do your heart good to see these kids enjoying themselves?
MR. CONKLIN: I'm so happy, I'm so goddam happy.
MRS. CONKLIN: Just think, Daddy. This is their salad days!
MR. CONKLIN: Salad . . . Bunny!

THEY *laugh.*

MRS. CONKLIN: Oh Daddy, you're so cute. Make me another drink, Daddy.
MR. CONKLIN: Speak to me, baby.

THE CONKLINS *exit downstage right.* ALVIN *and* BUZZ *are left on stage vomiting.* DAPHNE *is shouting at* DOT *as* DOT *exits centerstage right.*

DAPHNE *(Backing off centerstage left):* I told you the plots of the latest movies. I helped you with your math homework. I encouraged your interest in music. I had you over to my house for dinner. I helped pick out your wardrobe. I always treated you as a friend, Dot! (SHE *exits)*

BUZZ *and* ALVIN *have worked their way upstage left to pee. The last lines of "I Thought about You" are heard as all lights fade.*

Scene 11
Testimonials

Simple, repetitive synthesizer music with an eerie edge to it begins. The cyclorama and plaque lights come up blood red. The STAGEHAND, *carrying the rock, crosses the stage in silhouette from upstage right to upstage left;* HE *reenters from centerstage left, exits centerstage right. Meanwhile slides are projected, each one showing a year: 1959, 1960, 1961, 1962, 1963, 1964, 1965, 1966, 1967, 1968. The* STAGEHAND *reenters downstage right and is about to put the rock down.*

NARRATOR: No, not yet.

STAGEHAND *exits downstage left.*

One, two, three, four, five.

LULU, RUDY, DOT, ALVIN *and* DAPHNE *enter in that order from downstage left. Five specials come up, one for each character.*

Brax Hixton, please. (THEY *raise their arms parallel to the ground, then bring the index fingers of each hand toward each other until the tips of the fingers touch)* Very good. Lulu.
LULU: Yes?
NARRATOR: When was the last time that you saw Buzz?
LULU: Well. This was a while ago. I still had my Mustang. I picked him up at his apartment and we went to House of Hunan for dinner. We both love that place. I had the crispy duck, he had the noodles. And then we got fortune cookies and his said: The answer that you seek is in an envelope. Mine said: Your house is an infinite mystery. So—we took a ride up the coast and—just on a whim—I drove into a motel parking lot and checked us both in. He was a little stunned. He didn't say anything and . . . . Then when we got to the room, he just sat on the edge of the bed like he was waiting to have

his temperature taken. I slipped off my bra. I took off my panties. I said, "Is this all right, Buzz?" He nodded so I started caressing him, you know . . . but—when I tried to kiss him he wouldn't let me. So, I took his face in my hands and I said, "Buzz, look at me—look at me. I've loved you for all these years—couldn't you ever love me?" He shook his head. So I put my clothes back on and we drove back to the city. Neither of us said a word. And after that I had to go out of town to see someone, and—when I got back, he was gone. And I never saw him again.

LULU *hurries off in tears. Her special goes out as* SHE *exits downstage right.*

NARRATOR: Rudy, when was the last time that you saw Buzz?
RUDY: Buzz, oh Buzz, oh yeah. He was a nice guy, huh? A really pleasant fellow. Big guy. Yeah. Whatever happened to him?

RUDY *exits downstage right. His special goes out.*

NARRATOR: Dot.
DOT: Let's see. I ran into Buzz at the opera and afterwards we went to a cafe and had some espresso. Well, I had been through some pretty heavy changes and so had Buzz. Buzz was always such a trip. Anyway, we were talking about personal growth and—what do you do when you can't improve yourself anymore? I mean, you can alter your state for so long before you hit a wall. It happens to everyone. So, we were getting into a kind of a mock despair and playing "Can You Top This?" and I said that I would go off and become a hermit and he said that he would go and break all his opera records. Then I said I would go jump into a fast-flowing river and he said that he would put out to sea in a rowboat with no oars. Then I said I'd go hiking in the Grand Canyon with no food and he said that he would get into a car, drive cross-country with no money and a half a tank of gas. So then I said that I would climb Mount Everest in ballet slippers and he said he'd jump off Mount Everest. Well, by the time we got done talking it must have been about four in the morning, so I took Buzz in a cab to his home. Oh—and as he was getting out of the car, I asked him if he had seen Rudy lately and just as the door was closing I heard him smile.

DOT *exits downstage right. Her special goes out.*

NARRATOR: Alvin.
ALVIN: The last time I saw Buzz, he was riding by on a bus. I saw him sitting in the back. I said, "Hey Buzz!" I guess he didn't hear me. But it's funny you should ask me this question, because there isn't a day that goes by when I don't think about Buzz. You know, I'm still wondering what it was he had, why all the girls fell for him, what I didn't have. I bet he still has it.

NARRATOR: Anything else?

ALVIN: Ah . . . yeah. Yeah, there's something you might not know. He was one hell of a hockey player.

ALVIN *exits downstage right. His special goes out.*

NARRATOR: Daphne, when was the last time you saw Buzz?

DAPHNE: Oh . . . . The last time I saw Buzz. Hmmm.

Music tape cross-bumps with the sound of crickets. BUZZ *enters.* DAPHNE *walks over to him, greets him, sits on ground next to him, takes off her sandals. Looking at the night sky,* BUZZ *sees a shooting star.*

Oooh! (*Pause.* SHE *points*) Buzz . . . is that Cassiopeia right here overhead? (BUZZ *moves her arm over*) You know, I'm going to ask Dot to bring another six pack tomorrow—just to be safe. Do we have enough paper plates and cups? (SHE *stands up.* BUZZ *gets up and moves to another spot.* SHE *moves over and sits next to him*) Buzz, you're going to laugh . . . you know what I always think of on a night like this? I think of Beethoven, his third symphony where—

BUZZ *interrupts and draws "7" on ground.*

His seventh, you're right. Yeah, Beethoven's Seventh. (*Pause*) What d'you say? Think there's life out there?

BUZZ *disagrees.*

Well, not people necessarily, but something alive.

BUZZ *speaks.*

Not just kooks . . . a lot of serious scientists consider it a good possibility. (BUZZ *is sorrowful.* HE *gets up and moves to a third spot.* HE *is silent and looks up.* HE *moves to a fourth spot upstage left.* SHE *joins him*) Do we have enough knives?

BUZZ *asks a question.*

Oh, tons of barbecue sauce! (BUZZ *gets up as* HE *sees shooting star.* SHE *gets up to look but misses it*) I'm convinced of it. There's got to be life out there!

BUZZ *speaks.*

Why not? There could be two people gazing at the night sky, looking right down on us, asking all the same questions we're asking . . .

BUZZ *waves up at the imaginary people, makes a sound.* DAPHNE *waves.* BUZZ *exits upstage left. When* DAPHNE *sees* BUZZ *is gone,* SHE *follows him off in a hurry.*

Scene 12
At the Zoo

As BUZZ *and* DAPHNE *exit, the sound of crickets cross-bumps with sounds of a public park. The* STAGEHAND *enters upstage right with his rock and walks to centerstage right.*

NARRATOR: Yes, now. (STAGEHAND *starts to put rock down*) Not there. (STAGEHAND *moves rock*) No, not there. (STAGEHAND *moves it again*) Very good.

The STAGEHAND *brings on more rocks. When* HE *has finished, a diorama-like setting has been completed: a habitat for an animal. A rubber tire hangs from a rope centerstage left. A* GORILLA *enters. The* GORILLA *is played as realistically as possible.*

DAPHNE(*Off; from downstage left*): Oh honey, I thought you were packing extra Wash 'n' Dri's . . . . Chippy, do you have to throw up everything we give you to eat? Must've been that cheese.

DAPHNE *enters downstage with a baby carriage, followed by* BUZZ. THEY *are silhouetted against the brightly lit* GORILLA's *habitat upstage of them.* DAPHNE, *who appears completely uninterested in her own baby, stops to look for her compact in her bag.*

(*Looking in the mirror*) Look at the monkey, honey . . .

BUZZ *makes a sound to the imaginary baby, pointing toward the* GORILLA.

Yes, very big. And very ugly.

BUZZ *asks a question.*

I don't know, Buzz. It's already pretty late.

THEY *exit downstage right. Enter* BARKER.

BARKER: Souvenirs, get your souvenirs here, peanuts, popcorn, souvenirs, stuffed animals, peanuts, popcorn, souvenirs, balloons, Cracker Jacks.
DAPHNE (*From offstage*): Get him a snack, honey, some Cracker Jacks or something.

BUZZ *enters, buys Cracker Jacks from* BARKER, *exits again downstage right.* BARKER *tosses a peanut to* GORILLA.

BARKER: Here you are, chimp. (*Starts to exit downstage right*) Souvenirs, souvenirs, stuffed animals, peanuts, popcorn, Cracker Jacks, souvenirs, balloons.

The GORILLA *is left alone on stage. A scratchy old recording of a plaintive aria begins to play. The* GORILLA *pushes the peanut around, loses interest and goes to climb on the rubber tire.* HE *gets off, drags the tire back a ways, lets it go, jumps up on the highest boulder and watches it swing.* HE *comes back down and jumps on the tire. It swings offstage, then swings back on. It swings back off, then on again, but this time the* GORILLA *is gone. The tire is left on stage, swinging. Rain tape has snuck in under the aria. The aria fades out, leaving the sound of the rain. The tire swings, slowing down. The stage lights fade out, followed by the cyclorama and plaque lights and the sound of the rain.*

END OF PLAY

T Bone N Weasel
Jon Klein

About Jon Klein

Jon Klein is a native of Kentucky now living in Minnesota, where he is a member of The Playwrights' Center. His plays include *Losing It, Bluegrass, Private Places*, and two plays developed in collaboration with Illusion Theater, Minneapolis—*Southern Cross*, and *The Einstein Project* (co-authored with Paul D'Andrea). These plays have received productions at Off-Broadway, regional and university theatres, including Provincetown Playhouse in New York; Wisdom Bridge Theatre in Chicago; Actors Theatre of St. Paul; Alley Theatre in Houston; and, in Minneapolis, Illusion Theater, Brass Tacks Theatre and the Walker Arts Center. His plays have been developed at Midwest PlayLabs on three occasions, and at the Sundance Institute Playwrights Laboratory in Utah. Klein was the recipient of an FDG/CBS New Play Award for *Losing It*, and has received Bush, McKnight, Jerome and Minnesota State Arts Board fellowships.

About the Play

T Bone N Weasel was developed at Midwest PlayLabs, a program of The Playwrights' Center in Minneapolis. It was originally produced by Quicksilver Stage, Minneapolis, in December 1986. The play's professional premiere, under the direction of Steven Dietz, was at Actors Theatre of Louisville where it was presented as part of the Eleventh Annual Humana Festival of New American Plays March 6-22, 1987. Subsequent productions include those at Studio Arena Theatre in Buffalo, Victory Theatre in Los Angeles and Market Street Theatre in Philadelphia. The play was circulated as a *Plays in Process* script in the fall of 1987.

Playwright's Note

The reader will notice that this play contains no stage directions. My intention in writing the script in this way was to free directors and designers to use their own staging concepts rather than mine. At the same time, I wanted to suggest that the focus of the play in production should be almost exclusively on the actors and that whatever staging concept was used, it should be as simple as possible.

The scene titles (including *Intermission*) are an integral part of the play and are always incorporated into the production. At Actors Theatre of Louisville they were announced as voice-overs as the lights came up on each scene. At Studio Arena Theatre a visual device was used that suggested the destination scroll on a bus.

Finally, I hope that the humor in this play won't divert the reader from its serious implications. On one level, *T Bone N Weasel* is about the development of a friendship. On another, it's about the growing awareness of social injustice in two people accustomed to being its victims. This is why one actor plays nine of the roles: Injustice takes many forms but always has a familiar face.

Characters

T-BONE, black man, mid-30s.
WEASEL, white man, younger than T-Bone.

MR. FERGUS
HAPPY SAM
REVEREND GLUCK
LEMUEL CLAYBORNE
VERNA MAE BEAUFORT   }   all played by the same actor.
OFFICER KLAMP
DOC TATUM
BROTHER TIM
RAINCOAT

Time

The present.

Place

The backroads of South Carolina.

The Play

T Bone N Weasel

He swallows buildings, the universe, the whole planet
His mouth burns up when he drinks the sun like a Coke
He has three heads so he can see everywhere he goes
He has rubberband legs and one plastic leg
He's so round he can hardly hold himself to the ground
Gravity and ropes freeze him there
He's a good monster, for when someone robs the bank
before the thief can get caught he swallows the robber,
*   the building and the money.*

   Class poem, Grade 1, Mossy Oaks Elementary*

A Stolen Buick on U.S. 21

WEASEL: It aint me . . . it aint me . . . I aint no fohtunate son . . . naw naw naw . . .
T-BONE: Dont sing along man.

Long pause.

WEASEL: Sa good song.
T-BONE: Yeah but you suck.

Pause.

WEASEL: I know that.

Pause.

*From *Growing up Southern*, edited by Chris Mayfield. Copyright © 1981 by Institute for Southern Studies. Reprinted by permission of Pantheon Books, a Division of Random House, Inc.

T-BONE: Which way. We got four directions.

WEASEL: Head south. *(Pause)* The hell you doin.

T-BONE: Huh.

WEASEL: Watch it.

T-BONE: You tryin to say.

WEASEL: The way you drivin.

T-BONE: Whats wrong with it.

WEASEL: Jest that I be feelin a tad too familiar with the good folk in the neighborin lane. Close enough to shake hands an trade spit.

T-BONE: Aint use to power steerin.

WEASEL: How many times I gotta tell you. Only steal cars you know how to *drive*. But no, you keep goin after this uppity Buick shit. We shoulda grabbed that Chevette.

T-BONE: Pore mans car.

WEASEL: I know what you own, T-Bone. I saw you put it all in this here glove compartment.

T-BONE: Jest rest yer features. I got my pride.

WEASEL: Pride? Lessee. Map o South Caroline. Somebodys comb. Box o Trojans— what, you keep these for luck? Bout twenny-seven dollas and half a Moon Pie. Nope. Don't see no pride.

T-BONE: I said lay off.

WEASEL: Now where would a man like you hide his pride? I got it. In the gas tank.

T-BONE: I mean it Weasel you lay off or Im gonna cloud up and rain all over you.

WEASEL: I hear a lotta thunder but I dont feel a drop.

T-BONE: That chews it. You the expert you drive.

WEASEL: Whacha doin T-Bone get yer hands back on this wheel.

T-BONE: You doin fine without me. We gonna change seats.

WEASEL: I aint never drove before look at my hands shake.

T-BONE: Look to me like Im in the presence of a genuine ace long-distance road runner.

WEASEL: I dont know how.

T-BONE: Thass right you dont know how jest like you dont know how to read or write or clean your teeth once a year or put a piece o soap to yer face or spell yer own goddam *name* fer Chrissake.

WEASEL: Come own T-Bone take this wheel back we gonna end up somebodys hood ownament.

T-BONE: Say pleez.

WEASEL: Pleez you slapassed slack-twisted strut fart.

T-BONE: Awright jest member. Pays to be nice.

Pause.

WEASEL: Need a drink. My throat thinks my heads cut off.

T-BONE: Likker stoer near Blythewood. Saw the sign. "De Sto." Bout as funny as a three legged dog.

WEASEL: Hyeh hyeh hyeh hyeh.

T-BONE: I mean it aint funny.

WEASEL: Oh. (Pause) Whats the name o this sto?

T-BONE: De Sto.

WEASEL: Right whats it called.

T-BONE: Thass it. D, e, s, t, o. Hillbilly way o sayin the stoer. Downright condensational.

WEASEL: What is.

T-BONE: De Sto.

WEASEL: What bout it.

T-BONE: Hell you cant spell why I waste my time jawin I dont know.

WEASEL: Me neither.

T-BONE: Its an insult, thass what. Sayin folk go roun talkin like ignorant crackers.

WEASEL: Im hungry.

T-BONE: Godforsaken South Carolina sandlappers. Puttin up signs like that its a goddam insult to educative people.

WEASEL: What is.

T-BONE: The sign.

WEASEL: What sign.

T-BONE: De Sto.

WEASEL: What bout it.

T-BONE: Thass another thing Weasel seem like all I do with you is *explain* shit.

WEASEL: All I know is I aint the one goin into conniptions over some damn road sign. You ever read a book they gonna have to tie you down.

T-BONE: You pass right by that likker stoer if it wasnt fer me.

WEASEL: Hell I would.

T-BONE: How you gonna know yer there?

WEASEL: Got a system.

T-BONE: System.

WEASEL: Thass right. Little windows mean beer by the can. Big windows mean beer by the bottle. No windows an flashin lights mean beer on tap. But you might have to kill somebody to git it.

T-BONE: You learn to read you wont have to guess these things.

WEASEL: Aint guessin. Ive developed my observational powers. That, fer example, is a little girl. On her way to school Id say. On account o the books shes carryin.

T-BONE: Hell of a talent.

WEASEL: Jest takes a little concentratin. Now that theres a barn, an thats somebodys wash hangin out to dry, and up head a ways some kinda big tree, an thats a raven. Or else a crow.

T-BONE: Whats this?

WEASEL: Thats yer fist in my face.

T-BONE: You sure? You concentratin?

WEASEL: Aint causin no harm, T-Bone. Jest passin time.

T-BONE: Jest dont pass it my way. (Pause) This is it. De Sto.

WEASEL: What I tell you. Big windows.

T-BONE: No cars. Looks closed.

WEASEL: Saw somebody in there.

T-BONE: Think yer right.

WEASEL: Hey where you goin.

T-BONE: We comin back.

WEASEL: Im thirsty.

T-BONE: Said we be back. Dig out that black-eyed susan o yours.

WEASEL: Say what?

T-BONE: Your piece.

WEASEL: What you want?

T-BONE: Pull out your rod. Lets have a look.

WEASEL: You wanna see my dick?

T-BONE: The *gun*, dammit. Gimme the gun.

WEASEL: Well why dont you *say* so. Gimme this pull out yer *rod* shit.

T-BONE: Jest hand it here.

WEASEL: Minute there thought I was back in the penitentiary.

T-BONE: This thing loaded?

WEASEL: Hell I dunno.

T-BONE: Whens the last time you used it?

WEASEL: Aint never used it.

T-BONE: Never *used* it?

WEASEL: Im least as handy with that .32 as you are with this Buick.

T-BONE: You ever shoot anybody?

WEASEL: I dont keep track o them things. *(Pause)* Owww leggo leggo leggo.

T-BONE: Look here Weasel. You said you was my man.

WEASEL: I am I am leggo leggo.

T-BONE: I aint so sure bout you.

WEASEL: I gave you references.

T-BONE: They all servin time.

WEASEL: Aint my fault shit that hurts T-Bone.

T-BONE: Dont tell me. Dont tell me I aint spent two weeks lookin fer talent jest to end up with some kinda bum with a head fulla stump water.

WEASEL: I aint gonna tell you that ow.

T-BONE: Dont tell me my partner has feathers on his legs.

WEASEL: Im with you T-Bone.

T-BONE: Thass good Weasel. Otherwise I might be obliged to rearrange yer face.

WEASEL: No need fer that been done three times awready oww shit.

T-BONE: You tell me how I kin trust you I let you go.

WEASEL: I *been* shot does that help?

T-BONE: Where?

WEASEL: Greenville.

T-BONE: I mean where on you.

WEASEL: Left ear.

Pause.

T-BONE: Holy shit took a piece out dint they.

WEASEL: Got me runnin. *(Pause)* Thanks T-Bone.

T-BONE: Sokay.

WEASEL: Hell of a grip there.

T-BONE: Who shot you. The law?

WEASEL: My dad.

T-BONE: Wha for?

WEASEL: Tryin to member. Think I set fire to his car.

T-BONE: God damn.

WEASEL: It was a Buick.

T-BONE: I countin on you Weasel. We gonna go back an take De Sto.

WEASEL: It aint even lunchtime yet.

T-BONE: It jest waitin for us. Daylight dont matter to me.

WEASEL: That how you got sent to Black River?

T-BONE: How many times *you* been in prison?

WEASEL: Dunno. I try to arrange it roun the holidays.

T-BONE: What they get you for?

WEASEL: Lessee. Think the last time was attempted robbery.

T-BONE: Armed?

WEASEL: Hell no. Aint *that* fond o the pen. Like to keep my visits short.

T-BONE: Had to scare em somehow.

WEASEL: Sure did. They emptied all the cash drawers.

T-BONE: How you manage that?

WEASEL: Threatened to take off all my clothes. Hell they threw money at me.

T-BONE: Shit. I wanted skilled labor.

WEASEL: Im more of an idea man.

T-BONE: This dont go right you gonna be more of a dead man. Now heres the plan. I pack the heat.

WEASEL: Heat?

T-BONE: The gun. Now you go in to buy somethin an I keep the feller at the register entertained.

WEASEL: What do I buy?

T-BONE: I dont care. Jest dont act like a bum. Show some class.

WEASEL: Night Train.

T-BONE: Fine. Now bring it up to the register. Soons he opens the drawer, I flash my iron.

WEASEL: What iron.

T-BONE: The *gun*, dammit.

WEASEL: You got somethin gainst the word?

T-BONE: You dont call a gun a gun.

WEASEL: You dont.

T-BONE: It aint cool. Iffen I been reduced to a life o crime at least I gonna show some style.

WEASEL: Mebbe I should change my clothes.

T-BONE: We grab the cash an go. We keep the car runnin.

WEASEL: How you gonna keep this guy occupied.

T-BONE: I talk to him.

WEASEL: Bout what.

T-BONE: I dunno. Anythin. The weather.

WEASEL: Lemme hear you.

T-BONE: "Hot, aint it?" Hows that.

WEASEL: Jest fine. You gonna last alla three seconds fore you got ants crawlin up yer nose.

T-BONE: You got a suggestion.

WEASEL: Lemme do the talkin.

T-BONE: Ferget it.

WEASEL: You missin a golden oppotunity. Conversatin is my specialty.

T-BONE: Dont I know it. I wanna git outa there fore Saturday. *(Pause)* There she is. Still empty.

WEASEL: Hope they got Pearl Beer.

T-BONE: Grab that money. Lets go.

WEASEL: Hold on T-Bone.

T-BONE: Come on. Git out.

WEASEL: I been thinkin.

T-BONE: What.

WEASEL: I aint sure but this jest might be a parole violation.

T-BONE: *Out.*

Inside De Sto

MR. FERGUS: Come on in boys. Slow day so Im cleanin my rifle.

WEASEL: Lets go.

T-BONE: We be right back.

Back in the Buick

WEASEL: Id say this calls for a change of plans.

T-BONE: No it dont.

WEASEL: You crazy?

T-BONE: We can still do it. We got a .32.

WEASEL: Thass right. We can blow our own brains out an save him the trouble.

T-BONE: Look he said he was cleanin that thing. Means its empty. Least fer a while.

WEASEL: What you talkin bout. The mans got a firearm in his hands an you gonna stick him up.

T-BONE: Gotta hurry fore he loads it.

WEASEL: One thing, T-Bone. It ever dawn on you if the man aint had no business he probly got no cash in that drawer.

T-BONE: He gotta make change dont he. Gotta be least a hunnerd in there.

WEASEL: That worth you gettin shot?

T-BONE: I get shot you keep the car.

WEASEL: What if *I* get shot.

T-BONE: Awright Weasel. Guess you right. But jest lemme ask you this. What else you gonna do with yer life?

WEASEL: I tell you what I gonna do with my life. I gonna keep it alive fer one thing. I gonna give up this shit, spendin a week drivin roun South Caroline with one eye on the rear view an the other on easy marks, keepin outa sight o the highway patrol an sleepin in the back seat of a car you cant even operate. Met a man at Black River say he be happy to hep me out, mebbe washin dishes, somethin like that. I kin look him up see if he members me, get a job how bout that T-Bone, a bonerfide *job*, somethin you never even stopped to *consider* am I right. A steady paycheck an a roof over my head an reglar hours an holdin my head up as a law-abidin citizen.

Pause.

T-BONE: You ready?

WEASEL: Keep the car runnin. Lets take this sucker.

Back in De Sto

T-BONE: Fergot our money.

WEASEL: Keeps it in the glove compartment. Twenny-seven dollas.

MR. FERGUS: Dont wanna lose that.

WEASEL: No sir.

T-BONE: Why dont you jest go pick somethin out.

WEASEL: Will do.

T-BONE: Hot, aint it.

MR. FERGUS: Whats that.

T-BONE: Hot. Hot day.

MR. FERGUS: Wouldnt know. Got an air conditioner.

Pause.

T-BONE: Nice in here.

MR. FERGUS: That sight look straight to you?

WEASEL: Dont shoot! I dont even know him! Picked me up hitchin to Columbia!

T-BONE: He jest fixin the *sight*.

Pause.

WEASEL: I know that.

T-BONE: Dont let him bother you. Guns make him a little rabbity.

MR. FERGUS: No need for that. Theys a sayin, hows it go. Guns dont kill people. People kill guns. No that aint right. Well, guns, people, it all works out somehow.

T-BONE: You decide what you want?

WEASEL: Not yet. It all looks so *good*.

T-BONE: Put it in gear.

MR. FERGUS: Mebbe I can hep find what you lookin fer.

T-BONE: You stay right there. I see what we want from here. Right in front o his nose.

WEASEL: This thing?

T-BONE: Thass right. Bring it up here.

WEASEL: You say so.

MR. FERGUS: What the verdict. Why I declare I aint never sole one o these items. Imported pear brandy.

T-BONE: What the hell is that?

WEASEL: Thass what was in front o me.

MR. FERGUS: Straight from the still. No need to age it. You boys plannin a celebration?

T-BONE: Could say that. How much is it?

MR. FERGUS: Less see. Includin tax, that come to twenny-fo dollas an ninedy-five cents.

T-BONE: *How* much?

MR. FERGUS: Come from Switzer-land.

WEASEL: Look T-Bone why dont I jest put the damn thing back.

T-BONE: Pay the man. We gonna be makin a withdrawal anyway.

WEASEL: How we gonna do that we aint even got a bank acc-owww leggo leggo.

T-BONE: Pay him.

Pause.

MR. FERGUS: Outa twenny-five. *(Pause)* Doggone cash drawer. Been stickin for days. *(Pause)* Nope. Cant budge it. See if one o you can open it.

T-BONE: Glad to. *(Pause)* Son of a *bitch*.

MR. FERGUS: Shoulda had the man out yesteday. What I get fer puttin it off.

T-BONE: Mebbe if I had a rock.

WEASEL: He only owes us a nickel.

T-BONE: Shut up an find a rock Weasel.

MR. FERGUS: Weasel? Used to know a boy back in Greenville called himself Weasel.

WEASEL: Im from Greenville.

T-BONE: No you aint! He aint from Greenville!

WEASEL: Shore I am. Brought up on Palmetto Drive.

MR. FERGUS: William Weasler! Thought I recognized you!

T-BONE: You *know* him?

MR. FERGUS: Shonuff. Use to live cross the street from the Weasler family.

WEASEL: Not Mister Fergus.

MR. FERGUS: The same.

WEASEL: With them Porky Pig imitations.

MR. FERGUS: Uhh th-th-th-that-thats ri-ri-ri-ri-you bet.

WEASEL: I be dogged.

MR. FERGUS: Hows yer dad.

WEASEL: Dead.

MR. FERGUS: Lets see that ear. *(Pause)* Took a chunk out dint he.

WEASEL: Yes sir.

MR. FERGUS: Still. Shouldna burned his Buick.

WEASEL: I know it.

T-BONE: We got *bizness* here Weasel.

MR. FERGUS: Oh you kin spare a minute with an ole neighbor from Greenville. Hows yer mama.

WEASEL: She killed my dad. I think shes in Utah.

MR. FERGUS: You hear from her say hi from Mr. Fergus.

T-BONE: Hate to break up the social hour.

WEASEL: T-Bone.

T-BONE: Now if you wont mind movin way from the register.

MR. FERGUS: You gonna shoot it open?

T-BONE: Thass the idea.

MR. FERGUS: Preciate the thought boy. But Id rather jest call the serviceman.

T-BONE: You aint got the picture yet, do you.

WEASEL: T-Bone.

T-BONE: This aint for yer *benefit*.

WEASEL: T-Bone.

T-BONE: What the hell *you* want.

WEASEL: Take a listen.

T-BONE: What you talkin bout? I dont hear nuthin.

WEASEL: What I mean. The car aint runnin. The motor gave out. *(Long pause)* Wanna sip?

The Parking Lot

MR. FERGUS: Jest as I figgered.

T-BONE: What is it?

MR. FERGUS: Fan belt broke. New one cost you three fifty.

T-BONE: We aint got three fifty. Spent it all on that damn brandy.

MR. FERGUS: Then you cant afford to tow it. Thats a tough one. Nearest gas stations fifteen miles.

T-BONE: How bout a refund on the pear brandy.

MR. FERGUS: Not with that Greenville boy over there suckin on the bottle.

T-BONE: Damn it Weasel. Now we stuck with a dead car an less than two bucks cash.

WEASEL: This stuff . . . is worth it.

T-BONE: Now to top that off you drunk.

MR. FERGUS: Theys a car lot down the road a mile. Happy Sams. Mebbe he give you a belt.

WEASEL: No thanks . . . got plenty.

T-BONE: Get up Weasel you gonna push this car.

WEASEL: You gonna blow it out yer ass.

MR. FERGUS: Mebbe you oughta let him steer.

WEASEL: Thass right. I been practicin.

T-BONE: Get in the car.

MR. FERGUS: Almost forgot. Here you go.

T-BONE: Whats this.

MR. FERGUS: Your change. Had a nickel in my pocket. Looks like your lucky da-da-de-de-de-da-de-day.

Happy Sam's Used Cars

T-BONE: You can let go the wheel now.

WEASEL: Hot damn. Got this steerin *down*.

T-BONE: Here he comes. I do the talkin.

WEASEL: Fine by me. Gotta use the facility. Time to recycle my shorts.

Long pause.

HAPPY SAM: Give you a hunnerd.

T-BONE: What.

HAPPY SAM: Fer the Buick.

T-BONE: Aint fer sale.

HAPPY SAM: Then fuck off.

T-BONE: Hold on. Wheres Happy Sam.

HAPPY SAM: You got him.

T-BONE: Happy Sam?

HAPPY SAM: Got a problem with that? Oh I know what yer thinkin, you jest dont seem all that happy, Sam. Well it hard to be happy all the goddam time. You try spendin day after day dealin with the dregs o humanity, people so low they could wear a top hat and still walk under the belly of a snake. Like people who push busted Buicks on my lot.

T-BONE: I jest need a fan belt.

HAPPY SAM: Course you do every goddam car comes on this lot needs a fan belt an Im the one has to put em on.

T-BONE: You got one I can use?

HAPPY SAM: This look like a *garage* boy you can look around as far as the eye can see an you wont find no mechanic. Its jest me, two pimple-face boys couldnt sell a fly to a spider, an a doberman I keep on hand to chew the ass off people like you. Aint got no fan belts anyway.

T-BONE: Could you look?

HAPPY SAM: I know what I got here its *my* goddam lot. I got cars an calendars. An you dont get a calendar less you buy a car.

T-BONE: Look its an emergency.

HAPPY SAM: Lifes an emergency. You fucked up.

T-BONE: Awright what if I did. Can I jest borrow a fan belt off one o these ole cars?

HAPPY SAM: Thass the problem with this country too many handouts. Its a national disgrace an I aint gonna be no contributin facter.

T-BONE: Listen. We need some cash.

HAPPY SAM: Well dont that make you the wonder attraction o Richland County. People be linin up for miles jest to take a look at you.

T-BONE: Okay. The Buick.

HAPPY SAM: A hunnerd.

T-BONE: You know what I paid for this car?

HAPPY SAM: Probly a hunnerd less than my offer.

T-BONE: You sinuatin Im a car thief?

HAPPY SAM: Got the registration? *(Pause)* One hunnerd.

T-BONE: Please mister.

HAPPY SAM: Happy.

T-BONE: Happy. Check it out. Its gotta be worth a few grand at the least. Its prackly new.

HAPPY SAM: Its broke. Saw you push it on the lot.

T-BONE: Thats the fan belt!

HAPPY SAM: So get it fixed. Then I look at it.

T-BONE: I aint got the *cash*.

HAPPY SAM: Look you tryin to sell me a car that dont even *run*. You lucky I dont sic the doberman.

Long pause.

T-BONE: Two thousand.

HAPPY SAM: One hunnerd.

T-BONE: One thousand.

HAPPY SAM: One hunnerd.

T-BONE: Five hunnerd.

HAPPY SAM: One hunnerd.

T-BONE: Four hunnerd.
HAPPY SAM: One hunnerd.

Pause.

T-BONE: Three hunnerd.
HAPPY SAM: One hunnerd.
T-BONE: Two hunnerd.
HAPPY SAM: One hunnerd.
T-BONE: Hunnerd fifty.
HAPPY SAM: One hunnerd.

Pause.

T-BONE: Hunnerd twenny-five.
HAPPY SAM: One hunnerd.
T-BONE: Hunnerd twenny.
HAPPY SAM: One hunnerd.
T-BONE: Hunnerd ten.
HAPPY SAM: One hunnerd.

Pause.

T-BONE: One hunnerd *five.*

Pause.

HAPPY SAM: Awright Im a reasonable man. Here you go. Twenny, forety, sixty, eighty, one hunnerd an five dollas.
T-BONE: Dont I sign anythin?
HAPPY SAM: Shore if you want. Course that sends yer name to the state courthouse along with the record o transfer.
T-BONE: Never mind. Jest lemme ask you somethin.
HAPPY SAM: Fire away.
T-BONE: How much you gonna sell this car for?
HAPPY SAM: O Id say bout five thousand.
T-BONE: WHAT?
HAPPY SAM: Course I gotta fix that fan belt first. Thanks boy. You jest made Sam very happy.

Killian City Limits

T-BONE: Killian city limits.
WEASEL: You jest said that.

T-BONE: I did?

WEASEL: Hope theys a donut shop in town. My stomachs wamblin an my feet are draggly.

T-BONE: All that fool pear brandy.

WEASEL: Thass right, go head an critisize. Hope you notice how Im sidlin way from the fack that you done give way our only means o transport. Hope you preciate how I dont bring that up.

T-BONE: Yer bringin it up now aint you.

WEASEL: But I aint makin no judgment. I could be tellin you how that was dumber than takin a piss on a lectric fence.

T-BONE: Awright awright lemme have some o that Swiss pear juice.

WEASEL: Dont see why not you paid fer it.

Pause.

T-BONE: Boy that fix yer plumbin dont it.

WEASEL: Where is Switzer-land anyhow.

T-BONE: Some place in Yurp. They got lots o mountains an cheese an chocklit and clocks an shit. I seen pictures.

WEASEL: They got women?

T-BONE: You know that gal on those cans o powder coco? With the blonde hair an the puffed up shirt?

WEASEL: Right look like she be herdin goats or somethin.

T-BONE: Thass what they look like.

WEASEL: Shit. I gonna move there.

T-BONE: Lets do it Weasel.

WEASEL: Do what.

T-BONE: Go to Switzer-land.

WEASEL: You mean it?

T-BONE: You an me. Leave South Carolina to the sandlappers.

WEASEL: Now you talkin.

T-BONE: Put er there.

Long pause.

WEASEL: Aint got a chance do we.

T-BONE: Hell no.

WEASEL: Shit.

T-BONE: We outa pear juice.

WEASEL: Things come crashin down *fast* dont they.

T-BONE: Lets get some beer.

WEASEL: An donuts.

T-BONE: I wanna real meal. We go to the store an get us some Spam.

WEASEL: I jest now figgered it out. Its yer name.

T-BONE: What bout it.

WEASEL: Why Im hungry all the damn time. I keep thinkin bout steak. That really yer name?

T-BONE: Naw.

WEASEL: What is it.

T-BONE: Pends on the state.

WEASEL: State o what.

T-BONE: State o the country. In Geohgia Im Leland Johnson. In Loosiana Im Hakim Lefevre.

WEASEL: But whats yer *real* name.

T-BONE: Oh that. Dont rightly member. Use so many. I pretty much ruled out Bob. Aint many black folk name they kids Bob.

WEASEL: Where you git T-Bone.

T-BONE: Take a gander at my shin.

Pause.

WEASEL: Nasty lookin scar.

T-BONE: Folks owned a nearsighted rat terrier. Was playin on a swing set an he thought someone was throwin him a steak bone.

WEASEL: He chew yer leg?

T-BONE: Wouldnt let go. My daddy had to borry a bitch in heat from down the street jest to distract him.

WEASEL: He shoot the dog?

T-BONE: Naw. Jest fed him reglar.

WEASEL: Damn thing look like my ear.

T-BONE: Life aint easy.

WEASEL: Dont seem right.

T-BONE: Aint right.

WEASEL: Well it gotta stop sometime T-Bone. I mean ever since my mama grab that .32 and blew off the back o my dads head while he was eatin breakfast. Things jest dont seem to let up. Whacha stop fer.

T-BONE: She use this gun.

WEASEL: Yep. Talk bout a mess. Good thing the table was formica.

T-BONE: Dont tell me. Dont tell me I been carryin round a *murder* weapon.

WEASEL: Well if you wanna put it that way oww leggo leggo.

T-BONE: I almost *use* this thing back in Blythewood. I thought it was clean.

WEASEL: *Is* clean. Only been used once. Oww will you leggo.

T-BONE: How you git this thing.

WEASEL: Come UPS right after I got outa Black River.

T-BONE: She *mail* it to you?

WEASEL: Thass right now leggo o me.

T-BONE: We gotta git rid of it.

WEASEL: Wish you quit grabbin me like that. Give it here. *(Pause)* There. Now you happy?

T-BONE: Dont tell me. Dont tell me you jest threw it off a bridge with our finger-prints all over the damn thing. Dont tell me you threw that gun.

WEASEL: Okay. I dint throw no gun. I threw a *rod*.

A Ravine under County 555

T-BONE: You find it?

WEASEL: Not yet. Amazin all the artyfacks you find under a bypass. Look at this. A toilet seat.

T-BONE: Jest look fer that .32.

WEASEL: Heres a damn washin machine. An a dryer next to it. Could open a laundermat under this bridge.

T-BONE: We be needin one after we wade through this shit.

WEASEL: Hold on.

T-BONE: See it?

WEASEL: Some kinda tellygram.

T-BONE: Bring it here. *(Pause)* "You could already be a winner." Some kinda sweepstakes.

WEASEL: An somebody threw it *away?*

T-BONE: Junk.

WEASEL: Hey give it here.

T-BONE: Theys millions o those things. Only meant to get pore folks hopes up. See that word? That say "occu-pant." Mean they dont even care *who* gets it.

WEASEL: Then they dont mind I keep it. Might come in handy.

T-BONE: Suit yourself. *(Pause)* Somebody done settled down here. Campfire, wood shelter. Mus be a tramp nearby.

REVEREND GLUCK: Aint no tramp. Aint no vagrant, transint or ragpicker neither.

WEASEL: Thats my gun.

REVEREND GLUCK: Get yer hands up.

T-BONE: Mean no harm mister.

WEASEL: Jesus Mary an Joseph.

REVEREND GLUCK: Dont talk to me bout Jesus. I read the Bible ever day an I know what it take to save souls.

T-BONE: Course you do mister.

REVEREND GLUCK: Reverend. Reverend Gluck. Doctor o Sacred Theology an Minister o the Holy Church o the Ravine. The Lawd Awmighty bless you an preserve you now an forever.

WEASEL AND T-BONE: Amen.

REVEREND GLUCK: Now empty yer pockets.

WEASEL: But thats my gun. I threw it off the bridge.

REVEREND GLUCK: Then it aint yers no more. Anythin tossed off this bridge comes a sacrifisial offerin to the Lawd an church property. As Gods personally ordained minister its my duty to gather up these holy gifts. An to accept donations in His name.

T-BONE: Aint got nothin to give.

REVEREND GLUCK: That true Lawd? *(Pause)* Sorry. The Lawd say you holdin out on Him. He say fer me to look in yer shoes.

T-BONE: Its all we got.

REVEREND GLUCK: Have to give up earthly possessions if you gonna enter the gates o Heaven. Now take em off. *(Pause)* Theys a lotta hate in the world, my sons. Lotta injustice. Cruelty. Dishonesty. Sometimes it hard fer me to git up in the moanin an face another day. But jest when my spirits sink to the point where I begin to turn my back on the Lawd, there outa the sky come flyin a spiritual offerin. Some days its a dead cat. Some days its a rusted engine. Some days its some kind o poison chemical. But all things are precious in the eyes o the Lawd, an they give me the strength to go on. An that goes fer your—how much you got there?

T-BONE: A hunnerd an five dollas.

REVEREND GLUCK: The Lawd is pleased. Put it in the collection plate. Now you.

WEASEL: All I got is a card fer social security.

REVEREND GLUCK: Aint no such thing. Put it in the plate. Whats that in yer hand.

WEASEL: Sweepstakes offer.

REVEREND GLUCK: Keep it. Awready got one somewheres. Now lessee . . . William Weasler. And . . . dint ketch yer name.

T-BONE: Dint give it to you.

REVEREND GLUCK: Aint necessary. The Lawd members His chosen ones. Now off with you. *(Pause)* Run. *(Pause)* Thass it. Spread the word. Service on Sunday! Nine o clock sharp! Come early! The car seats fill up fast!

The Basement of St. Boniface

T-BONE: Cant sleep there.

WEASEL: Dont worry bout it.

T-BONE: All the beds taken. Gotta use the floor.

WEASEL: Had a chat with the head nun. Said I could use this one till the guy gits back from the blood bank.

T-BONE: What then.

WEASEL: I worked it out.

T-BONE: Dont say I dint warn you.

WEASEL: Not a bad meal. Coulda done without the Kool Aid.

T-BONE: Its humiliatin. Never spent a night in a shelter an I hope I never do again.

WEASEL: Got a lead on a job. Woman in Lugoff need help.

T-BONE: We go there tomorrow.

WEASEL: Time fer a change in luck. That preacher was past strange.

T-BONE: Shoulda taken Happy Sam. Would have without the doberman.

WEASEL: Countrys gone to shit ever since Creedence Clearwater broke up.

T-BONE: You an that damn band. Theys other bands jest as good.

WEASEL: Name one.

T-BONE: I dunno . . . the Beatles.

WEASEL: T-Bone. Look at me. *(Pause)* Tell me you dont mean that.

Pause.

T-BONE: Awright I hate the Beatles.

CLAYBORNE: Hey. You. Thass. Mmmmy. Bed.

T-BONE: Now you in fer it.

WEASEL: Yer name Lemuel Clayborne?

CLAYBORNE: Yeah. Sssso. What.

WEASEL: Been waitin fer you. To deliver this tellygram.

CLAYBORNE: Fer. Mmmme?

WEASEL: From yer sister.

CLAYBORNE: Aint. Got. Nnnno. Sis. Ter.

WEASEL: I mean yer brother.

CLAYBORNE: Nnnna. Than?

WEASEL: Thass right. Nathan. Here you go.

Pause.

CLAYBORNE: Whats. It. Ssssay?

WEASEL: Give it back. I read it to you. *(Pause)* "Brother Lemuel. Stop."

CLAYBORNE: Sssstop. What.

WEASEL: Thass jest tellygram talk. I leave out the stops. "Brother Lemuel. Come home now. Important."

CLAYBORNE: To. Nnnnight?

WEASEL: "Leave tonight. Nathan."

CLAYBORNE: He. Throwed. Mmmme. Out.

WEASEL: Guess all is fogiven. Better skedaddle.

CLAYBORNE: Thanks. Mmmmis. Ter.

WEASEL: Best o luck. *(Long pause)* That boy was *slow.*

T-BONE: Thass a terrible thing to do.

WEASEL: Folk belong with their fambly.

T-BONE: He jest git throwed out agin.

WEASEL: Mebbe. Mebbe not.

T-BONE: You slicker than goose shit, you know that?

WEASEL: Night T-Bone.

T-BONE: Night.

Long pause.

WEASEL: T-Bone.

T-BONE: What.

WEASEL: You miss yer home.
T-BONE: No.
WEASEL: You sure.
T-BONE: Shut up an go to sleep.

Long pause.

WEASEL: T-Bone.
T-BONE: What.
WEASEL: What yer name really.
T-BONE: Dunno.
WEASEL: You gotta know.
T-BONE: Dammit Weasel you dont pipe down I come over there an rip yer arm off.

Long pause.

WEASEL: T-Bone.
T-BONE: *What.*
WEASEL: How bout a good-night kiss oww leggo leggo.

Verna Mae Beaufort's Farm

WEASEL: Pardon us maam. This here the Beaufort place?
VERNA MAE: Thass right.
WEASEL: We was hearin as to how you might could use a coupla hired hands.
VERNA MAE: Take off yer shirts.

Pause.

WEASEL: Scuse me maam?
VERNA MAE: Yer shirts. Both o you. *(Pause)* Awright. Youll do.
WEASEL: Whats the job.
VERNA MAE: Need some bird minders.
WEASEL: Hens what I tell you T-Bone that right up our alley.
VERNA MAE: No hens. Bobolinks. Gotta chase em outa the rice field. Youll git yer feet wet.
WEASEL: That all there is? Chasin rice birds?
T-BONE: Whats the pay.
VERNA MAE: Show some respeck boy. Miss Beaufort.
T-BONE: Sorry. Miss Beaufort.
VERNA MAE: Three dollas an hour. Work sunup to sunset an the rest o the nights yours to do as you please. Plus johnny cake fer lunch an chicken bog fer supper. An a place to bed down in the barn.

WEASEL: Chicken bog you say. Sounds reasonable.

VERNA MAE: Course yer boy eats outside.

T-BONE: I aint his—

WEASEL: We preciate it Miss Beaufort. We shore do need the work.

VERNA MAE: Gotta be here through harvest. I expeck seven mortars a day from each o you.

T-BONE: Now hold on.

WEASEL: That fine by us.

VERNA MAE: Awright then. Can both start out in the paddy till I ring the bell.

WEASEL: That mean lunchtime?

VERNA MAE: That mean I want you come see me personal. Got another task. Yer boy can stay with them birds.

T-BONE: Miss Beaufort.

VERNA MAE: Yes?

T-BONE: My name . . . my name is Tom.

Pause.

VERNA MAE: Dont need yer name boy. Aint ever gonna use it.

8:00 in the Paddy

WEASEL: Chicken bog. Hot damn.

T-BONE: Dont care what she feeds us. Aint gonna be no womans slave. She stomp-down ugly to boot.

WEASEL: She aint that bad.

T-BONE: I tell you she could turn a train down a dirt road.

WEASEL: Look at them rice birds. Fly you birds! Eeeaayyaaa!

T-BONE: Yaaahooo!

WEASEL: Yaaawwww!

T-BONE: Hoooo birds! Git!

WEASEL: These little fellers some kinda brave. Keep comin back fer more.

T-BONE: Haaaahh!

WEASEL: Grab up some rocks.

T-BONE: Weasel.

WEASEL: Got one in the wing see that.

T-BONE: Weasel. Askin you somethin.

WEASEL: Yeeeeehawwwww what.

T-BONE: I wanna know where you stand.

WEASEL: Right here what kinda fool question—

T-BONE: I mean on color. *(Pause)* Talkin bout this *thing* man. What people *say* bout it.

WEASEL: What you goin on bout T-Bone.

T-BONE: Im askin what it *mean* to you.

WEASEL: Aint never thought bout it.

T-BONE: *Course* you aint man that cause you the white man you dont have to give it no *thought* see what Im sayin.

WEASEL: What the hell is *with* you. We got work to do.

Pause.

T-BONE: Hyyaaaaaaaaaahhh you rice birds!

WEASEL: Jesus T-Bone slow down you got the whole day head o you.

T-BONE: Yaaaaaaaaaaaawwwwwwwwww!

WEASEL: *Stop* it.

Pause.

T-BONE: Theys the bell.

WEASEL: You all right?

T-BONE: Go on see what she wants.

WEASEL: I be back soons I can.

Long pause.

T-BONE: God damn birds.

10:30

WEASEL: T-Bone? T-Bone! Where the hell are you. Damn bobolinks. Hyaaah! What the—T-Bone? Get up yer face outa that mud fore you drown. Come on. Roll over. *(Pause)* Jesus Mary an Joseph.

Pause.

T-BONE: Yiiiiii!

WEASEL: Aiiiieee!

T-BONE: Hee hee hee the look on yer face.

WEASEL: Damn it T-Bone.

T-BONE: That set yer hair dint it.

WEASEL: Aint in the mood for yer shenanigans.

T-BONE: Damn Weasel you look like somethin the hogs left behind. What she got you doin anyhow.

WEASEL: Dont wanna talk bout it.

T-BONE: Whatever it is you shore dont look dirty. What kinda job—*(Pause)* Weasel.

WEASEL: What.

T-BONE: You *servicin* that woman.

WEASEL: Said I don wanna discuss it.

T-BONE: Weasel. That woman could gag a maggot.

WEASEL: I tell you T-Bone you lemme alone or else I gonna—whats that.

Pause.

T-BONE: The bell.

WEASEL: No. God no.

T-BONE: Lets get outa here Weasel. Theys hair in the butter.

WEASEL: Cant leave.

T-BONE: Why not.

WEASEL: Chicken bog. *(Pause)* The bell.

T-BONE: Weasel. If you gotta do this.

WEASEL: My mind is made.

T-BONE: Dont let her get on top. An think bout Switzer-land.

11:45

WEASEL: T-Bone.

T-BONE: Over here.

WEASEL: Cant make it over there. My legs are shot. *(Pause)* No. No. Tell me Im hearin things.

T-BONE: Its the bell.

WEASEL: Kill me now T-Bone. Slit my throat.

T-BONE: Could jest be the johnny cake.

WEASEL: Aint ever gonna eat. Just gonna shag her till I die. *(Pause)* T-Bone.

T-BONE: Why you lookin at me like that.

WEASEL: You gotta take my place.

T-BONE: Have you lost yer ever lovin *mind*. You couldnt get me in there with a cattle prod. *(Pause)* Dont cry Weasel. *(Pause)* Shit. Whats that woman gonna do when a black man walk into her bedroom.

11:52

T-BONE: Lets go Weasel.

WEASEL: Where you off to?

T-BONE: I got her purse and shes got a shotgun. Come *own*.

WEASEL: Why you always pull this shit at mealtimes.

T-BONE: Run!

A Back Corner Booth in the Pontiac Snack House

WEASEL: Eatin a double cheeseburger be like starin in the face o God.

T-BONE: One could say that.

WEASEL: Wonder they got cheeseburgers in Heaven.

T-BONE: Hard to know.

WEASEL: Aint goin if they dont.

T-BONE: Mama use to say God be havin fish fries on Friday an fried chicken on Sunday.

WEASEL: How bout rest o the time.

T-BONE: Dont eat. No matter since no one ever get hungry.

WEASEL: That hashes it. They gonna have to drag me in screamin.

T-BONE: Aint goin to Heaven so why worry bout it.

WEASEL: Why you so negatory.

T-BONE: Gotta be in a church. We aint mean nuff for the Baptists or rich nuff for the Catlicks.

WEASEL: Theys the Lutherans.

T-BONE: Day they let a black man in be the day God holds Open House.

WEASEL: Might have a better chance if we dint go round robbin folk.

T-BONE: Dont think they heard you in the next county.

WEASEL: I mean it jest dont settle with me takin that purse.

T-BONE: We done *earn* this money Weasel. Dont see you keep from crammin yer jowls with the profits.

WEASEL: Dont mean I *like* it. Say girl. Back here. Hot fudge sundae. With nuts.

T-BONE: You sufferin all right.

WEASEL: It my *conshus* that botherin me T-Bone. All I know is we had a chance at some honest work for a change.

T-BONE: I was her nigger an you was her whore. That what you call honest?

WEASEL: You an me got a different way o lookin at right an wrong. Pass the ketchup.

T-BONE: Hush up. The law comin this way.

Long pause.

OFFICER KLAMP: How do boys. Mind I set a spell. That is if it dont ill convenience you.

WEASEL: Cose not officer. We jest passin through town an came across this pleasant little rest stop.

OFFICER KLAMP: Travellers are you. Roy Klamp. My pleasure. How bout them onion rings house specialty.

WEASEL: Past excellent.

OFFICER KLAMP: Mind if I.

WEASEL: Hep yourself.

OFFICER KLAMP: By chance that wouldnt be your Buick out there.

Pause.

T-BONE: Buick.

WEASEL: We be explorin the fine countryside on foot officer.

OFFICER KLAMP: Jest as well. That back tire mighty low. Well. Better ask roun.

WEASEL: Thanks for the drop in. Take another onion ring with you.

OFFICER KLAMP: Dont mind if I do. By the by, you bein visitors must explain why you boys sittin in the wrong booth.

WEASEL: Wrong booth. Dint realize it be reserved.

OFFICER KLAMP: So you boys wont mind movin to the other section.

WEASEL: Course not officer. What sections that.

OFFICER KLAMP: The colored section. *(Pause)* Jest kiddin boys haw haw haw haw haw haw haw.

WEASEL: That ones a knee slapper aint it T-Bone. *Aint* it.

T-BONE: Funny.

OFFICER KLAMP: Now thats what I like to see. Good sense o humor.

WEASEL: Nice talkin to you but we better mosey along while the lights good.

OFFICER KLAMP: Now that bring up another little matter. Here I am at the counter enjoyin a mud flop sandwich when I happen to notice these two boys in the back corner. Course I know ever body in Pontiac so a strange face sorta stands out roun here. An it hits me like a bolt from the blue that these two boys come awful close to matchin a radio scription from the sheriff o Lugoff. Seems Verna Mae Beaufort run into some trouble end up misplacin bout two hundred thirty dollas. Now Lawd knows Verna Mae could make a bull freeze in his tracks an his piss turn to ice but still the law *is* the law an you know the rest of it. So now I be faced with a perdickament. One thing I can do is take these boys back to face the wrath o Verna Mae, a sitchyation which make my eyes water jest to think of it. The other choice be to let these boys jest hand over the money they found to Officer Klamp fer safekeepin. That way ever body gets saved from certain unpleasant consequences. Now heres my trouble. I jest caint make up my mind what I should do. Thought you boys might could give me a little *hep.*

Pause.

T-BONE: How much.

OFFICER KLAMP: No need to split it up. Wouldnt want any o them bills gettin lonesome. *(Pause)* I do declare. An here I figgered Verna Mae was exaggeratin. Well I hope to ketch up with them purse snatchers soon. You boys have youself a good trip. Tell you what Im in a generous mood. Lunch is on me. An heres some money fer a coupla bus tickets outa Richland County. Cause the next time I see you Im gonna find a reason to bust yer ass. *(Pause)* These boys gotta run Ruthie. I can take that sundae.

On the Greyhound

WEASEL: I done had all I can take o this T-Bone.
T-BONE: Jest rest yore eyes Weasel. I sense somethin comin.
WEASEL: What you think it is.
T-BONE: Aint sure. But we be due for a break.

Intermission

Edisto Beach at 3 AM

WEASEL: Unh? Wha? Pfffft. Pffffffftt.
T-BONE: Some folk tryin to sleep.
WEASEL: Pfffft.
T-BONE: Quit makin like a cat.
WEASEL: Sand in my mouth.
T-BONE: What happen when you roll off the blanket.
WEASEL: Ohhhhh. Oohhhhhhhhhhhh.
T-BONE: Feelin sick?
WEASEL: Stomach.
T-BONE: Nother thing wrong with you Weasel never can hold yer likker.
WEASEL: Likker is one thing. Rubbin alcohol an grape juice another matter.
T-BONE: It was Sunday. Now what you trying to do.
WEASEL: Put on my pants.
T-BONE: Thass yer shirt.

> *Pause.*

WEASEL: I know that.
T-BONE: You still drunk Weasel.
WEASEL: Am not.
T-BONE: Are so look at you caint hardly stand soun like a camel when you talk.
WEASEL: I got *poison* in my system T-Bone poison that you concocted an poured
down my throat like it was some kinda damn motor oil. Probly used a funnel.
T-BONE: No body forced you.
WEASEL: Coulda given me a little *warnin*, somethin like "Hey Weasel, what say
we drink some o this shit gonna make us die an go into mortar riggis." But
no jest cause you in this *mood* to pack it in an visit Charleston Bay face down
I gotta go along. Ohhhhhh.
T-BONE: You trying to say.
WEASEL: Sayin you on a *slide* T-Bone you tryin to take me with you got another
thought comin. I got *plans* you know lotta stuff I could be doing stead o

sleepin on beaches, drinkin cheap wine an panhandlin people from Milwaukee while they be playin volleyball.

T-BONE: Like what.

WEASEL: Like going to Columbia an findin a *job* T-Bone. A way to live. Vocation counselor at Black River tell me they got a company there called Service Industry always lookin fer people.

T-BONE: Aint no company Weasel. Service industry mean minimum wage work. Means takin a job where you sell other folk things you never gonna have youself. They turn it to shit an you clean it up.

WEASEL: Aint like that T-Bone.

T-BONE: Wise up Weasel you live in a dream.

WEASEL: Rather live in a dream than not at all. Somethin in my damn pants what the owww shit owww somethins got me. Look at that look at that T-Bone a crab a damn *crab* in my pants.

T-BONE: Tole you to roll yer pants legs tight.

WEASEL: Dont you sit there actin like a newborn *chile* you put it there you put it in my pants. Probly hopin it would bite my pecker off so you could use it fer soup.

T-BONE: You bout to have a dog fit Weasel. Sit down.

WEASEL: No Im leavin.

T-BONE: No you aint.

WEASEL: Jest watch me.

T-BONE: You caint last an hour out there. You in some kinda breakdown fever.

WEASEL: Get outa my fuck you *face*.

T-BONE: Caint even cuss right.

WEASEL: Dont touch me. I aint afraid to use this.

Pause.

T-BONE: Where you git that Arkansas toothpick.

WEASEL: This is a *knife*. Aint a Texas sewin needle, a Mississippi pig sticker or a Kentucky back scratcher. Its a knife a knife a knife a knife a knife now what you gonna do bout it.

T-BONE: Not a damn thing.

WEASEL: Thass good.

T-BONE: See you later.

Pause.

WEASEL: You goin back to sleep.

T-BONE: Might as well.

WEASEL: Dark out there aint it.

T-BONE: Usually is this time o night.

WEASEL: Mebbe I should wait till morning.

T-BONE: Mebbe you should.

WEASEL: Hell T-Bone you really gonna settle fer this?

Pause.

T-BONE: I dont settle fer *nothin* man. *(Pause)* Went fer a swim yesterday. Water was clean blue. Specks o coral washin through my toes. Winnebago pulls up on shore. Family gits out. Man, woman, two little kids with bony knees an big bright eyes. They all dressed up in swimmin outfits, headin fer the water. An the little ones start bouncin on the sand, lettin the waves carry em back an forth an trying to ketch the seagulls. All of a sudden the mama calls em in an they climb right back into the trailer. Couldn figger this out. I mean they was havin plenty o fun, why cut it short. Then jest fore the mama climb in with the baskets an shut the door, she stop, turn an look straight at my face.

Pause.

WEASEL: What this got to do with me.

T-BONE: Dont give me that man you was right there on the beach.

WEASEL: I dint notice.

T-BONE: This what I talkin bout Weasel. Things go on all the time, right front o yer nose, an you dont ever *see* nothin. Why is that?

WEASEL: Dunno T-Bone. Hard to say.

Pause.

T-BONE: Guess you right. Time to move on.

A Construction Site in Frogmore

WEASEL: Hell of a crowd here.

T-BONE: Yellin an carryin signs. Dont like the looks of it.

WEASEL: Lets check it out.

T-BONE: Could be the Klan.

WEASEL: Naw theys black folk too.

T-BONE: Whats that they sayin.

WEASEL: Sounds like no nukes, no nukes.

T-BONE: Whats a nuke.

WEASEL: You know. Them little Oriental fellas, come here after the war.

T-BONE: An they gainst them. What I tell you. Ever way you turn another damn biggot.

WEASEL: Man climbin the platform.

DOC TATUM: Friends an noble citizens o the esteemed municipality o Frogmore. For those who dont know me, I be jest a country doctor. A pore doctor whose only fee is the welfare an safety o the residents along Port Royal Sound. So what, you may well ask yourself, is a country doctor doin on top the stump spoutin off like some kinda know-it-all bout nookular power. What am I doin here.

T-BONE: Beats the fuck outa me.

WEASEL: Let him talk T-Bone mebbe you *learn* somethin.

T-BONE: Only thing I wanna know is where folk findin this corn on the cob.

WEASEL: Fine go look fer it I wait here.

DOC TATUM: What are any of us doin here, soakin ourselves with sweat an sea air, tired an hungry. How bout you young man.

WEASEL: Who me.

DOC TATUM: Thass right come on up here where we kin all see you. *(Pause)* Tell us yer name son. *(Pause)* Go head we aint gonna bite you.

WEASEL: Weas . . . William.

DOC TATUM: Where you from Bill.

WEASEL: Greenville.

DOC TATUM: Greenville thass a long journey. What brings you to our fine community.

WEASEL: Lookin fer work.

DOC TATUM: You hear that folks. The man is *looking for work.* Find anythin yet.

WEASEL: Well not exactly—

DOC TATUM: Course not you know why not I tell you why not. *Indifference.* Plain an simple. Who the hell cares bout you.

Pause.

WEASEL: Dunno.

DOC TATUM: I do. I care bout you Billy. An I wanna do my best to find you a job.

WEASEL: How bout somethin in sales.

DOC TATUM: Gotta git elected first Bill. You kin step down now.

WEASEL: Thanks Doc.

DOC TATUM: Now I—

WEASEL: An thanks to the city o Frogmore. Its a pleasure to be passin through sech a nice town.

DOC TATUM: Fine fine git youself some corn while its hot. *(Pause)* Now I hear you askin, whats wrong with the district representatives we awready got. What makes *you* so different. Well all I got to say is its bout time we had a feller in the Statehouse who knows somethin bout *disease.* I aint jest talkin bout the putrefaction o the flesh. Im talkin bout a disease o the spirit. The kind o disease that leads to nookular waste in your neighborhood. Dont let that disease infect the glorious land o Port Royal Sound. Vote for Doctor Lyle Tatum. Thank you.

T-BONE: He done?

WEASEL: Where you been.

T-BONE: Workin the crowd. Looky here. Two wallets an a bracelet.

WEASEL: You missed somethin lemme tell you. I gotta talk to this feller.

T-BONE: Wha for the man could pop corn in his mouth.

WEASEL: You wrong T-Bone hey Doctor Doctor.

DOC TATUM: Lyle Tatum. Glad to meet you thanks fer comin out showin your support proud citizens like you gonna bring bout brighter days in the tidelands. Will you help us in our noble efforts by takin up one o these plexiglass protest signs.

T-BONE: Whats it pay.

DOC TATUM: Thass a good point my friend but Im sorely afraid all I have to offer is the eternal gratitude o the good common folk o South Carolina.

T-BONE: Hell even the unions pay a dolla a day.

WEASEL: See Doc we aint been eatin too reglar an a little bit o sustinance could go a long way with us. We might could even spread the word long to a whole slew o folk aint got no permanent address. Theys a lotta folk like us be glad to vote fer a feller like you.

DOC TATUM: My friend you have touched my conscience down to its very core. The plight o the homeless is one o the central thrusts o my campaign. Please be my guests at my house tonight for the Virginia end of a ham an cornbread.

T-BONE: *Awright.*

WEASEL: We dont wanna take advantage.

DOC TATUM: Not at all.

T-BONE: Caint say no to a man as hospital as you.

WEASEL: Any nuke shows his face roun here gonna have to deal with *us*.

Doc Tatum's Porch

DOC TATUM: You boys git yer fill?

T-BONE: Yessir. That hit the spot all right.

DOC TATUM: Got some news fer you boys.

WEASEL: Whats that.

DOC TATUM: A surprise. You gonna git yer picture took.

T-BONE: By who.

DOC TATUM: City paper. They gonna do a story on you. You boys gonna have jobs fore you know it.

WEASEL: Hear that T-Bone what I tell you bout this feller. How kin we thank you proper.

DOC TATUM: Jest enjoy yourselves.

WEASEL: Thank the man T-Bone whats wrong with you.

T-BONE: Dont want my picture took.

WEASEL: Course you do.

T-BONE: Dont want nobody lookin at me.

DOC TATUM: Fine fine we discuss it later have some more Jack Daniel. Now tell me true what you think o the speech.

T-BONE: You done raise the devil all right.

DOC TATUM: But what did you think. I wanna know yer perspective as a coupla citizens abused an betrayed by society.

T-BONE: That us?

DOC TATUM: The way I see you. How do you see yourself.

T-BONE: A car thief.

DOC TATUM: You are a creature o God.

WEASEL: T-Bone dont believe in God.

T-BONE: God aint got no use fer the likes o me.

DOC TATUM: He looks after each an ever one o his creations.

T-BONE: You ever see a possum git squashed by a semi.

WEASEL: Last piece o pie.

DOC TATUM: Take it I git the phone. (Pause) Tatum. Where you at Skippy tole you to be here eight sharp with photographers. (Pause) Nother assignment you tell me what they got thats better than Doc Tatum feedin a coupla bums week fore election. They keep askin fer human interest soon as you give em some where the hell are they. Four-alarm fire hell gotta be somebody left. (Pause) God no not that cross-eyed fool last time he took my picture I looked like a burn victim. Okay Skippy you done right jest line it up fer tomorrow night I make sure they still be here hold on. (Pause) Hey boys if you not too busy why not stay a coupla days. Free room an board till you feel good an refreshed cant beat that now can you.

T-BONE: Dont know bout this Weasel.

WEASEL: Whats on the menu.

DOC TATUM: Hell I dunno how bout some nice veal hold on whats that Skippy. (Pause) Right veals too ostentatious how bout fried chicken. Good boys how does fried chicken an mashed potatoes sound.

WEASEL: Jest dandy.

DOC TATUM: Right eight o clock tell em I gonna take em in that should git their asses over here. (Pause) Sorry boys a little campaign bizness now where were we.

T-BONE: Talkin bout yer speech.

WEASEL: I liked it.

DOC TATUM: You did now.

WEASEL: Liked it a bunch. Minded me o that feller on the 700 Club.

DOC TATUM: I got plans fer this state boys. Big plans.

WEASEL: Kin tell that jest by lookin at you. Whatcha plannin to do.

DOC TATUM: Lookin fer some Jim Beam. Here it is.

WEASEL: I mean when you git elected. You gonna turn things roun aint ya.

DOC TATUM: You damn right I gonna turn things round. I give you my solemn promise that I aint gonna let up till I wipe out ever pocket o poverty in this district. I tell you how come. As God is my witness I mean what I bout to say from the bottom o my heart. I *hate* poor people. I hate lookin at em an I hate livin near em. I hate the way they look the way they smell an most of all I hate that pathetic look o dejection and humiliation on their faces. Gives me a headache jest to think bout it. Disturbs my sleep.

WEASEL: I know what you mean.

DOC TATUM: Speakin o which its bout that time. You boys make yourself comfy spare room down the hall bathroom next to it. Tomorrow we give some reporters a call an they can watch me give both o you thorough medical examinations for free. Either o you got hookworms?

WEASEL: No sir.

DOC TATUM: Damn. You sure? Tell you what I check yer stools in the mornin an mebbe we get lucky. Night now.

Pause.

T-BONE: I got his car keys. Lets go.

WEASEL: Put them back T-Bone.

T-BONE: Whats wrong with you.

WEASEL: Not him. This is different.

T-BONE: What is.

WEASEL: He cares bout us. Wants to hep us.

T-BONE: He *gonna* hep us. That Chrysler gonna hep us get to Florida. Time he shakes off that Jim Beam we be in Key West.

WEASEL: Aint gonna do it T-Bone.

T-BONE: Dont be a fool Weasel we be *nothin* to this man talkin bout us like some kind o damn *animal.* Settin right there in front of us saying how bad we stink.

WEASEL: He dont mean us.

T-BONE: He mean ever one but *him.*

WEASEL: Dammit T-Bone we gettin fed at last an you wanna fuck it up.

T-BONE: You jest hearin what you wanna hear.

WEASEL: I gettin sick o you T-Bone so proud o sayin how nothin matters, givin up fore you even try.

T-BONE: Thass right. Comin or aint you.

WEASEL: Not with you.

T-BONE: You rather kiss ass all yer life.

WEASEL: An you rather be an empty sack. A *loser.* (*Pause*) Ahhhhhhhhhhh!

Long pause.

T-BONE: You hurt me Weasel. Why you wanna hurt me.

WEASEL: Look at this blood. Shit.

T-BONE: I break yer nose?

WEASEL: Probly.

T-BONE: You shouldna said that.
WEASEL: Git out.
T-BONE: Yeah. *(Pause)* See you.

In the Dark

WEASEL: Doc Tatum. *(Pause)* Doc. Doc Tatum. Wake up.
DOC TATUM: That you Skippy.
WEASEL: No sir. Its me. Weasel. You took us in, member? Fed us some ham.
DOC TATUM: What the hell you want. Dont you try nothin I got a gun right here.
WEASEL: No no it aint nothin like that. Look kin I turn on the light. Its somethin important.

Pause.

DOC TATUM: Go head. *(Pause)* You woke me up cause of a nosebleed.
WEASEL: No sir.
DOC TATUM: Tilt yer head back an put ice on it. Good night.
WEASEL: Its bout T-Bone. He borrowed yer car.

Pause.

DOC TATUM: Borrowed it.
WEASEL: Cept he might ferget to bring it back.
DOC TATUM: Lemme git this straight. He attacked you an stole my car.
WEASEL: He didnt attack me.
DOC TATUM: He didnt.
WEASEL: Naw. He jest . . . hit me.
DOC TATUM: I see.
WEASEL: I said something stupid. I deserved it. This is all my fault.
DOC TATUM: Hand me that phone.
WEASEL: He dont even know where he be goin. He jest headin fer more trouble.
DOC TATUM: Thass fer sure.
WEASEL: I cant let him do that to hisself. Know what Im sayin Doc Im worried about him.
DOC TATUM: You did the right thing son. We gonna bring him back here dont you fret.
WEASEL: He aint a bad man Doc. He jest needs a little . . . what you call it . . .
DOC TATUM: Rehabilitatin.
WEASEL: Yeah thass it. You gonna help him aint ya? Dont send him back to Black River.
DOC TATUM: I wont press charges. You have my word.

A Prison Cell

T-BONE: Hunh? Who there.

BROTHER TIM: Just me.

T-BONE: A preacher. Dont want no preacher.

BROTHER TIM: Brother Tim.

T-BONE: Dont care if you Father Time git outa my cell.

BROTHER TIM: Wanna cigarette?

T-BONE: No I dont wanna cigarette I wanna know why you preachers gotta assume ever body lying in a jail cell caint wait to feast they eyes on a man o the cloth. This gonna be hard fer you to unnerstan but I dont want you. I want a woman. Git me a woman or ask God to send me one. While you at it tell him I want a few answers to some questions disturbin my mind. Sech as if God be so disgusted with the human race that he set up places like this why dint he just wipe us all out with the Flood in the first place. Or is it all some kinda game with him like the one he played with Abraham. Some angel come down an tell me to sacrifice *my* son I whip that angels ass. An Job what a sorry son of a bitch standin round thankin God ever time he gits kicked in the nuts. I wont put up with that shit an you can go tell that to God. An where the hell did Jesus go, up there watchin the dog races ever day whens he plannin to come back anyway. Maybe he jest plain *forgot*. An whats God got to offer a feller like me? He gonna stick me in some place where all I do is sit around worshippin *him*? Got news fer you Brother Tim that might be *yore* idea of eternal bliss but it jest dont cut it with me. Tell you something else. I seen them pictures o God when I was in school an the cat is *white*. So what you got to say Brother Tim I be all ears lay the Word on me.

Pause.

BROTHER TIM: Wanna cigarette?

Clayborne Construction Company

WEASEL: Howdy do sir. William Weasler at yer service. I heard bout yer ad an jest wanted to quire bout the bricklayin job.

CLAYBORNE: I. Knnnow. You.

WEASEL: Lawd in heaven you the man back in that church basement.

CLAYBORNE: You. Gave. Mmmme.

WEASEL: A tellygram right well theys a proper explanation fer that see Western Union done mixed up the wires. Course I took the blame an fore you know it I be outa the messenger service you dont believe a word o this do you.

CLAYBORNE: Nnnno.

WEASEL: I be on my way now.

CLAYBORNE: Hold. On. You. Got. The. Job.

WEASEL: I do?

CLAYBORNE: I. Won. The swee. The swee.

WEASEL: The sweepstakes? You won the sweepstakes?

CLAYBORNE: Nnnnow. Immmm. Rich.

WEASEL: I had it in my hands. In my very hands. An now you work here. Wait a minute. Clayborne Construction. You own it.

CLAYBORNE: Mmme. And. Nnnna. Than.

The Prison Cell

T-BONE: Hunh what now who are you.

REVEREND GLUCK: The Lawd Awmighty bless you an preserve you now an forever.

T-BONE: Reverend Gluck.

REVEREND GLUCK: Kind sir you member the man I was only pretendin to be. But alas it was only a disguise to cover a multitude o sins. I stand afore you one William Weasler, former resident o Greenville, now yer cellmate for the heenous crime o patricide.

T-BONE: What you sayin. They took you in fer killin Weasels daddy?

REVEREND GLUCK: I give up peaceful. They have all the evidence they need. The murder weapon. Identification. Fingerprints. Motive.

T-BONE: What motive?

REVEREND GLUCK: I hated my daddy.

T-BONE: But he aint yer daddy. They got the wrong man.

REVEREND GLUCK: Beg to differ son. I confessed to the murder.

Pause.

T-BONE: You total crazy now aint you.

REVEREND GLUCK: Crazy . . . is a Willie Nelson song. I like Willie Nelson. You like Willie Nelson?

T-BONE: Listen Reverend you aint William Weasler. You jest think you are.

REVEREND GLUCK: Thass where you wrong. I think Im Reverend Gluck. Thank heaven the authorities found me in time. They gonna send me to a place where they got drugs to help me member.

T-BONE: You dint kill him.

REVEREND GLUCK: You just said I was crazy.

T-BONE: You are. But William Weasler is my friend.

REVEREND GLUCK: Thank you son. You my friend too. I jest pray I dont strangle you in yer sleep.

Weasel's Bedroom

T-BONE: Weeeeasel. Wake up Weasel.

WEASEL: Go way T-Bone. You still in prison.

T-BONE: We got some bizness Weasel.

WEASEL: You aint even real. You jest a nightmare.

T-BONE: You been havin this nightmare a lot.

WEASEL: Look what do you want.

T-BONE: To beat the stuffin outa you.

WEASEL: Dammit T-Bone git outa here I gotta be up at six.

T-BONE: They lettin me out next month. Aint you fraid I gonna be lookin fer you?

WEASEL: Course I aint afraid. I gonna drive to Black River to pick you up.

T-BONE: Who gonna pick *you* up?

WEASEL: Where the hell are you.

T-BONE: In yer pillowcase. You been sleepin on my face.

WEASEL: You caint scare me.

T-BONE: What say I twist yer head off an use it fer a basketball.

WEASEL: Stay way from me T-Bone I mean it owwww leggo leggo my head no dont tear it off you pullin me outa bed stop it shit. *(Pause)* Where you at now.

T-BONE: Still in yer pillow. Night Weasel.

WEASEL: Look I doin fine without you. Got my own place, food on the table, gonna buy a *car* what you think o that T-Bone a car you dint even *steal*. When you git out I gonna hep you git back on yer feet then I kin sleep agin.

T-BONE: Think so.

WEASEL: Thass right now I gonna go back to sleep an I dont care if you in my pillow or not.

T-BONE: You need a shave.

The Gates of Black River Penitentiary

WEASEL: I swear T-Bone its damn good to see you agin. What say we put this place behind you.

T-BONE: Still dont know how they found me on the road to Florida.

WEASEL: Best not to think bout it no more.

T-BONE: Where you learn to drive.

WEASEL: Triple A Drivin School.

T-BONE: Git yer money back.

WEASEL: Like my car?

T-BONE: Its a *Chevette*.

WEASEL: Thass right you got somethin gainst compacts.

T-BONE: Jest Chevettes. You git that piece I ask for?

WEASEL: Why you need somethin like that T-Bone you jest got *out* for Chrissakes.

T-BONE: Where is it.

WEASEL: Aint got the need fer one now I got a job all lined up for you in Columbia.

T-BONE: The *piece* Weasel.

WEASEL: Under the seat.

Pause.

T-BONE: This it?

WEASEL: Course what you think.

T-BONE: Kin barely *see* this thing. I got fingers bigger than this barrel.

WEASEL: Its a snubnose.

T-BONE: Its a piece o shit.

WEASEL: Look I lost my ole contacts I did what I could.

T-BONE: Good thing I dont have a hole in my pocket.

WEASEL: Guess you heard Doc Tatum won the election. *(Pause)* Oww leggo leggo I tryin to drive.

T-BONE: Two things I dont wanna hear agin. One is the name o Doc Tatum. The other is the word "loser."

WEASEL: Got you.

T-BONE: Good. Now git off the highway take the county road.

WEASEL: Where we goin.

T-BONE: Gonna pay somebody a visit.

WEASEL: Look I went to a lotta trouble to git you this job.

T-BONE: Sorry Weasel we gonna take a little detour. Got a score to settle.

Happy Sam's Used Cars

WEASEL: Place all boarded up T-Bone. Lets go.

T-BONE: I dint come all this way fer nothin. He gotta be here.

WEASEL: Anybody there!

HAPPY SAM: Go to hell!

T-BONE: Thass him.

HAPPY SAM: I be tryin to sleep here. We aint open. Aint buyin aint sellin.

T-BONE: Aint leavin till we see you.

HAPPY SAM: Whos we.

WEASEL: T-Bone an Weasel.

HAPPY SAM: This look like a butcher shop boy now hit the highway.

T-BONE: Aint sellin meat.

HAPPY SAM: Had weasel once dont even make good stew.

WEASEL: Look T-Bone what you got in mind here anyhow.

T-BONE: Open up or we force the door.

Pause.

HAPPY SAM: There you happy now what the hell you want.

T-BONE: Wanna talk to you.

HAPPY SAM: Bout what.

T-BONE: Dont you member me.

HAPPY SAM: What is this shit now you gonna make me *guess.*

T-BONE: We done bizness with you bout a year ago.

HAPPY SAM: That narrows it down dont it.

T-BONE: You bought a Buick from me fer a hunnerd five dollas.

HAPPY SAM: No kiddin musta circled that day on my calendar.

T-BONE: Mebbe this hep you member.

HAPPY SAM: What the hell you call that dont even look like a real gun.

T-BONE: Try me.

WEASEL: Now you done it we gonna go right back to prison.

HAPPY SAM: Now I suppose you gonna kill me.

T-BONE: Thinkin bout it.

HAPPY SAM: Thinkin bout it you mean you dont even *know.* I supposed to stand aroun in my shorts while you make up yer mind.

T-BONE: Shut up.

HAPPY SAM: Oh I know its the *suspense* of it aint it. You want me to stand here shakin while I wonder what you gonna do to me.

T-BONE: Aint afraid o nothin are you.

HAPPY SAM: Hell I had so many guns an knives stuck in my face I lost count. Folk try to poison my food. Hit me with their cars. Somebody put a cottonmouth in my mailbox jest last week. Hell my own dog tried to kill me till I had him shot.

WEASEL: Mebbe its yer attitude.

HAPPY SAM: Who asked you dickface. Now shoot me or git out.

T-BONE: We want our money back. Five thousand.

HAPPY SAM: Fine jest take yer popgun to the county attorney an rob *him.* He took everthin I own cept my teeth.

T-BONE: You sayin the law shut you down.

HAPPY SAM: Cuzed me o sellin stolen property. Course now *they* git to sell it dont they.

WEASEL: We wastin time here T-Bone.

HAPPY SAM: So long boys. *(Pause)* What the hell is that a *Chevette.*

Long pause.

T-BONE: Awright Weasel lets check out this job o yours.

WEASEL: You wont be sorry T-Bone jest wait till you feel that steady paycheck in yer pocket. Whole new life fer you earnin some *respeck* fer yourself.

T-BONE: Now dont *push* me. I say I try it. Thass all.

Future Home of Columbia Trust

T-BONE: What first.

WEASEL: See that stack o tile.

T-BONE: Yep.

WEASEL: Start in the corner an lay it out.

T-BONE: Okay. What then.

WEASEL: Do the next room.

T-BONE: No I mean what else I git to do.

WEASEL: You aint even started this job an now you want another one.

T-BONE: Aint saying that.

WEASEL: Then what you want.

T-BONE: Jest dont wanna do the same thing all day. I like a little variety.

WEASEL: I tole them this be your *specialty* T-Bone. Once you git a specialty you gotta stick with it. I do bricks. You do tile.

T-BONE: An thass all I do. Forever an ever.

WEASEL: Thass right. You a free man now. Take advantage of it.

T-BONE: Shit.

WEASEL: Now git started an I check back on you.

T-BONE: Hey Weasel.

WEASEL: What now.

T-BONE: Somebody sleepin here behind the tile.

WEASEL: Hell not again wake up you.

T-BONE: Hey dont you scarin him.

WEASEL: Thass the point.

T-BONE: Aint wearin nothin but a raincoat. Who is he.

WEASEL: Some derelict thinks he got the right to spend the night here. Cant tell you how many times I have to kick him out.

T-BONE: I dont see him hurtin nobody.

WEASEL: He aint right in the head. Look at him throwin his arms around.

T-BONE: Look like a dog been beat too much.

WEASEL: He gotta go fore they find him here an we git in trouble.

T-BONE: Mans got some demons to fight. Who you swingin at feller. I be able to hep you if you tell me who to ketch.

WEASEL: Dont *talk* to him T-Bone you jest encouragin him.

T-BONE: Whats wrong with that. Gimme a sandwich.

WEASEL: No way Jose this gotta git me through the day.

T-BONE: You got two sandwiches there.

WEASEL: I *work* T-Bone. I *burn* this food.

T-BONE: I say give it here. (*Pause*) Here you go feller. Like some tuna salad. (*Pause*) Nice raincoat. Too bad you got paint on it.

RAINCOAT: Blood.

Pause.

T-BONE: Wanna bite?

Pause.

RAINCOAT: I guess.

WEASEL: Jesus T-Bone now we never git rid of him.

T-BONE: You got a name feller.

RAINCOAT: Nope.

T-BONE: Me neither. How bout I call you Raincoat.

RAINCOAT: I guess.

WEASEL: Look its my ass on the line you know. I *got* you this job I be responsible fer you.

T-BONE: Well I be relievin you o that Weasel.

WEASEL: Guess you want us both out on the street agin that what you want.

T-BONE: Keep this shit up I gonna quit.

WEASEL: Now aint that smart. Go head run away like you did with Doc Tatums car. See if I bring you back this time.

Pause.

T-BONE: What you mean bring me back.

WEASEL: I always lookin out fer you T-Bone keepin you outa trouble. I woke up Doc Tatum tole him you stole his car.

T-BONE: You set me up fer Black River.

WEASEL: Now that aint my fault. Tatum said he wouldn press charges.

T-BONE: An you believed that.

WEASEL: Hell I gotta believe in *somethin* dont I.

Pause.

T-BONE: Someone callin yer name.

WEASEL: Shit thass the foreman I be in fer it now. Make sure you git him outa here I be right back.

Pause.

T-BONE: Dont mind him jest rest yer legs awhile. Taste good dont it.

RAINCOAT: I guess.

T-BONE: Used to git in a lot of fights myself. In the State Reformatory. Thirteen years old. You ever there.

RAINCOAT: Nope.

T-BONE: You lucky. *(Pause)* Ran away once. They sent some dogs out an caught me. Took me back to this big room with a mattress on the floor. Had to lie face down while they hit me with a strap. Had little holes cut in the leather so it would tear strips o skin off. An if I cried they start all over. But I dint cry. I jest lay there. An took it. *(Pause)* Few days later I took a knife in the shin.

WEASEL: You tole me it was a rat terrier.

T-BONE: I know. *(Pause)* You feel like gettin up now Raincoat? Cause I gotta git at this tile soon. I be a company man now.

WEASEL: No you aint. Foreman jest let you go.

T-BONE: How come.

WEASEL: He say I never tole him you was colored.

T-BONE: Fergot that little fact now did you.

WEASEL: Like I tole you before T-Bone I dont think bout them things.

T-BONE: Now you see where that gits you.

Pause.

WEASEL: What you gonna do now.

T-BONE: I be hittin the highway.

WEASEL: Where you goin.

T-BONE: What you care.

WEASEL: You off to git youself arrested agin aint you.

T-BONE: Mebbe.

WEASEL: Or killed.

T-BONE: Look you got somethin to say then say it.

WEASEL: Lemme come with you.

Pause.

T-BONE: You expeck me to take you along. Somebody I thought was my *friend.*

WEASEL: I am yer friend.

T-BONE: You sent me to *prison.*

WEASEL: I aint always a *good* friend.

Pause.

T-BONE: You got a good thing goin here Weasel.

WEASEL: They fired you T-Bone.

T-BONE: That dont bother me.

WEASEL: It bothers me.

Pause.

T-BONE: Could be dangerous.

WEASEL: Okay by me.

T-BONE: I dunno Weasel.

WEASEL: You kin hit me if you want.

T-BONE: Dont wanna hit you.

WEASEL: Shore you do go head you know it make you feel better. Grab me twist my arm.

T-BONE: Dont have to do that.

WEASEL: How come.

T-BONE: I git *him* to do it. Hey Raincoat. He all yours.

Another Highway

WEASEL: I tell you we be headin fer trouble T-Bone.

T-BONE: Hey Raincoat. Do we git yer word you aint gonna rob or kill us tween here an the state line?

RAINCOAT: I guess.

T-BONE: There you go, Weasel.

WEASEL: That good nuff fer you?

T-BONE: The most we kin ask for.

RAINCOAT: Im hungry.

WEASEL: *Live* with it. Look T-Bone I still wanna be prepared.

T-BONE: Okay I got a pen out. Dont take all night.

WEASEL: This be the last will an testament o William Weasler, formerly o Greenville, South Carolina. Bein o sound mind—

T-BONE: That be the day.

WEASEL: You mind yourself. This a sacred document.

T-BONE: What the hell you gonna leave anybody.

WEASEL: In the event o my death, I would like my mama to have all the money left over at the moment o my departure.

T-BONE: Anythin else.

WEASEL: To my best an only friend T-Bone—

T-BONE: Shit Weasel—

WEASEL: Take it *down*. To T-Bone I leave my most prized possession—my car.

T-BONE: You gonna give me a goddam Chevette an thirty-two car payments?

WEASEL: You dont want it.

T-BONE: Hell no I dont want it.

WEASEL: How bout a tape containin Creedence Clearwater greatest hits.

T-BONE: *No.*

WEASEL: How bout you Raincoat you like CCR.

RAINCOAT: Proud Mary.

WEASEL: Thass the one.

RAINCOAT: Green River.

WEASEL: Yep.

RAINCOAT: Keep on Chooglin.

WEASEL: Hear this T-Bone.

RAINCOAT: Ramble Tamble.

WEASEL: Damn right.

RAINCOAT: Ooby Dooby.

WEASEL: Thass right thass right you like em *too* doncha.

RAINCOAT: Nope.

Pause.

T-BONE: You done.

WEASEL: Now your turn.

T-BONE: Come off it Weasel.

WEASEL: You be surprised. It give you some piece o mind.

T-BONE: For Chrissake. This here be the last will an testament o T-Bone.

WEASEL: Gotta use yer real name.

T-BONE: I dont have a damn thing an I never did. But if I do happen to own anythin at the time o my death . . . nobody gits to have it. Signed an witnessed, Thomas J Bone. *(Pause)* You right Weasel. I feel a whole lot better.

WEASEL: Which way T-Bone. We got four directions.

RAINCOAT: Head south.

END OF PLAY

Tent Meeting
Larry Larson, Levi Lee
and Rebecca Wackler

About the Playwrights

Larry Larson was born in Minneapolis and attended the University of Minnesota before moving to Atlanta in 1970. After work in advertising, rock-and-roll and local radio, he joined the company of Academy Theatre in 1972. He performed in over 40 plays at the Academy, as well as directing the company's Lab Theatre, teaching in its school and creating plays for its Youth and Children's Theatre program. Since leaving the company in 1980, he has worked at Alliance Theatre, Theatre Emory, Actors Theatre of Louisville, and most notably at Southern Theater Conspiracy, where *Tent Meeting* was developed. He has also acted in films and TV. In addition to his many collaborations with Lee and Wackler and STC, Larson's writings include songs, poetry, and the plays *Christmas at the Palace, Far from the Peaceful Shore* and *Hardware Jim*.

Born in Atlanta and a graduate of Western Kentucky University, Levi Lee has been acting, writing and directing since 1961. He has appeared in nearly one hundred productions, primarily in Atlanta at Alliance Theatre, Academy Theatre and Theatre under the Stars, as well as at Actors Theatre of Louisville. He has directed at these theatres and has also appeared in films and TV. In 1979, with Rebecca Wackler, he founded Southern Theater Conspiracy, for which he has written, directed and acted, serving as its artistic director through the present time. Works he wrote and produced for STC include the book and lyrics of the musical *Outlaws*; several one-act plays; and, with Larry Larson, *Mirandolina Unchained, The Blood Orgy Trilogy*, and *Some Things You Need to Know Before the World Ends: A Final Evening with the Illuminati*, which was presented at Actors Theatre of Louisville's 1986 Humana Festival of New American Plays and is to be published in *American Theatre* in the spring of 1988. In collaboration with Larson and Wackler he wrote *Nicholas DeBeaubien's Hunchback of Notre Dame*; and *Isle of Dogs*, commissioned by Louisville and performed at the theatre's 1985 SHORTS festival and at the Edinburgh Festival. The three also collaborated to write *The Gatherer* for PBS. Lee and Larson's plays for young people, *Tales of Rat Alley* and *The Grubb Chronicles*, written for Alliance Theatre, have found several other productions around the country.

Rebecca Wackler was born in Anchorage, Alaska. A graduate of Florida State University, she now lives in Atlanta. Besides acting and directing with Southern Theater Conspiracy, she has been acting for many years with Atlanta's Alliance Theatre, Academy Theatre, Proposition Theatre, Theatrical Outfit and Theatre Emory. She has also worked in film and TV. In addition to her collaborations with Larson and Lee, she has co-authored with Lee *The Gospel of St. Mary*, a musical about Mary Magdalene presented in Atlanta in 1982, and *Moonlily*, a children's play produced by Theatrical Outfit. Her play *Wild Streak* was produced by Actors

Theatre of Louisville in 1986. Most recently she has been commissioned, with Lee, to write an "adult" version of *Alice in Wonderland* for Atlanta's Center for Puppetry Arts.

About the Play

Tent Meeting was developed by Southern Theater Conspiracy in Atlanta and was originally presented in workshop productions there at Nexus Theatre (1983) and Alliance Theatre (1984). Part of Actors Theatre of Louisville's Humana Festival of New American Plays in 1985, the play was subsequently performed at the Spoleto Festival USA in Charleston, S.C.; the Kennedy Center in Washington, D.C.; and the Dublin International Festival. It was produced by Philadelphia Drama Guild, under the direction of Patrick Tovatt, in November 1985. In the spring of 1987, it was presented by ERB Productions, Joan Stein, the Seco Production Company and John Roach at the Astor Place Theatre in New York City, directed by Norman René. In all these productions, the play's three roles were performed by the authors. *Tent Meeting* was circulated as a *Plays in Process* script in the summer of 1986.

Characters

THE REVEREND EDWARD O. TARBOX, an evangelist.
DARRELL, his adult son; wears a Purple Heart at all times.
BECKY ANN, his adult daughter.
VOICE ON RADIO
VOICE OF CUSTOMS MAN
VOICE OF DRIVER

Time

1946.

Place

The primary setting for the play is the interior of a makeshift house trailer, vintage 1930s-40s. The trailer is seen outside a laboratory at the University of Arkansas, in Moose Jaw, Saskatchewan, and on the road in between.

The Play

Tent Meeting

ACT ONE

Scene 1

Night. Outside a laboratory at the University of Arkansas. Dim light on a high balcony. REVEREND EDDIE and DARRELL stand in front of the trailer, carrying large flashlights and a wicker basket. THEY look up at the balcony and speak in hushed, urgent tones.

REV. ED: This is it!

DARRELL: How do you know?

REV. ED: Because God told me this is it.

DARRELL: Oh.

REV. ED: He has led our footsteps to this place. This is it. Up there. *(Shines his flashlight on the balcony)*

DARRELL: Way up there?

REV. ED: It's not that high.

DARRELL: Not that high! If I had a good leg, I would go up, which I don't . . .

REV. ED: Darrell . . .

DARRELL: So I'll just stay here . . .

REV. ED: Darrell, you're going up.

DARRELL: Yes sir.

Dog barks.

REV. ED: Hand me the rope.

DARRELL: What rope?

REV. ED: The rope to get up there with! You haven't got the rope?

DARRELL: No.

REV. ED: Then how do you aim to get up there?

DARRELL: Well, I don't have no rope.

REV. ED: I hear you saying that! I am simply asking you how you aim to get up to that window?

DARRELL: I'll go up the fire ladder.

REV. ED: And what about the rope?

DARRELL: What rope?

REV. ED: The rope, the rope, the rope! We gotta have a rope! How's the rope gonna get up there? It can't just climb up there magically by itself!

A rope comes tumbling from the balcony. THEY *are startled.*

DARRELL: Jesus!

REV. ED: Shhhhhh!

We hear humming from the balcony. THE REVEREND EDDIE *shines his flashlight up on the balcony, illuminating the face of* BECKY ANN. SHE *is leaning over the railing, with large wads of cotton stuck in her ears.*

Becky Ann!

DARRELL: Jesus!

REV. ED: Don't say Jesus!

DARRELL: You say Jesus.

REV. ED: I'm praying when I say it. *(Looks up at balcony)* Becky Ann, I thought I told you to wait in the car. Get down here!

DARRELL: Someone's gonna hear that hummin.' We're all gonna go to jail for a hundred years . . .

REV. ED: Becky Ann!

DARRELL: She can't hear you. She's got that cotton in her ears.

REV. ED: I know she does. Becky Ann! Take that cotton out! Becky Ann!

REV. ED AND DARRELL *(Ad-libbing, overlapping)*: Take the cotton out . . . take it out . . . etc. *(Yelling)* TAKE THE COTTON OUT!

BECKY ANN *(Removes the cotton from one ear)*: Huh?

DARRELL: Jesus.

BECKY ANN: What?

REV. ED: Get down here!

BECKY ANN: Okay. *(*SHE *stuffs the cotton back in her ears and starts down, humming)*

REV. ED: All right. You go up. I'll stay down here and tie the rope.

DARRELL: Daddy, I've got an idea. I've got a good idea. Here's my idea. See, Becky Ann is already up there, right? She's already up there. And I'm down here. See what I mean. Why don't Becky Ann just stay up there since she's already up there and I'll just stay down here, since I'm already down here. I'll just stay here and help you. Isn't that a good idea? I'll tell Becky Ann.

HE *turns and comes face to face with* BECKY ANN.

BECKY ANN: Hi.

DARRELL: Hi. Okay, I'm going up there now, at the risk of my own life.

REV. ED: Hold this flashlight on the knot, Becky Ann. Knot! (HE *hands her the flashlight*) Stop humming. Now hold your finger there . . . *finger*, Becky Ann. (HE *puts her finger in the knot*) Okay . . . stop humming . . . stop humming, Becky Ann. Someone will hear you . . . stop humming . . . (HE *snatches the cotton out of one ear*) Becky Ann!

BECKY ANN: Huh?

REV. ED: Stop humming.

BECKY ANN: Okay.

REV. ED: Darrell, are you up there? Darrell?

DARRELL *appears at the edge of the balcony.*

DARRELL: What?

REV. ED: Are you up there?

DARRELL: Yeah!

REV. ED: Are you ready for the basket?

DARRELL: I guess.

REV. ED: Pull it on up.

DARRELL: Yes sir. (HE *begins to pull the basket up*) Daddy! It's caught on something!

REVEREND EDDIE *shines his flashlight on the basket.* BECKY ANN's *finger is still in the knot.*

REV. ED: Becky Ann! Take your finger out of the knot! Finger! Finger!

SHE *does so.* DARRELL *pulls the basket up.* BECKY ANN *disappears.*

DARRELL: Okay, I got the basket up here. Now what?

REV. ED: Go get him.

DARRELL: Where is he?

REV. ED: Just look around. There ain't no two like him.

DARRELL: That's the truth (*Pause*) Wait. I think I see him.

REV. ED: Well fetch him and put him in the basket. *(Pause)* What's takin' so long?

DARRELL: There's all kind of tubes and wires hooked up here . . . I got to pull them out . . .

REV. ED: Hurry!

DARRELL: Okay, I think I got 'im out.

REV. ED: Put him in the basket.

DARRELL: Yeccch! Yeccchhhh!

REV. ED: Hurry up!

DARRELL *brings the basket to the edge of the balcony.*

DARRELL: Okay! I got 'im in the basket. I'm gonna lower it down, now. You gonna catch it?

REV. ED: No, I'm gonna let if fall splat at my feet! Just lower it down!

DARRELL *lowers the basket and* THE REVEREND EDDIE *takes it, unties his end of the rope.*

I got it. (HE *walks away from the balcony and kneels over the basket, praying)*

DARRELL: Bombs away! We did it! We did it, didn't we Daddy? Where are you goin'? Daddy what are we doin'? Why don't you answer? (HE *runs to the kneeling* REVEREND EDDIE) C'mon let's go.

REV. ED: . . . and John the Baptist. Thank you Lord. Thank you in Jesus' name. Amen.

DARRELL: We better get out of here.

REV. ED: Start the car.

DARRELL: What if it won't start?

REV. ED: Darrell start the car! The car ain't gonna start magically by itself!

Sound of the car starting. THEY *are startled.*

DARRELL: Becky Ann.

Loud car horn honking.

REV. ED: Jesus!

DARRELL: See, you said Jesus.

REV. ED: I was praying.

THEY *exit.*

Scene 2

In the darkness, we hear a radio: old-time programs from the '40s; the sound of someone switching the dial, moving from program to program. Lights up on the family in their trailer. DARRELL *is frantically switching stations.* THE REVEREND ED-DIE *is standing beside the baby basket, reading his Bible.* BECKY ANN *is at the stove, the cotton in her ears, cooking and humming. In this scene and throughout the play, whenever* BECKY ANN *has the cotton in her ears, it should be assumed that* SHE *is humming, in various degrees of loudness and energy, according to how it affects the focus of the scene.*

REV. ED: Turn off that radio.

DARRELL: Nothing. There's nothing about it on my radio. I've tried every station.

REV. ED: I told you God would look after us.

DARRELL: Yeah, well I just wish God could do the driving with his headlights off, in the middle of the night, pullin' this trailer in one-thousand-degree heat, and a carburetor that coughs like an ol' coal miner with black lung and TB . . .

REV. ED: Sit down and eat your breakfast.

BECKY ANN serves food and continues humming. DARRELL *sits at the table.*

DARRELL: I don't like eatin' breakfast at ten o'clock at night. I don't see why we can't eat and sleep like normal people.

REV. ED: I told you. We sleep during the day and drive at night.

DARRELL: I wouldn't mind so much if I didn't have trouble sleepin' because of my war memories . . .

By this time BECKY ANN *is seated at the table,* DARRELL *is beginning to sit.* REVEREND EDDIE *reaches up and places his hands on their shoulders. Silence.* THEY *bow their heads.*

REV. ED: Amen.

The humming resumes.

DARRELL: . . . which I do. I don't know this whole thing just seems kinda crazy.

REV. ED: Crazy? Crazy? I suppose you think Daniel was crazy. I suppose you think Job was crazy. I suppose you think God was crazy.

DARRELL: Here it comes. Here it comes.

REV. ED: Everybody at this table who thinks God is crazy, raise your hands. *(Pause)* I suppose I was crazy when I had my affliction. I just imagined it. What caused the itching. The rash. The oozing sores. (HE *rolls up his sleeves and shows his bare arms*)

DARRELL: Poison ivy.

REV. ED: It was *not* poison ivy! I have never been allergic to poison ivy a single day in my life. The day we gave this baby away, blisters popped out under my arms. Then the creeping plague of God spread to my legs and feet. My feet swole up so big I couldn't lace my shoes. Then it infested my eyes. I couldn't see nothing but dark and light. Then . . . then it spread into my mouth. My mouth filled with pus. My tongue blistered, and my lips swole so big that I couldn't speak God's name.

DARRELL: Poison ivy.

REV. ED: It was *not* poison ivy! It was a sign from God. He was telling me that we had to get the child back. That we all sinned, all of us, in giving away one of our own. The baby was a gift from God!

DARRELL: Yeah, well it was Becky Ann's gift, why didn't she get poison ivy?

REV. ED: You know, Darrell, I feel sorry for you. Because you're blind. Not in your eyes, but in your soul. The glory of God is in front of you in all its majesty and splendor and you're too blind to see it. If you weren't my own son, I would cast you out to wander the earth in darkness.

DARRELL: Why don't you just cast me out, then?

REV. ED: Because family is in the flesh and in the blood. And because I swore on your momma's Bible that I would bring you to Jesus. And by God I aim to do it. (*Hits* DARRELL *with Bible several times, accenting the last sentence*) "The Son of Man goeth as it is written of him: But woe unto that man, by whom the Son of Man is betrayed! It had been good for that man if he had not been born!"

REVEREND EDDIE *exits, after grabbing his plate and greasy bacon.* DARRELL *sits for a moment, then rushes over to get his Bible.*

DARRELL: I'll bet that's not even in there. He makes most of that stuff up! He thinks nobody will call him on it. . . . He thinks just because he says a few "thees" and "thous" and stuff that nobody'll call him on it . . . well, I'll call him on it.

REV. ED (*Yelling from offstage*): Matthew 26:24.

DARRELL (*Pauses for a moment, starts to throw the book down angrily, then places it softly on the table*): Well, he makes some of it up. Momma wouldn'a let 'im get away with this.

DARRELL *puts on a baseball glove and smacks a ball into it.* BECKY ANN *stacks dishes and hums.* THEY *go on like that for a while, smacking and humming, smacking and humming. Finally,* DARRELL *stops and turns to* BECKY ANN, *whose humming has built to a loud tuneless symphony.*

Becky Ann? (*No response*) Becky Ann? (*No response*) Becky Ann? (HE *places himself in front of her face and waves.* SHE *looks up.* HE *points to his ears*)

BECKY ANN (*Takes the cotton out*): Huh?

DARRELL: You were hummin' again, Becky Ann. Did you know that? That you were hummin' again?

BECKY ANN: Was I?

DARRELL: Yes you were, Becky Ann. Hummin' up a storm, and not no tune that I ever heard, neither.

BECKY ANN: It weren't?

DARRELL: No, no tune at all. Now, Becky Ann, some people would get real bothered by that constant loud hummin' but not me, no sir, because you're my sister, and I know you've been under a lot of worry what with the . . . baby . . . and all. But maybe . . . and I would take this as a personal favor . . . if you could just stop that hummin'.

BECKY ANN: But I don't know I'm hummin'. How can I stop it if I don't know I'm doing it?

DARRELL: Maybe if you left the cotton out of your ears . . .

BECKY ANN: Oh, I'm sorry, Darrell, I can't do that. (Picks up her knitting and the baby basket)

DARRELL: Why not?

BECKY ANN: Well . . .

DARRELL: What are you trying to keep out, Becky Ann?

BECKY ANN (Laughs): I ain't trying to keep nothing out. I'm just trying to keep it in.

DARRELL: What? What are you trying to keep in?

BECKY ANN: The music. I'm really sorry it don't sound to you the way it does to me. Maybe if I hum better. I'll try it for you again.

DARRELL (Protesting): No, no, that's all right . . .

SHE puts the cotton back in her ears and hums loudly. SHE takes the cotton out of her ears.

BECKY ANN: How was that?

DARRELL: That wasn't no better, Becky Ann.

BECKY ANN: Oh, I know! You put the cotton in your ears.

DARRELL: No, I don't want no cotton!

BECKY ANN: But I want you to hear the music! (Despite DARRELL's protests, SHE stuffs the cotton in his ears. HE resigns himself and sits for a moment, listening) Darrell? (DARRELL just sits with a blank look on his face) Darrell? (No response) Darrell? (No response. SHE takes the cotton out of his ears)

DARRELL: Huh?

BECKY ANN: Did you hear it?

DARRELL: What?

BECKY ANN: The music.

DARRELL: No, I can't hear nothing with cotton in my ears.

BECKY ANN: I know, you just need more cotton. (SHE goes and opens a kitchen cabinet. The cabinet is stuffed to overflowing with cotton) I once tried putting corn silk in my ears, but it didn't work as good.

DARRELL: No, Becky Ann, no. I don't want no more cotton in my ears. I don't think I'm gonna hear it no matter how much cotton I put in my ears. 'Cause I don't think it's really there. (SHE *looks at him, hurt. Stuffs cotton back in her ears*) I'm sorry, Becky Ann. I'm sorry. (HE *takes the cotton from her ears*) Sure, it's there. I know it's there. I think I heard it a little bit!

BECKY ANN: Really? What did it sound like?

DARRELL: Well . . . it was . . . real nice . . . kind of faint . . . but nice . . .

BECKY ANN: Then you understand.

DARRELL: Sure. Sure I understand. Tell me when did you first hear that music Becky Ann? Do you remember?

BECKY ANN: Oh, I remember. I remember the exact moment.

Pause. DARRELL *waits expectantly.*

DARRELL: When was that moment?

BECKY ANN: It was almost a year ago. We were still living at the farm, in that old house. I'd gone to bed early the night before, 'cause it was rainin' real hard. And it was real dark outside and the wind was blowin' so hard like it would take the sides of the house off. I was all alone in the house. Daddy was off in Little Rock, and you was at the war . . . and the awful loudness of the wind kinda scared me. So I got in bed and crawled way down low under the quilt.

DARRELL: And that's when Daddy came home.

BECKY ANN: No, that's when I stuffed cotton in my ears, to keep out the beating of the rain and the roaring of the wind. I finally fell asleep. I don't know for how long, but when I woke up, it was daylight, and it was unearthly quiet. I'd forgot I had the cotton in my ears. Then I got up . . . and I felt dizzy . . . real good dizzy . . . purposeful dizzy . . . not Ferris-wheel dizzy . . . and I knew right then and there that I had been filled. (SHE *pats her stomach*) And that's when I heard the music.

DARRELL: Filled. Then, nine months later you had this little . . . rascal here, is that right?

BECKY ANN: That's right.

DARRELL: You know, Becky Ann, it don't look nothing like you. It must look more like . . . uh . . . what was the daddy's name again?

BECKY ANN: I didn't say.

DARRELL: Oh, I'm sure you did, Becky Ann. I'm sure I've heard you mention it.

BECKY ANN: I never.

DARRELL: Oh, you never . . . well, just for the record, what was the daddy's name? (SHE *puts the cotton back in her ears and begins to hum*) Don't do that, Becky Ann. I'm talkin' to you! I'm askin' you a question! I'm your brother. I have a right to know! (SHE *puts up her knitting and moves away*) Stop hummin'! Stop that! (*Her humming gets louder*) You might as well tell me now, Becky Ann, because I'm gonna find out one way or another! Becky Ann! (*Pause*) BECKY ANN!

SHE *washes the dishes.* DARRELL *looks disgusted and finally sits at the radio.* HE *turns it on.* HE *turns the dial and gets static and music. Suddenly, we hear the voice of a newscaster.*

RADIO: " . . . In his speech, he praised the integrity of General Douglas MacArthur and defended his own order to drop the atomic bomb on Japan last year. The President went on to say the effects of atomic power have not begun to be measured. In state news, authorities at the University of Arkansas are still baffled by the apparent kidnapping of a seriously deformed infant from the university laboratories . . . "

DARRELL *(Jumping up and running to the door)*: DADDY! IT'S ON! (HE *runs back and turns up the radio)*

RADIO: "State police working on the case say the infant was apparently abducted sometime during the night a few days ago from the laboratory where scientists were studying it. The window of the second-story lab showed signs of a break-in, police said."

THE REVEREND EDDIE *enters.* DARRELL *motions to the radio.*

DARRELL: Jesus, the state police!

RADIO: "Authorities pleaded with the abductors to return the birth-defective infant, saying that it could not live without special care. Elsewhere in the state, it looks like a good year for hog farmers. Barrows and gilts were up . . . "

DARRELL *turns the radio off.*

DARRELL: There! You said God would look after us! You said God was watchin' us! Well, I wonder if God is goin' to jail for a hundred years, 'cause that's where we're going. God God God God God God, that's all I hear around here. Sometimes I think you love God more than you do me! (REVEREND EDDIE *looks at him and laughs)* Well, you heard the radio. That baby needs special care. If that baby had a chance of living, I would stay and help Becky Ann out, which it don't. (HE *starts to throw his clothing into a duffel bag)* You know what they do to kidnappers? They don't even bother puttin' 'em in jail. No sir. They *fry 'em!*

REV. ED: Darrell, this is not kidnapping.

DARRELL: What do you mean?

REV. ED: The baby is our own flesh and blood. We are simply reclaiming what is ours.

DARRELL *(Intensely)*: Ours. What do you mean, ours? This baby is none of mine and I ain't gonna fry for this baby. I'll tell you who oughta fry. We oughta put this baby out of its misery. And then we oughta bury it alongside this godforsaken road, then go somewhere and live like normal people!

REV. ED: You want this baby to fry, Darrell? (HE *goes to the stove and grabs the skillet full of hot grease.* HE *crosses to* DARRELL*)* Well, Darrell, do you think this is what's best for this family? Do you think this is what God wants? To kill our own flesh and blood? Just say the word Darrell.

Pause.

DARRELL: If I hadn't already seen so much death . . . it would've been easy . . . which I did . . .
REV. ED *(Handing the skillet to* BECKY*)*: Get your Bibles! We need to be going.
DARRELL: Where?
REV. ED: Get your Bibles.

DARRELL *and* BECKY ANN *fetch their Bibles.* THE THREE *gather together. During the reading,* BECKY ANN *alternately comforts the baby and stares daggers at* DARRELL.

Open to Matthew 2:14. "When he arose, he took the young child and his mother by night and departed into Egypt. And was there until the death of Herod; that it might be fulfilled which was spoken of the Lord by the prophet saying, out of Egypt have I called my son!" Amen?
BECKY ANN: Amen.

REVEREND EDDIE *turns to* DARRELL.

DARRELL: Amen.

Blackout. Sound of motor.

Scene 3

Lights up on trailer. DARRELL *is alone in the trailer.* HE *is lying on the bed, snoring loudly. It is several days later.*

REV. ED *(Offstage)*: Darrell! Becky! Becky! Darrell! (HE *bursts through the door, still yelling. Glancing frantically around the trailer,* HE *sees* DARRELL *asleep)* Darrell! (DARRELL *continues snoring.* HE *slams the door loudly)* Darrell!

DARRELL *continues snoring.* REVEREND EDDIE *goes to the sink and fills a glass with water. Striding to the bed,* HE *throws the water in* DARRELL's *face.* DARRELL *starts awake sputtering.*

DARRELL: I was coming back . . . I was coming back, sergeant . . . I got lost . . .
REV. ED: Darrell, rise and shine buddy!
DARRELL: Oh! I coulda drowned! You coulda killed me! Jesus!
REV. ED: Don't say Jesus.
DARRELL: Well, Daddy, you coulda drowned me. If I could breathe underwater,

I'd be all right, which I can't! Were you trying to drown me? Who woulda drove the trailer then . . .

REVEREND EDDIE *has retrieved a map from a drawer and spreads it on the table.*

REV. ED: Darrell, you better take a look at this map.

DARRELL *(Starts back to the bed)*: I don't need to see no map. I got a perfect sense of direction.

REV. ED: We've got a long way to go to a place you've never been.

DARRELL *(Crawls under the cover)*: I been most everywhere.

REV. ED: Am I to assume then that you've been to Canada?

DARRELL *(Leaping up)*: Canada! I thought you said we was just going to hold up here across the state line! When did you get this idea?

REV. ED: It was not my idea. *(Pulls out letter)* It was God's idea!

DARRELL: Another letter! *(HE goes to brush his teeth at the sink)*

REV. ED: That's right, Darrell, a letter . . . a sign from God! This time, He found me on the banks of the moving water. I had gone down by the creek to perform my morning ritual. As you know, for the past three days, my morning ritual has gone . . . unrewarded.

DARRELL: I know.

REV. ED: Well, this time, I was squatting amongst some rocks, gazing at my image in a crystal stream, when suddenly, the earth . . . and my bowels . . . moved! After three days! Then the miracle happened. I reached for the Sears and Roebuck catalogue and it was gone! And this was in its place. I tore it open and read it. It tells us to get out of here as quick as we can and get up to Canada . . . the promised land!

DARRELL: The promised land! Daddy, if you think Canada is some kind of promised land, then this is dumber than I thought it was. There ain't nothing up in Canada but ice . . . and seals . . . and Eskimos.

REV. ED: Sounds to me like maybe you don't know the way.

DARRELL: Huh! Canada. That's easy. Lemme see . . . Canada . . . that's Arkansas . . . Missouri . . . Kansas . . . Nebraska . . . South Dakota . . . North Dakota . . . Canada! That's how you get to Canada.

REV. ED *(Laughs and puts his arm around DARRELL's shoulder)*: That's right, Darrell. That's good!

DARRELL: Yeah, I can get us to Canada and I don't need no map.

BECKY ANN *enters sans cotton.*

REV. ED: Becky Ann!

BECKY ANN: Hi.

REV. ED: Get everything packed. We're going to the promised land . . . *(Puts finger on the map)* Moose Jaw . . . Saskatchewan . . . Canada!

DARRELL: Moose Jaw!

Blackout. Motor noises.

Scene 4

In the blackout, we hear BECKY ANN *singing "Softly and Tenderly." Lights up on trailer.* THE REVEREND EDDIE *is playing a ukelele.* BECKY ANN *sings "Softly and Tenderly" sweetly and simply. There is no cotton in her ears. Before* SHE *can finish the song,* REVEREND EDDIE *interrupts her.*

REV. ED: That was very pretty, Becky Ann. But it's gonna have to be different if you're going to do it when the time comes in the tent, in front of all those people.

BECKY ANN: I don't want to do it in front of all those people.

REV. ED: You want to do it right for the baby, don't you?

BECKY ANN: Yeah.

REV. ED: Then let's do it again. Come here.

SHE stands facing the audience. SHE *beings to sing.* REVEREND EDDIE *interrupts her.*

You know, Becky Ann, that's better, but there's a certain way we sing hymns in church. Let's clasp our hands together. (HE *illustrates,* SHE *imitates him*) Smile. (SHE *smiles awkwardly*) Look up. (SHE *looks straight up*) No, not that far up, Becky Ann. About there. (HE *adjusts her face*) Like you're looking at God.

BECKY ANN: Why is God always up there?

REV. ED: Because He is. Because it's in the Bible.

BECKY ANN: Oh.

SHE drops her hands each time HE interrupts her.

REV. ED: Now, go ahead and sing. Clasp, smile and look up.

BECKY ANN: "Softly and tenderly Jesus is calling . . . "

REV. ED: That's so much better! Now let's add a little something. Maybe a little gesture on "calling." (HE *punctuates the word "calling" with a sharp stab of his fingers*) Shall we? Let's start again. Clasp, smile, look up . . .

SHE sings. When SHE reaches the word "calling," SHE stabs the air sharply as HE did. HE hangs his head in frustration.

I didn't mean that exact gesture, Becky Ann. I had in mind something like . . . "calling." (HE *makes a gentler, Las Vegas singer's gesture*) Did you see that? Let's try it. Clasp, smile, look up.

SHE sings. When SHE gets to "calling," SHE makes the same gesture, mechanically.

There now. You see how natural that is?

Blackout. Motor noises.

Scene 5

Lights up on trailer. Except for the glow from BECKY ANN's *flashlight as* SHE *sits at the kitchen table studying the map, the interior is dark.* THE REVEREND EDDIE *is asleep on the cot. Suddenly, there is a pounding on the door—three blows.* BECKY ANN *starts, freezes.* SHE *runs to her sleeping father, but, as* SHE *reaches the bed, the knocks come again, as before.* BECKY ANN *slowly approaches the door, debating whether or not to open it. The door opens slowly. There is the sound of loud rushing wind and eerie music.* SHE *looks fearfully into a blinding white light. It is as if the wind is talking to her.*

BECKY ANN: Uh, yes, yes he does, but he's asleep. A what? It can't be! (*Clipboard drops magically into the doorway*) He can't sign anything. He's asleep. (*Pause*) Well, why do I have to sign? (*Pause*) Oh. Okay. (SHE *signs and takes a letter from the clipboard. The clipboard ascends*) Oh . . . thank you. Would you like something cold to drink?

The door slams. BECKY ANN *looks at the letter, turning it over in her hands.* SHE *takes it to the table and looks at it in the light.* REVEREND EDDIE *begins to stir awake.*

REV. ED: Becky Ann? (BECKY ANN *thrusts the letter in her pocket and moves away from the table*) Becky Ann?

BECKY ANN: What?

REV. ED: Who was that at the door?

BECKY ANN: A salesman.

REV. ED: A salesman. (HE *gets up and goes to the door*) What was he selling?

BECKY ANN: I'm not sure.

REV. ED: He must not have been a very good salesman.

BECKY ANN: You want breakfast?

REV. ED: No. I won't eat breakfast till ten o'clock. Where's Darrell?

BECKY ANN: He's out fixin' the generator.

REV. ED: That's good. It's good for him to keep busy. (SHE *searches for the cotton in her pocket and starts to put it in her ears*) Don't do that, Becky Ann. You won't be needing that. (SHE *returns the cotton to her pocket*) Tell me some more about the salesman, Becky Ann. What did he look like?

BECKY ANN: Well, he was *real* tall, and . . . he had a mustache.

REV. ED: A mustache.

BECKY ANN: Yes. And he had a real kind face and a leather suitcase. And he said he traveled everywhere all over the United States and even to Canada where we're going.

REV. ED (*Angrily*): You told him where we were going?

BECKY ANN: No, I didn't tell him. I just listened.

REV. ED: Good. That's good. (HE *goes to the basin and washes up*)

BECKY ANN: He said that he had a little baby at home just like mine. Well not *just* like mine . . . and . . . uh . . . his little baby likes to run and play and he reads stories to it and he takes it fishing with him and even though it's just a little bitty baby it knows everything that people are saying to it and everything that's happenin' around it . . . and it really loves its mommy and it wants to take care of its mommy and protect its mommy.

REV. ED: Sounds like you had quite a conversation.

BECKY ANN: I just listened.

REV. ED: That was a big mistake, Becky Ann. You should have just sent him on his way. You should have slammed the door in his face. Those fellows who travel from town to town are Godless. They leave their families behind and traipse around the country with no responsibilities or any thought for anybody but themselves. They only want one thing from someone like you, Becky Ann. First, they worm their way inside the door. They act sweet and charming and sugar wouldn't melt on their tongue. And they find a way to snake close to you and touch you. Maybe they touch your hair, or your dress, or they just happen to brush up against your breasts. And they say, oh I'm sorry, I didn't mean to, but all the time they are looking for another chance to press their flesh against your flesh. (*With growing anger*) They want to wind themselves around you and get inside you and possess you. They want to turn flesh into filth. They make you unclean. The only thing they're selling is sin. Is that what he was selling, Becky Ann, with his kind face and his leather suitcase?

BECKY ANN (*Almost crying*): It weren't no salesman.

REV. ED: What? It weren't?

BECKY ANN: No.

REV. ED: You lied to me, Becky Ann?

BECKY ANN: I didn't mean to.

REV. ED (*Falls to his knees*): God, give me strength. Help me, now, in my hour of need. How sharper than a serpent's tooth is a thankless child. I can't have you lying to me, Becky Ann.

BECKY ANN: I know.

REV. ED: Not now.

BECKY ANN: Daddy, I know.

REV. ED: There's no time for that now. (HE *reaches into a cabinet and pulls out an old wooden box*)

BECKY ANN: I know. I know there isn't. (SHE *sees the box*) No, Daddy, no . . .

REV. ED: Pull down your dress Becky Ann.

BECKY ANN: No, Daddy. Please.

HE *opens the box and pulls out a crude wooden cross, to which are attached long leather thongs, and a crown of thorns.*

REV. ED: Pull down your dress, Becky Ann. NOW!

BECKY ANN (*Frantically*): It was another letter! (SHE *hands the letter to him*)

REV. ED: A letter? Why did you keep it?

BECKY ANN: Because there's no telling what might be in it.

REV. ED: It's another one of the letters. Look at it. Typed on the same machine as the other ones. It's another sign. Another instruction. Thank you, Jesus. Thank you, Jesus. (HE *opens it and reads it silently.* HE *looks puzzled*)

BECKY ANN (*Watching him intently*): Daddy, what does it say?

REV. ED: What?

BECKY ANN: The letter, Daddy, what does it say?

REV. ED: Oh . . . never mind. Never mind what it says. It don't matter. (*There is the sound of a generator kicking in. The lights blink on*) It's a sign. It's a sign.

DARRELL *enters, covered with grease.* HE *sees the box on the table.* HE *looks at* REVEREND EDDIE *and* BECKY ANN *suspiciously.*

(*Holding up letter*) Darrell! So you fixed the generator, that's fine boy, that's fine. Look Darrell another letter. Found us in the wilderness. (HE *puts the crown and cross back in the box*) You can't say God isn't looking after us. You can't say that God isn't giving us a road map (DARRELL *goes to wash*) God's on his highway and all is right with the world. We'll celebrate God's goodness. Tonight we'll drive two hours with the headlights on. You'd like that wouldn't you Darrell? (*Pause*) I say you'd like that wouldn't you Darrell? (*Pause.* HE *crosses to* DARRELL) Or maybe you're unhappy. (HE *shoves* DARRELL's *face down into the basin and holds it there.* DARRELL *gurgles loudly*) That would be odd. Becky's happy, I'm very happy, we're happy to be doing God's work. (HE *releases* DARRELL) You know if you're unhappy, Darrell, I think you should just pack your bag and get out of here. (HE *gets* DARRELL's *duffel bag and throws it at him*) I think you ought to, Darrell, hitch a ride . . . back to Fort Chaffee. Anybody would be happy to give a ride to a war hero. I'm sure they'd be real happy to see you back at Fort Chaffee. Why don't you just leave?

DARRELL *sits.* BECKY ANN *puts the cotton in her ears and begins to hum. Blackout. Motor sounds.*

Scene 6

Lights on the trailer. BECKY ANN, REVEREND EDDIE *and* DARRELL *are at the table playing cards.* REVEREND EDDIE *is very cheerful.* BECKY ANN *is leaning over the baby, humming, her cards dangling loosely from her hand.*

REV. ED: Okay, Darrell, give me all your . . . fives. (DARRELL *angrily throws three cards on the table*) Aha! Okay, got yer fives, got yer fives. Lemme see, lemme see, Becky Ann, give me all your . . . jacks.

BECKY ANN, *of course, cannot hear.* REVEREND EDDIE *raps on the table.* BECKY ANN *looks up.* REVEREND EDDIE *draws a large "J" in the air.* BECKY ANN *looks through her cards.*

BECKY ANN: Daddy, go fish.

REV. ED: Okay, go fish, go fish. Wonder what I'm gonna get. (HE *draws a card*) Very interesting, very interesting all right. Darrell, it's your turn.

DARRELL (*Laughing with anticipation*): Yessir, give me all your . . . jacks.

Pause.

REV. ED: Well, I reckon you're just gonna have to go fish. (DARRELL *looks confused*) I hope you got your wadin' boots on! (*Laughs*) Hope you got a good net, Darrell, hope they're bitin' today . . . what do you say, Darrell, I hope they're bitin' today . . . what do you say, Darrell, I hope they're bitin' today, eh? (HE *pokes* DARRELL *in the ribs*)

DARRELL: All right, all right. I get it. (HE *draws a card*)

REV. ED: Becky Ann, it's your turn.

HE *raps on the table.* SHE *looks up.* HE *points at her.*

BECKY ANN: Daddy, give me all your queens. (*Resumes humming*)

REV. ED: Well, Becky Ann, I guess I'm gonna have to tell you what I told Darrell. I hope they're bitin' today . . . I hope you got your wading boots on, right Darrell? (BECKY ANN *looks at him blankly.* HE *makes a rod-and-reel motion.* SHE *draws a card*) Okay, I guess it's my turn. Guess the game's in my hands . . . okay . . . I hope I won't have to put on my . . . what?

DARRELL: Wading boots.

REV. ED (*Laughs*): That's right, wading boots. But something tells me I'm not gonna have to do that. Just one more card and I can go out, win all the matches. I wonder what that card could be? Maybe I'm gonna ask for a six. But no, Darrell laid down the sixes, that's the only book he's got. (DARRELL *is in an agony of impatience*) Well, that don't leave much. What do you think I'm gonna ask for, Darrell?

DARRELL: If my memory wasn't shot up, I could guess what you got, which it was.

REV. ED: Well, I'm gonna tell you, Darrell. Yes sir, here it comes. The big moment. Could we have a drumroll please?

HE *lays his cards down and plays a drumroll on the table.* BECKY ANN *looks up.*

BECKY ANN: Is it my turn?

DARRELL: Jesus take me now.

REV. ED: For all the matches, and the Go Fish championship of the entire world . . . he asks for JACKS! (DARRELL, *surly, takes a card out of his hand and starts to slam it down.* HE *pauses.*) Could that be a jack? Praise God! (HE *takes the card, makes his book, and takes in the matches*)

DARRELL: I asked for jacks last time it was my turn, and you said you didn't have any!

REV. ED: I must've drew one.

DARRELL: You got three jacks! How could you draw three jacks! That's impossible!

REV. ED: Nothing's impossible with the Lord.

DARRELL: You tellin' me the Lord lied about havin' three jacks?

REV. ED: Darrell, it's only a game. And I don't appreciate your yellin' durin' family time. (DARRELL *throws his cards down angrily and crosses to the radio*) Now I have something tremendously important. The flight from Egypt is almost over . . . (DARRELL *switches on the radio*) Darrell, turn off the radio.

DARRELL: I'm trying to find out if they're still lookin' for us.

REV. ED: We do not play the radio durin' family time.

DARRELL: To hell with family time.

REVEREND EDDIE looks at DARRELL, who for a moment continues to turn the dial. Suddenly, in one swift movement, REVEREND EDDIE moves to the table, picks up the radio, and smashes it to the floor. DARRELL looks at it, stunned.

REV. ED: There's where your hell is . . . right there.

DARRELL picks up the pieces and returns them to the shelf.

DARRELL: You broke it. That was my radio! And you broke it.

REV. ED: We don't need a radio. It has no information that we need. Now as I was saying that . . .

DARRELL: No, you'd rather play Go Fish! I don't see why we have to play the same dumb game every night! And you always win! Why can't we do something else during family time? We're family, too!

REV. ED: Son, come here.

DARRELL: No. (REVEREND EDDIE *reaches out a loving arm for him.* HE *relents and comes closer. Suddenly,* REVEREND EDDIE *grips him in a vicious hammerlock*) Ow!

REV. ED: Darrell . . . when our Lord gathered Simon Peter and his brethren on the rocky shores of the Sea of Tiberias, they were so afraid that their simple way of life was over . . . that they would no longer cast their rough nets to reap the harvest of the salty sea. But our Lord took Simon Peter aside and sat him upon a rock. (HE *sits* DARRELL *down*) He looked him in the eye . . . and what did our Lord say to Simon Peter?

DARRELL: Go fish.

REV. ED (*Releases him*): That's right, Darrell. Go fish. Be ye fishers of men! That's why Go Fish is the only card game not considered sinful in the eyes of God.

DARRELL: Aw, come on. That's not in there! God never said anything in the Bible about Go Fish! Where did you read that? Did you read it in one of your letters? What's in 'em Daddy? How come you don't read 'em to us anymore? We used to have to sit and listen to 'em over and over again. Signs from God! Why don't you read 'em to us now! (*Snatches cotton out of* BECKY ANN'S *ears*) Ask him Becky Ann! Ask him why he don't read us no more letters!

BECKY ANN: I hear the baby.

DARRELL: That's another thing. How can you hear the baby? It don't never make no sound. It *can't* make no sound. It ain't got no mouth.

BECKY ANN: The baby needs me.

DARRELL: What does it need? It don't ever seem to need nothing. It just lays there.

> BECKY ANN *takes the baby from the basket. Though seen only as a shapeless lump wrapped in a blanket, the baby is able to move and squirm. This is accomplished by using a remote-control airplane motor, operated from offstage.*

BECKY ANN: Hi, baby.

DARRELL: It can't hear you. How can it hear you? It ain't got no ears.

REV. ED: Hold it! Just hold it a minute! Now, for this entire trip I have heard this baby being called "it" and "baby." Don't nobody call him by name?

DARRELL: It ain't got no name.

REV. ED: Exactly. That's exactly my point. He don't have a name. And it's time. I've been waiting for the right time. And this is it. This is the time. The flight from Egypt is almost over. (DARRELL *starts out*) You stay and hear this. The flight from Egypt is almost over. The child is about to enter his father's temple. He baffles the elders.

DARRELL: He baffles me. (HE *sits*)

REV. ED: In generations to come, all mankind will praise His name. Will glorify *His* name. Will exalt *His* name! Of course, in order for this destiny to be fulfilled, the child must actually have a name. Now I have a name in mind. But this will be a family decision. We will all make our suggestions. Darrell why don't you go first? What do you think the little baby's name should be?

DARRELL: What difference does it make? You're gonna decide anyway.

REV. ED: Darrell, I am giving you an opportunity to partake in a moment that mankind will long remember. Now what do you think the baby's name should be?

> *Long pause.*

DARRELL: Bubba.

REV. ED: Bubba?

DARRELL: Yeah, Bubba or what about squash or turnip or eggplant? 'Cause it ain't nothin' but a vegetable anyway.

REV. ED: Darrell, you, by your blasphemy, have forfeited your right to take part in this moment. Henceforth you are erased from the recorded history of this event. Now, Becky Ann, you're the child's mother. I am sure you have given this much thought. What do *you* think your little baby's name should be?

BECKY ANN: Arlene Marie!

> *Pause.* DARRELL *snorts.* REVEREND EDDIE *gives him a warning look.*

REV. ED: Becky Ann . . . Arlene Marie is a very lovely name.

BECKY ANN: Thank you!

REV. ED: But it is a little girl's name.

BECKY ANN: It could be a girl.

REV. ED: It could *not* be a girl!

DARRELL: How can you tell, it ain't got no . . .

REV. ED: Shut up, Darrell! Becky Ann, I will ask you again for a suggestion and give you the opportunity to put forth an appropriate name.

BECKY ANN: Arlene Marie. (SHE *jams cotton in her ears*)

REV. ED: Becky Ann, don't do that!

BECKY ANN: Arlene Marie!

REV. ED (*Snatches the cotton out of her ears*): Becky Ann!

BECKY ANN (*Pulls more cotton from her pocket and stuffs it in her ears*): Arlene Marie!

REV. ED (*Snatches the cotton from her ears*): Becky Ann, stop it!

BECKY ANN: Arlene Marie.

REV. ED: It's a boy!

BECKY ANN (*Puts more cotton in her ears*): Arlene Marie Arlene Marie Arlene Marie . . . (HE *snatches the cotton out. This happens a few more times, until suddenly* SHE *is out of cotton.* SHE *rummages around in her pockets.* SHE *is panicky. Suddenly,* SHE *claps her hands over her ears*) Arlene Marie Arlene Marie Arlene Marie . . .

REV. ED: Becky Ann! Stop it!

HE *grabs at her arms and tries to jerk them away from her ears, but* SHE *holds fast, repeating the name over and over. Suddenly,* SHE *bolts from him.* HE *gives chase.* SHE *gets the table between them as* HE *grabs at her.* SHE *runs from the trailer.*

Darrell! Help me!

THEY *run outside and around the trailer,* DARRELL *close behind* REVEREND EDDIE. REVEREND EDDIE *stops and turns to* DARRELL.

Don't get after me, get after her!

DARRELL *runs after* BECKY ANN *to head her off.* HE *and* REVEREND EDDIE *chase her back into the trailer.* THEY *struggle around the room, knocking over furniture,* REVEREND EDDIE *and* DARRELL *screaming and* BECKY ANN *shouting "Arlene Marie!" over and over.*

Tie her to this chair!

DARRELL *and* REVEREND EDDIE *tie her in an armchair and stuff a gag in her mouth.* THEY *catch their breath. Silence.* REVEREND EDDIE *walks to the basket.*

I have had a revelation. I have decided on a name for the child. He shall be called Prince of Peace, Wise Counselor, Blessed Redeemer, Savior Anointed. He shall be called as he was in his first incarnation, when he promised to all those who kept his covenant that he would return in glory. From henceforth, the child's holy name shall be linked with the distinguished name of our family. The child shall be called Jesus. *(Raises his arms)* Jesus O. Tarbox. (HE *takes out a pocket watch and looks at it)* Well, family time is over.

Blackout.

Scene 7

Lights up on REVEREND EDDIE *at the typewriter.* BECKY ANN *and* DARRELL *are asleep.* REVEREND EDDIE *looks to heaven.*

REV. ED: God . . . I've done everything you've asked. I've followed all your instructions. I've never questioned you. But God . . . in a few days, we're gonna raise that tent, and cover ourselves in glory, and I've got to tell those people . . . (HE *gestures to the typewriter)* something. Won't you please help me? See God, I'm confused. I'm talking about the letters. In the beginning, your voice was clear. (HE *gets the old letters)* In the beginning, you said . . . and I quote . . . *(Reads)* "You should not have give the baby away. Shame on you, you should not have did it. Blood is thicker than water. Shame." Or this one . . . "This baby may not look like much, but it is family. Go get it as quick as you can, or you will burn in Hell." Or . . . "You are like a fly on the kitchen table. If you do not go get that child, you will surely . . . be swatted." I have listened to these letters, Lord, I have followed the signs. Fortunately, I was able to interpret them correctly. I saw your plan for my salvation . . . I saw my seat in glory. God . . . your son is in my hands. But now . . . I am bewildered. I don't understand what you're telling me with these *new* letters. (HE *holds up a stack of new letters, and opens one)* What does this mean? "We have come from the light, where the light originated through itself." *(Pause)* That makes no sense to me. Or this . . . "Knock on yourself as upon a door . . . and walk on yourself as upon a straight road." (HE *shrugs; looks at the third letter for a few seconds)* "Make no friendship with an elephant keeper . . . if you have no room to entertain . . . an elephant." God, I've never *seen* an elephant! These letters just don't fit! God, we're close so close. Why do you abandon me now? I have endured hardship and persecution in your name. I've lost my church, I've lost my home, I have been accused of a horrendous crime against you . . . people have took up rocks against us, and now this! It's just not fair! Are you testing me, God? I can pass the test. Speak to me through this baby. I will use this baby. He will have his thirty-three years of glorious ministry. I will see that your prophecy is fulfilled, even unto death and resurrection. (*Holds up letters*) But what do I do with these? I'm not think-ing of myself, Lord. I'm thinking of you. I'm thinking of how you will look if I read these letters at the tent meeting . . . especially the one about the elephant! What do I do with these? What do I do? What do I do? (*Pause*) What did you say, Lord? Yes, I hear you. I *hear* you! I think that is the right idea. (HE *takes the new letters and throws them into a bucket.* HE *strikes a match and holds it to the corner of an envelope*) And the Lord said . . . "The fire next time . . . "

HE *leaves the letters burning in the bucket.* HE *watches them burn for a second then exits. There is a pause. We hear the crackling of the flames. Then the baby basket begins to glow. It gradually slides across the stage until it is in front of the table. A light comes up on the typewriter. By itself, it begins to type in rhythm with the pulsing light in the basket. The typing continues, picking up speed, as the lights fade.*

END OF ACT ONE

ACT TWO

Scene 1

We hear a car idling. In the blackout, the following conversation is heard on tape.

CUSTOMS MAN: What is your destination?

DARRELL: Who cares?

REV. ED: Saskatchewan. Moose Jaw, Saskatchewan.

CUSTOMS MAN: How many in the car?

DARRELL: Four, if you count the . . .

REV. ED: Three! There are three of us, officer. Only three.

CUSTOMS MAN: Do you have any fruits or vegetables?

DARRELL: We're not sure.

REV. ED: No, officer, no fruits or vegetables.

CUSTOMS MAN: How long do you plan to stay in Canada?

REV. ED: Not long, officer. Two weeks from this very day, we will hold our tent meeting, then we will leave your lovely country, basking in the glory of that event. I hope you will be able to attend, officer, and hear my message.

CUSTOMS MAN: I'll try.

Lights up. The trailer is empty. The basket is glowing. It moves to the smashed radio. Then a light begins to glow inside the radio. It begins to play Fibber McGee and Molly. *The dial begins to switch stations until it arrives at the news.*

RADIO: " . . . have given up the search for the infant abducted from the University of Arkansas. Scientists at the university were experimenting with the child, who was born without vital organs. Doctors said that the infant needed special care, and must be presumed dead. In other news . . . a giant chicken . . . "

The dial switches stations, arriving at a bouncy verse of "If I Knew You Were Coming, I'd Have Baked a Cake." The baby's light bounces in rhythm to the music. DARRELL *bursts through the door, but the radio has stopped playing and the lights have ceased glowing.* HE *walks over to the radio and shakes it suspiciously. Disgusted,* HE *puts it down.* HE *starts to go out, but turns and walks slowly to the basket.* HE *has his ball and glove.* HE *looks into the basket. Reaches in and moves the blanket slightly.* HE *recoils from the sight.*

DARRELL: Yecch! Boy you sure are ugly. Hell, we'd have to hang a pork chop around your neck to get the dog to play with you. If we had a dog and you had a neck which we don't and you don't. You hear me? Of course you can't hear me. You need ears to hear. Can't see me either can you? Wait a minute, maybe that's an ear. Yeah, that could be an ear. Or maybe it's a hand. Nah! I don't see what's so special about you anyway. Where were you during the war, Jesus O. Tarbox? I didn't see you out where I was on the front lines in

France, Europe, where it was so freezin' cold out there in the field that we had to stuff newspapers in our uniforms to keep from freezing to death! I bet you are wondering about this medal. *(Fingers his Purple Heart)* This is called the Purple Heart, and except for the Congressional Medal of Honor, it's the best medal a person in the armed forces can get. I could've got a lot of other medals, but I wanted this one. They gave it to me for valor, bravery, courage and getting stuck with a bayonet. Oh yeah?! You want to see my war scar? (HE *raises his shirt)* There it is, right there. And that's why I'm not playing professional baseball to this day. If them krauts hadn't of stuck me, I'd still have my fastball. Which they did, and I don't. But I'm still better off than you. I got a good nickel curveball which is more than you've got. I got a spitball, which is more than you got. I got spit, which is more than you got. You couldn't throw a baseball if your life depended on it, which fortunately for you it don't. Hell, you can't even catch. You know, I bet if I was to take this baseball right here and throw it as hard as I can right in your . . . your . . . face, I'd probably kill you. I'd probably splatter you all over this trailer. End all this craziness forever. No more hearin' how special you are. So maybe that's what I ought to do. Put you out of your misery. End all this craziness. Course if you really was Jesus, like Daddy says, you could stop me . . . you could stop this baseball in midair, or turn it into a rabbit or something. Is that what you're gonna do? Come on, Jesus O. Tarbox, what'll it be? You're the catcher, give me a sign. Curve or spitball? Just give me a sign.

HE *raises his arm to throw. Pauses, lowers his arm and sits by the basket.* BECKY ANN *enters carrying groceries.*

BECKY ANN: Darrell! What're you doing?

DARRELL: I wasn't doing nothin'! I wasn't hurtin' your precious baby! I was just showing it my war scar.

BECKY ANN: Oh, she don't want to see any old scar from your hernia operation.

DARRELL: Hernia!

BECKY ANN: It's all right, baby. I don't like no ugly old scars either.

DARRELL: Hernia, hell. What'd you get to eat? Eggplant? Becky Ann, I told you no more eggplant. What's this?

BECKY ANN: A letter.

DARRELL: Another letter. How many of these we git today?

BECKY ANN: Five or six since this mornin'.

DARRELL: Five or six? How are all these letters finding us? How did this one get here?

BECKY ANN: It was waitin' for me at the market.

DARRELL: At the market? How the hell did anyone know you was goin' to the market?

BECKY ANN: Well, Darrell, we gotta eat.

DARRELL: No, no. How did anybody know you was going there today? (SHE *shrugs)* Has he seen this yet?

BECKY ANN: No.

DARRELL: Where is he?

BECKY ANN: He stayed in town to nail up leaflets.

DARRELL: Leaflets! I wonder what it says.

BECKY ANN: It says, "Big Tent Meeting Sunday night at 8:00."

DARRELL: No, Becky Ann, the letter, not the leaflets! I know what the leaflets say!

BECKY ANN: Oh.

DARRELL (*Reads*): "Reverend Edward O. Tarbox, c/o Scofield's Market, Moose Jaw, Saskatchewan, Canada." No stamp. No return address. No nothin'. Hmmmm. What's in it, Becky Ann?

BECKY ANN: I don't know.

DARRELL: Come on, Becky Ann. What's in it?

BECKY ANN: I don't know what's in it.

DARRELL: Let's open it.

BECKY ANN: Ain't addressed to you. It's addressed to Daddy.

DARRELL: He'll never miss it. He burns 'em all now anyway.

BECKY ANN: It's against the law.

DARRELL: The hell with the law. I'm gonna open it. (HE *looks around as if* THE REVEREND EDDIE *might be looking over his shoulder and rips the envelope.* HE *reads.* HE *looks puzzled*)

BECKY ANN: Darrell, what does it say?

DARRELL: Oh, now you want to know what it says. I thought you said it was against the law.

BECKY ANN: Darrell . . .

DARRELL: Why are you asking me?

BECKY ANN: Darrell . . .

DARRELL: All right! (*Reads*) "We wrote a hundred letters, and you did not answer. That, too, is a reply." What the hell does that mean?

BECKY ANN: I don't know.

DARRELL: Aw, come on! What's it mean?

BECKY ANN: I don't *know* what it means!

DARRELL: Becky Ann, I ain't stupid! I didn't just fall off the damn turnip truck! I've seen you from the time you was a little girl! I know you'd do anything to get that baby back. You wrote the letters! You wrote all those letters and sent them to him so's he would think they was signs from God! You think I couldn't tell you wrote all that stuff about how sinful it was to give away the baby, and how it was our own flesh and blood. How he was gonna burn in hell. How he was like a fly going 'round the kitchen table and was surely gonna get swatted. What was it you rubbed on his skin so's he would have an "affliction" like Job?

BECKY ANN: Lye.

DARRELL: I knew it. Lye. I knew it. (*Laughs*)

BECKY ANN: And Darrell, you know what?

DARRELL: What?

BECKY ANN: Sometimes, late at night, when he was asleep, I'd sneak into his room and whisper things in his ears, holy things like Bible verses, so's maybe he

would think it was the blessed Virgin Mary come to him in his dreams. . . .
He must not have heard me though, or if he did, he didn't mention it.

DARRELL: He'd kill you if he found out.

BECKY ANN: Well, he won't find out. Unless you tell him. (*Very frightened*) You ain't gonna tell him, are you?

DARRELL: Aw, I wouldn't tell him. He wouldn't believe me, if I did. But he's gonna get wise if you keep sendin' him those letters! I don't understand why you keep doin' it.

BECKY ANN: I ain't doin' it, cross my heart and hope to die!

DARRELL: Aw . . . Becky Ann.

BECKY ANN: I swear!

DARRELL: You swear! On what?

BECKY ANN: On Jesus' Holy Name!

DARRELL: Which Jesus? The real Jesus or Daddy's Jesus?

BECKY ANN: On my own life.

DARRELL: Ain't good enough.

BECKY ANN: I'm tellin' the truth. I'll swear on anything you want!

DARRELL: If that's true, if that's really true, you swear right here on our momma's Holy Bible.

HE *gets Momma's Bible and holds it in front of her.* SHE *places her hand on it.*

BECKY ANN: I swear on Momma's Holy Bible that I ain't wrote any of the letters since we got Arlene Marie back. Oh, except for the one about Moose Jaw. Sorry Momma.

DARRELL *takes his momma's lock of hair from the Bible and holds it out to* BECKY ANN. SHE *kisses it.* SHE *then holds it for him to kiss.* HE *lovingly returns it to the Bible, and returns the Bible to its place.*

DARRELL: Then who the hell is writin' these letters?

BECKY ANN: I don't know!

DARRELL: Wait . . . maybe he's writin' 'em himself.

BECKY ANN: Why?

DARRELL: I don't know. So he'll keep gettin' signs from God!

BECKY ANN: Then why would he burn them?

DARRELL: Because he's *crazy!* He thinks he's God. Don't you see how this whole thing's backfired on you?

BECKY ANN: What are you talking about?

DARRELL: Ain't you heard him? Don't you know what his plans are? Don't you know what he thinks God has prophesied for that baby?

BECKY ANN: Darrell, ain't nothing bad gonna happen to this baby! (SHE *begins to knit*) This baby makes Daddy real happy and she makes *me* real happy! Can't you just leave it alone?

DARRELL: You think that baby is yours, Becky Ann? That baby ain't yours. He thinks that baby is the second coming of Christ! (SHE *stuffs cotton in her ears and begins to hum*) He's gonna fulfill the prophecy. That's what this tent meeting is for, don't you know that? Little Jesus O. Tarbox is gonna be baptized under the big top next Sunday night! . . . And then you know what's gonna happen? He said it, Becky Ann! Even to death and resurrection! He ain't talkin' about his own death. He's talking about your precious baby! (*Gets right down in front of* BECKY ANN's *face*) Is that what you want, Becky Ann? IS IT? IS IT? (HE *snatches the cotton out of her ears*) Is it?

BECKY ANN: Did you say something, Darrell?

DARRELL: Becky Ann . . . we gotta get outta here. You and me and . . . Arlene Marie.

BECKY ANN: But what would happen to Daddy?

DARRELL: Who cares? He don't care about us!

BECKY ANN: He needs us.

DARRELL: Sure he needs us! Who else would drive his car without no headlights? Who else would cook his breakfast at ten o'clock at night? Who else would take care of that baby! Who else would go along with a lunatic that thinks that God is talking to him by way of the U.S. Mail?

BECKY ANN: Where would we go?

DARRELL: Back home.

BECKY ANN: Darrell, I can't go there . . . they would take her away from me again.

DARRELL: Maybe that's for the best.

BECKY ANN: No!

DARRELL: Maybe they wouldn't. Maybe we could talk to them.

BECKY ANN: No!

DARRELL: Maybe they'd let us take care of the baby together.

BECKY ANN: NO!

DARRELL: Becky Ann, we got to get out of here! That maniac is gonna kill us all! We're all gonna fry! (HE *starts to pack his duffel bag*) I ain't gonna let him do that. I'm going whether you go with me or not, I'm going. If he was right here now, I'd tell him right to his face . . .

The door bursts open. It is THE REVEREND EDDIE. HE *is dressed up, in a seedy kind of way.* HE *carries an armful of leaflets.*

REV. ED: This . . . has been . . . a very interesting day.

BECKY ANN: What's wrong, Daddy?

REV. ED: Nothing's wrong. God is still with us. He can do no wrong.

BECKY ANN: That's good.

REV. ED: I'll tell you what's wrong. Satan has arrived in the town of Moose Jaw. He has taken control of this town.

BECKY ANN: What did he do, Daddy?

REV. ED: He got a law passed that nobody can put up advertising without a license. I went to the city hall to get a license. They asked to see my ministerial credentials. Credentials! When Jesus spoke to his disciples, he told them to go out and preach the word. He did not tell them to go out and get six years of college and preach the word!

BECKY ANN: Well Daddy, did you show them your Bible?

REV. ED: They spit upon the Bible!

BECKY ANN: Well I'll wipe it off for ya. (SHE *takes it and starts to wipe it off*)

REV. ED: They spit on it *spiritually!* (HE *snatches it from her*)

BECKY ANN: Oh. (SHE *resumes knitting*)

DARRELL: What about the permit to set up the tent?

REV. ED: Do you think I'd soil my purpose by continuing in conversation with agents of the devil?

DARRELL: So you didn't get the permit.

REV. ED: Permit! Permit! Who gives God a permit? Who tells God what to do and what not to do? Who gives God leave to conduct his business? Who dares to do that?

DARRELL: You ain't God.

REV. ED: *IT'S THE SAME THING!*

DARRELL: Well, Daddy, whatcha gonna do? You know if we set up that tent without a permit, they're gonna arrest us. They're gonna put us in jail . . . they're gonna try to find out if we got any other kind of record. Probably gonna get on the phone to them authorities back in El Dorado, them authorities are gonna get out our permanent records and find them "black marks" on our permanent records—mine and yours. Then, them authorities back in Arkansas, they're gonna expedite us back to Arkansas. And we're gonna stand trial, and that judge is gonna bang down his gavel and say "I find you guilty as sin and I sentence you all to fry." Of course, if we was to fry because that's what God wanted, it would be one thing . . . but maybe God is trying to tell us that he don't want us to fry. Maybe he's tryin' to tell us to get our butts out of Moose Jaw. Maybe he's trying to tell us to give the baby back. It's still alive as far as anyone can tell. We ain't hurt it any. They'll probably take the baby back and just forget the whole thing.

REV. ED: Maybe . . . maybe . . .

DARRELL: Maybe that's the right answer . . . the right reply!

REV. ED: What?

DARRELL (*Pulls out the letter*): God says that He ain't heard no reply. You ain't answered His letters. Maybe the reply He wants is for us to get our butts . . .

REV. ED (*Interrupting*): What's that?

DARRELL (*Stunned pause*): What?

REV. ED: Is that a letter?

DARRELL: This? I don't think so . . . I . . . uh . . .

REV. ED: Give me that!

DARRELL: Oh, you don't want to see this . . .

REV. ED: *Give me that!* (DARRELL *reluctantly hands him the letter.* HE *takes it out of its envelope and reads it.* HE *puts it back in the envelope*) You opened my letter. You read it.

DARRELL: No! No I didn't. I swear I didn't. It was open when it got here. It kinda just fell out of the envelope . . . I couldn't help but see what it said . . . it was just laying there open . . . I didn't open it. I swear to you I didn't. Becky Ann, tell him. *(Pause)* Tell him, Becky Ann!

BECKY ANN: You did. You did, Darrell. You opened Daddy's letter and you read it.

DARRELL: Becky Ann . . .

BECKY ANN: And then you tried to get me and the baby to run away with you.

REV. ED: Is that right, Darrell? Is that what you did?

DARRELL: I was only kiddin'.

REV. ED: Is that right, Judas? You were only kidding were you? What else did he say, Becky Ann?

BECKY ANN: That you was crazy.

DARRELL: I never said that.

BECKY ANN: And you thought you was God and he wanted to give my baby away and he didn't fall off the damn turnip truck.

DARRELL: Becky Ann . . .

REV. ED *(Picks DARRELL up and throws him across the room)*: Satan! You are erased. I have erased you. Your name is dust. Your body is ashes. God will no longer recognize your face. Get out of my house.

DARRELL: No Daddy, no.

REV. ED: Get out!

DARRELL: I'll do anything!

REV. ED: Get out of my house and go back to your father in hell!

REVEREND EDDIE *throws* DARRELL *out the door.* HE *throws some of* DARRELL's *things after him.*

DARRELL *(Offstage)*: I could tell you something about your precious letters, but you wouldn't believe me. And I know what you did! I know what both of you did! And I ain't gonna be the one who's gonna burn in hell!

BECKY ANN: We've upset the baby. It's all right, baby.

REVEREND EDDIE *paces about angrily. Suddenly,* HE *falls to his knees.*

REV. ED: Becky Ann.

BECKY ANN: What?

REV. ED: The Holy Ghost is in this trailer.

BECKY ANN: Where?

REV. ED: The moment I drove Satan out that door, the Holy Ghost came in and my mind cleared. I can see everything like it was crystal.

BECKY ANN: What do you see, Daddy?

REV. ED: I see a vision. I'm in the vision. And you're in the vision.

BECKY ANN *(Fearful)*: Is the baby in the vision?

REV. ED: Yes, Becky Ann. The baby *is* the vision! In my vision he stands tall and straight and he has limbs of ivory and his eyes are as bright as brass and his mouth speaks with a tongue of fire. And all mankind bow down to him and worship his name. And he wants us to help him.

BECKY ANN: How?

REV. ED: Here's what I'm going to do. I'm going to find a way to get this tent up! I am going to go to the house of every farmer in this Godforsaken territory. I will ask them for permission to put our tent up on their property. I will ask them in God's name and explain to them that we are doing God's work. I will get down on my knees and beg them if I have to. After dark, I will return. Then, you will take the leaflets and spread them all over town. And then, together, we will bask in God's glory.

BECKY ANN: Is that what you see in your vision?

REV. ED: Among other things.

BECKY ANN: And am I the mother in the vision?

REV. ED: Yes, Becky. You are the blessed Virgin.

BECKY ANN: Will I always be the mother?

REV. ED: Yes, Becky Ann. You will be revered through all eternity. You are the vessel of glory. And you will be there as God's plan is fulfilled, even unto death and resurrection.

BECKY ANN (*Looks down at the baby*): Oh.

Blackout.

Scene 2

In the blackout, we hear the taped voice of BECKY ANN *singing to the tune of "Jesus Loves Me."*

BECKY ANN: Happy birthday, baby girl.
I love you more than all the world
You are sweet and you are purty
You don't even get things dirty.

Yes, Arlene's one month old
It's the happiest story ever told
Yes, Arlene's one month old
One month old today.

Lights up on the trailer. BECKY ANN, *wearing a party hat, is sitting at the table holding the baby, who is squirming.* SHE *lights the lone candle on the birthday cake.* SHE *looks at the cake.*

Make a wish. Blow it out. (*Pause*) Oh, that's all right. (SHE *blows out the candle*) Ain't it a pretty cake? I didn't have no food colorin' for the icin', so I had to write your name in grape jelly. (SHE *puts the baby in the basket*) Look at this birthday girl! She's so purty. (SHE *stands and bats the balloon that's tied to the edge of the basket.* SHE *bats it again)* Ain't birthdays fun? Oh! You want your present? I made it just for you. (SHE *goes to her knitting bag and pulls out a lopsided rectangular piece of knitting.* SHE *shows it to the baby)* I hope it fits. (SHE *lays it on the baby)* There. That fits perfect. (SHE *picks the baby up)* Oh my, I love you, Arlene Marie. They always said I couldn't take care of a baby, but you ain't no trouble at all. You never wet, or cry, or nothin'! You are such a good baby. (SHE *talks to the right end of the baby)* Ol' Darrell, he makes fun of you all the time, (SHE *talks to the left end of the baby)* but he's just jealous because he wants to be special. Always remember, Arlene Marie, no matter how hard life gets, you are special. And your daddy was special. I'm gonna tell you something, Arlene Marie, that I ain't ever told nobody. It's about your daddy. I didn't know at first that it was happenin'. I thought it was a dream. It happened so sudden and so forceful that I got really scared. But I guess it was good . . . 'cause I got you. And I was filled with this music . . . an unearthly kind of music that I never even heard before. I can't even sing it for you. I wrote you a song, though! Yeah, for your birthday! (SHE *fetches the ukelele and plants her foot on the chair.* SHE *plays and sings)*

I'm gonna tell you 'bout your daddy and me
How you was born, how you came to be
You're a big baby now, old enough to know
Wasn't like they tell you in the picture show
Lots of fear
It was his idear
Raped by God

You know it's kinda hard for even me to understand
I guess you know your daddy's not an ordinary man
I wanted to scream but I didn't have a voice
I wanted to run but I didn't have a choice
I guess you could say
He had to have his way
Raped by God.

(SHE *moves the chair away)* And now this part I learned at the picture show. You ready, here I go. (SHE *begins to hum, play the ukelele, and do a very bad soft-shoe to the tune of the song* SHE *has written. During this the baby basket begins to spin to the verse.* SHE *stops and looks at the baby)* Arlene Marie! That was really good! How'd you learn to do that? (SHE *begins to dance again)* Doodle li doodle li doo. Hi! Doodle li doodle li doo. Boo! I'm just gonna have to teach you all the songs and dances I know. I wish I could remember everything to tell you exact but there was all this wind and fire and fog and stuff. He whispered to me though. He said, "I'm gonna give to you what the eye has not seen, what the ear has not heard, what the hand has not touched, and what has not yet risen up in the heart of man" and "ye who are near to me are near to the fire," and then he said something about an elephant. And then the wind and the fire and the fog was gone. I'm really sorry no one else remembered your birthday. Happy birthday, Arlene Marie.

SHE *begins to sing and dance with the baby.* REVEREND EDDIE *bursts through the door.* SHE *freezes.*

REV. ED: Hallelujah! God has opened the door. What are you doing?

BECKY ANN: It's the baby's birthday . . .

REV. ED: Never mind. (HE *rips the party hat off her head and throws it on the floor)* I have something important for you to do. Get your coat on.

BECKY ANN: Why?

REV. ED: Because God's wheels are in motion. His train is pulling into the station. I have been through this Godforsaken territory from one end to the other, hoping I could convince God to spare this barren Sodom by helping me find one good man. Well, I found him, not two miles from where we speak. He will allow us to raise our tents in his pasture for only a modest fee. God's plan is working! It is inevitable!

BECKY ANN: What does He want me to do?

REV. ED *(Hands her the pamphlets):* He wants you to spread them as far and as wide as you can before daylight.

BECKY ANN: What if someone tries to stop me?

REV. ED: Tell them you are doin' God's work. Anyway, they will be loath to detain a woman. Go, do God's will, and hurry back.

REVEREND EDDIE *ushers her out the door.* HE *joyfully whoops and claps his hands. In his exuberance,* HE *suddenly pops the baby's balloon.* BECKY ANN *bursts back through the door.*

BECKY ANN: I think I'll take the baby . . .

REV. ED: No, leave the baby where it is. You will have your hands full enough.

BECKY ANN *(Trying to get to the baby, but blocked by* REVEREND EDDIE): I think the baby needs fresh air . . .

REV. ED: Fresh air could be the worst thing in the world for that child. He might get the croup.

BECKY ANN *(Struggling):* I'll dress it real warm . . .

REV. ED: No! Leave the baby here. I will look after the baby!

HE *grabs her by the arm and pushes her roughly out the door. Pause.* HE *hangs his jacket up, then notices the cake. Casting the single candle aside,* HE *scoops up some icing with his finger and licks it.* HE *looks into the basket.* HE *begins to croon "The Old Rugged Cross." As* HE *sings,* HE *picks the baby up from the basket and cradles it awkwardly.* HE *sits.*

On the Old Rugged Cross, stained with blood so divine
A wondrous beauty I see . . .
For 'twas on that old cross Jesus suffered and died
To pardon and sanctify me . . .

As HE *reaches the end of the verse, the door behind him opens with a squeak.* HE *freezes.* DARRELL *appears in the doorway, wearing army fatigues and a helmet.* HE *carries a bayonet.* HE *lets the door slam.* REVEREND EDDIE *turns.*

Darrell! You scared the hell out of me . . .

DARRELL: I hope so, Daddy . . . I hope so. (HE *plunges the bayonet into the countertop*)

REV. ED: I was just singin' the baby to sleep.

DARRELL: I know you were.

REV. ED: That's a mighty sharp bayonet you got there. Is that the one they stabbed you with during the war?

DARRELL: What do you think, I'm crazy? I got it at the army surplus. (HE *pulls the bayonet from the counter*) I know where I got it.

REV. ED: Of course you do, Darrell. The same place you got your war medal.

DARRELL (*With a swift movement,* HE *cuts* REVEREND EDDIE *on the neck*): We weren't talkin' about my war medal.

REV. ED: You cut me.

DARRELL: Well, you better wash it off. Cuts can get infected.

Silence. REVEREND EDDIE *does not move.* DARRELL *lowers the bayonet.* HE *laughs maniacally.*

What did you think I was gonna do with this bayonet, Daddy? What did you think? I was gonna kill you?

REV. ED: No, Darrell, I know you're not gonna kill your father.

DARRELL: Well, you're wrong. I was gonna kill you. And I still am. (HE *suddenly grabs his father by the hair and puts the bayonet to his throat*)

Pause.

REV. ED: Some fun, huh Darrell? Look . . . we can talk about this. Just let me put this baby down.

DARRELL: Why do you want to put the baby down? I thought that baby was Jesus. I thought that baby was your salvation. Well, let's see him save you now. Come on, Jesus, save my daddy. (*Pause*) We're waitin'. (*Pause*) Well, Daddy, it looks like that baby ain't gonna save you. (HE *releases his father*) I wonder who's gonna save you now. Anybody in this trailer who can save my daddy, raise your hand.

REV. ED: I just don't understand what I've done that's so wrong that would make you want to kill me. Was it beatin' you at cards?

DARRELL: You cheated!

REV. ED: Well, Darrell, if it makes you feel better to think that I cheated, then . . . yes, I cheated, and I beg your forgiveness . . .

DARRELL: You broke my radio.

REV. ED: Son, I'll fix your radio. We'll take it into town. I'll buy . . .

DARRELL: I don't care about no radio!

REV. ED: Was it because I cast you out?

DARRELL: You erased me!

REV. ED: I'd have taken you back with open arms . . .

DARRELL: I'm erased!

REV. ED: All you'd have to do is come back and apologize . . .

DARRELL: Oh, all I'd have to do is come crawlin' back on my hands and knees! You'd really like that, wouldn't you?

REV. ED: You're wrong, Darrell. I don't like it when you crawl. *(Starts to rise)*

DARRELL: Sit down! You know what you did. To that poor simple girl, who didn't have mind enough to know what was happenin'. And I want to hear you say it.

REV. ED: What?

DARRELL: That that baby ain't from God, and this whole thing is crazy!

REV. ED: So that's what you think . . . that I fathered this child . . .

DARRELL: I'm gonna kill you whether you say it or not, so you might as well say it.

REV. ED: Then after you've killed your father, what'll you do?

DARRELL: Then I'm gonna take Becky Ann and that baby and we're gonna get out of here.

REV. ED: Where will you go?

DARRELL: Somewhere. While you're rotting in your grave, we're gonna go somewhere and live like normal people.

REV. ED: Listen!

DARRELL: What?

REV. ED: Hear that?

DARRELL: What?

REV. ED: The devil! Satan is laughin' and dancin' on your soul.

DARRELL: Stop it! I know what you're doin'.

REV. ED: Darrell, it doesn't matter what the truth is. It only matters what you believe.

DARRELL: Say it.

REV. ED: All right Darrell, the truth. (HE *stands*) Hand me your mother's Bible.

DARRELL: Why?

REV. ED: Shall I get it myself?

DARRELL: No.

REV. ED: I thought you wanted to hear the truth. Darrell, I'm putting the baby down. And now, I'm going to get your momma's Bible (HE *picks up Momma's Bible, moves away from* DARRELL, *and kneels*) Jesus, to manifest the truth, and to bind the devil I swear on this Holy Bible that I have only wanted for this family.

DARRELL: That's a lie.

REV. ED: I swear I have repented for all my sins!

DARRELL: Lie.

REV. ED: And I swear . . . on this Bible . . . and in Jesus' holy name . . . that I did not father that child . . .

DARRELL (*Drops the bayonet and falls on his knees, grabbing the Bible*): Don't swear that! Don't swear on my momma's Bible!

REV. ED (*Closes his hands over* DARRELL's): And I swear Darrell, on this Holy Bible . . . with Jesus and your momma looking down from Heaven . . . that this child is Christ come again . . . and that every word I speak is the gospel truth. (*Pause.* HE *looks to Heaven*) Jesus, give me my son back. What is loosed on earth shall be loosed in Heaven. Jesus, I bind the devil! (HE *strikes* DARRELL *on the head with his palm*) I bind the devil and cast him out in Jesus' name. I cast him out in Jesus' name. Get out Devil! Get out! (HE *slaps* DARRELL *on the forehead and sends him sprawling*)

DARRELL: What do I do?

REV. ED: What you do Darrell is you think upon your sins.

DARRELL: I don't know what to think . . . 'cause I always thought . . .

REV. ED: Judge not that you be not judged.

DARRELL: I'm sorry.

REV. ED: Don't say you're sorry to me, Darrell. It was God who you offended.

DARRELL: I'm so sorry.

REV. ED: You beg forgiveness?

DARRELL: Yes . . .

REV. ED: From who?

DARRELL (*Reaches for* REVEREND EDDIE): From you . . .

REV. ED (*Slaps his hand away*): From God . . .

DARRELL: From God . . .

REV. ED: From his mercy . . .

DARRELL: From his mercy . . .

REV. ED: From his grace . . .

DARRELL: From his grace . . .

REV. ED: I have sinned . . .

DARRELL: I have sinned . . .

REV. ED: I have sinned against God . . .

DARRELL: I have sinned against God . . .

REV. ED: I have sinned against man . . .

DARRELL: I have sinned against man . . .

REV. ED: I am a coward . . .

DARRELL: No!

REV. ED: Say it!

Pause. DARRELL *weeps*.

DARRELL: I am a coward . . .

REV. ED: I am a traitor . . .

DARRELL: I am a traitor . . .

REV. ED: I am a deserter . . .
DARRELL: I am a deserter . . .

REVEREND EDDIE *picks up the fallen bayonet and walks up slowly behind the kneeling* DARRELL.

REV. ED: I am empty . . .
DARRELL: I am *so* empty . . .
REV. ED: Unworthy of life . . .
DARRELL: Unworthy of life . . .
REV. ED: I do not deserve to live . . .
DARRELL: I do not deserve to live . . .
REV. ED: I deserve to die . . .
DARRELL: I deserve to die . . .

Suddenly REVEREND EDDIE *grabs* DARRELL, *throws him down on the table and holds the bayonet to his throat.* DARRELL *screams.*

REV. ED: Oh, God, thy servant Abraham laid his lamb upon the altar. God make manifest thy will. God's will be done! *(Jerks* DARRELL's *hair)* God's will be done!
DARRELL: God's will be done . . .
REV. ED: I am the lamb . . .
DARRELL: I am the lamb . . .

REVEREND EDDIE *looks to the heavens and raises the bayonet.* HE *pauses.*

REV. ED: What God? What? I hear you. Yes . . .
DARRELL: No . . .
REV. ED: Yes . . .
DARRELL: No . . .
REV. ED: Darrell, you know what God has told me?
DARRELL: No, what?
REV. ED: Your life . . . has been spared!

REVEREND EDDIE *throws the bayonet aside.* DARRELL *flings himself to the floor.*

DARRELL: Oh God . . . thank you, thank you.
REV. ED: Thank you, Jesus . . .
DARRELL: Thank you, Jesus . . .
REV. ED: Thank you, Lord . . .
DARRELL: Thank you, Lord . . .
REV. ED: Thank you, Jesus . . .
DARRELL: Thank you, Jesus . . .
REV. ED: Jesus, I am empty . . .

DARRELL: Jesus, I am empty . . .

REV. ED: But I want to be filled!

DARRELL: I want to be filled!

REV. ED: With the Holy Ghost . . .

DARRELL: With the Holy Ghost!

REV. ED: Come in to me, Holy Ghost!

DARRELL: Come in to me, Holy Ghost!

REV. ED: Come in to me, now!

DARRELL: Come in to me, now!

REV. ED: Now!

DARRELL: Now!

> DARRELL *falls to the ground ranting in tongues and twitching spasmodically. Gradually,* HE *comes out of it and lies on the ground, exhausted, with a beautiful smile on his face.* REVEREND EDDIE *kneels beside him.*

REV. ED: Pray with me, Darrell. Pray with me. (DARRELL *repeats the prayer after him*) God . . . you have seen my only son become lost and turn away from God. And you have seen fit to return him to me in glory. Now, together we can go forth and do your will, and glorify thy Son. In the name of Jesus. Amen.

DARRELL: Amen. Is it all true?

REV. ED: Yes, Darrell.

DARRELL: Is it really in there?

REV. ED: What?

DARRELL: Go fish.

> *Pause.*

REV. ED: Yes it is, Darrell!

DARRELL: Amen . . .

REV. ED (*Reaches in the basket and picks up the baby*): Darrell, do you know why God has saved your life?

DARRELL: No, Daddy.

> BECKY ANN *enters the trailer as* REVEREND EDDIE *puts the baby in* DARRELL's *arms.*

REV. ED: Because God has sent another lamb to die in your place. And now, God wants you to help to glorify and bless that lamb even unto death and resurrection.

DARRELL: I know, Daddy. (*Pause*) I know.

> BECKY ANN *takes in the scene. Blackout.*

Scene 3

The scene changes to the tent meeting. BECKY ANN *rolls in the podium, then the baptismal pool. Over the loudspeakers we hear the congregation singing the hymn "Washed in the Blood of the Lamb." After the first verse, we hear* THE REVEREND EDDIE *exhorting, "Come on, everybody, you all know this one . . . sing along!" Hopefully, by the time the scene is set up, the audience will be singing along. When the lights come up,* REVEREND EDDIE *is in the audience singing and shaking hands.* BECKY ANN *is leading the singing.* THEY *are both dressed in white. After the hymn is over,* THE REVEREND EDDIE *shouts.*

REV. ED: Are you washed in the blood of the lamb! I hope you are. I wish there was thousands more of you here tonight to be washed in the blood, but those of you who *are* here tonight, are in fine, fine voice, and GOD . . . is blessing us all here tonight! Can I hear an amen? *(Response)* It's wonderful to be with you here in this glorious country full of so many holy, God-fearing people. I have never felt so welcome. I would especially like to thank your wonderful city officials of Moose Jaw for their marvelous cooperation. I am so . . . HAP-PY . . . tonight! Why? Because tonight is a very special night. More special than you can possibly imagine! What could be so special? What could be so monumental? Well, I'm not gonna tell you. You know, this meeting kinda reminds me of something that happened a few years ago back in a little town where I come from, in Arkansas. In this little town, one day a sign went up in the town square . . . and all it said was, "It's comin'." Well folks didn't pay much attention to it. Well, the next day, that sign was gone, and another was in its place. It said, "It's comin' soon." Well, now people was beginnin' to get a little curious . . . so every day, a new sign showed up. "It's comin', don't miss it." "It's comin' . . . Thursday." Then, the night before the big event, there was a huge sign and it said, "It's comin' tomorrow . . . two dollars." Well the next day there was a tent in the town square and people was lined up for miles. There was now another sign that said "It's Here." They all plunked down their two dollars, and crowded into that tent. Hundreds of 'em. And after they was all in there the lights went down, went up . . . and there was a sign. And it said . . . "It's Gone". . . . I want you to think about that while we listen to that lovely old hymn, "Softly and Tenderly." It will be sung by that vestal flower that has been blessed by God's Holy Spirit, my lovely daughter, Becky Ann. (BECKY ANN, *looking frightened, does not budge*) Becky Ann! "Softly and Tenderly." *(Sotto voce)* Clasp, smile, look up.

BECKY ANN *comes forward and sings "Softly and Tenderly."* SHE *carries* REVEREND EDDIE's *idea of "gestures" to a literal, and comic, extreme.*

Thank you, Becky Ann. You know, you're a wonderful group of people, a special group. I'd like to share something with you. Becky Ann, will you come forward? (BECKY ANN *hesitates*) Becky Ann! (SHE *comes forward, tentatively*) Some months ago, Becky Ann had a child. A son.

BECKY ANN: No, it was a . . .

REV. ED: Now! . . . Ordinarily, the birth of a son is a happy event in the life of any family. But this was no ordinary child. Becky Ann, would you tell these people about the birth of your baby?

BECKY ANN: Daddy!

REV. ED: Go on!

BECKY ANN: Well . . . uh . . . there was a lot of wind and fog and fire and stuff . . .

REV. ED: No, Becky Ann, we want to hear about your reaction after the baby was born.

BECKY ANN: Oh. Well, I was laying in the bed at our house near El Dorado, Arkansas. And the doctor came in the door with a little bundle and laid it on my chest. I pulled back the blanket and I looked at it. And I went (*Blood-curdling scream.* REVEREND EDDIE *starts, dropping his Bible*) and the doctor took the baby away . . .

REV. ED: Becky Ann screamed because she had seen a hideous sight. Her son was deformed, defective, and misshapen. I was in despair. I said, "Father, I have always been your loyal servant, how could this have happened to me? To my family?" And then, in a moment of shame and guilt, I told the doctor to take the baby, to take it out of our sight. And so he did. I did not know then what I know now. I did not know what you are going to know in the space of a few minutes. I doubted God. And I was punished. I was visited by an affliction that looked like poison ivy, but was certainly *not* poison ivy because I have never been allergic to poison ivy a day in my life! My daughter refused to eat or speak for a number of weeks. Satan visited my home in the body of my own son, Darrell. But then a miracle happened. And I'm gonna tell you about it. But first, let's join together in song. Becky Ann. (BECKY ANN *looks puzzled*) "Shall We Gather at the River."

BECKY ANN *leads the audience in singing "Shall We Gather at the River." During the song,* THE REVEREND EDDIE *removes his coat and rolls up his sleeves.* HE *gestures toward the back of the auditorium. A white light reveals* DARRELL, *dressed in a white baptismal robe and beaming, holding the basket, which has been painted for the occasion and has festive ribbons on the handles. In time with the music,* DARRELL *marches down the aisle, transported.* HE *joins* REVEREND EDDIE *and* BECKY ANN *on the stage.* REVEREND EDDIE *puts his arm around* DARRELL'*s shoulder.*

Well . . . who is this handsome young man? This is my son Darrell. Darrell, as I told you, was filled with Satan. But now, hallelujah, he is filled with the spirit of the Holy Ghost! He has come back to God's bosom, and he has been born again. Born again! Hallelujah, praise God! It's like in the words of the old hymn, "When the pain and grief would start, Jesus pardoned me! He took the evil from my heart . . . Jesus pardoned me!" Say amen, somebody!

(Response. HE *is almost crying)* Darrell! (DARRELL *steps forward)* I think Darrell has something he wants to say to all of you. Darrell, step forward.

DARRELL: Before I was born again, when the devil was still inside me, I committed sins against my father . . . and my family . . . and God . . . and the United States of America. Then I took Jesus Christ as my personal savior.

REVEREND EDDIE *applauds.*

REV. ED: Praise God, Darrell?

DARRELL: Praise God.

REV. ED: Thank you, Jesus?

DARRELL: Thank you, Jesus.

REV. ED: And *this* wasn't the only miracle. My daughter . . . is at peace. And all of my oozing sores are gone. And who caused these miracles? (HE *takes the basket from* DARRELL *and brings it forward)* Jesus. Now, I know what you're thinkin'. Is this what he's been leadin' up to? Is this what all of this is about? Is he sayin' that Jesus Christ is here in the flesh? Yes. That is *exactly* what I'm sayin'. In a moment of horrible despair, we gave Jesus away, and pestilence come upon us, and the sky darkened. We got Jesus back, our bodies and our souls were healed and light poured down on us from the sky like honey. . . . He was gone. But now he's here. And tonight, Jesus begins his new ministry. How lucky . . . how lucky you people are. For someday it will be written that you were present at the baptism of Jesus Christ at his second comin'. You were there when God came down like a dove to say, "This is my beloved son, in whom I am well pleased." Darrell. (DARRELL *steps forward)* Darrell, will you take the infant to the river of his baptism?

DARRELL *takes the basket.*

DARRELL: I will.

THEY *wait for a moment.*

REV. ED: Will you perhaps do it now?

DARRELL: Yes sir.

DARRELL *walks to the edge of the baptismal pool.* REVEREND EDDIE *steps forward.*

REV. ED: Now, before this wondrous moment of consecration and baptism takes place, let's bow our heads in prayer. (HE *kneels and holds up the letters)* Father, we thank you for your signs. We thank you that you have given your prophet the wisdom to interpret them correctly. . . . And we thank you, almighty God, for the gift of water. Because the Holy Ghost is in it. Just as it was in the Jordan River in which John the Baptist baptized your son as the Messiah who led us all to everlasting life through his death and resurrection. And now, Father, I will baptize your son in his second comin' and he will lead a new age to everlasting life through *his* death and resurrection! (*Suddenly,* DARRELL *plunges the baby beneath the water*) Father, let the blood of his lamb wash away our sins and our iniquities, and make our souls as clean and pure as the crystal stream and let the Holy Ghost descend upon us. (DARRELL *is still holding the basket underwater. There is a determined, transported look on his face.* HE *raises the basket and plunges it in again*) Bring us into glory, bring us unto the mountain. Bring us unto the throne. Let us look upon the throne like a jasper, or a sardine stone, and a rainbow be in sight around the throne like unto an emerald, and around the throne let there be crowns of gold! (DARRELL *plunges the basket in a third time*) Let there be lightning, and thunderbolts, and voices! And let those voices say, this is my Prophet! This is my Prophet, without sin! Bathed in Glory! Came to the throne! Followed the signs! This is my Prophet! This is my Prophet. He who has ears! Let him hear! Let him hear! (HE *begins to speak in tongues*) Thank you God. (HE *rises*) And now, the moment has arrived. According to his commandment, we will baptize the infant Jesus.

DARRELL: I did it. I did it, Daddy.

REV. ED (*Turns and sees him*): You did what?

DARRELL: Even unto death and resurrection . . .

REV. ED: NOOOO! (HE *pushes* DARRELL *away from the basket.* HE *grabs him by the neck and begins to choke him*) What did you do! What! What! WHAT! (HE *drops* DARRELL *and takes the basket from the water, whimpering*) No . . . no . . .

DARRELL: Even unto death and resurrection, like you said . . .

Slowly, THE REVEREND EDDIE *looks up.* THEY *notice the audience. Silence.* REVEREND EDDIE *allows* DARRELL *to take the basket from him.* DARRELL *slowly opens the basket and looks inside, dread on his face.* HE *reaches into the basket and removes a bundle, wrapped in a soggy baby blanket.* HE *slowly unwraps it. With surprise and awe,* HE *holds up . . . an eggplant.*

Daddy . . . it's an . . . I thought it was the baby . . . (THE REVEREND EDDIE *stares into space*) Daddy, what happened to the baby? (THE REVEREND *continues to stare*) Daddy, what happened to the baby? Daddy? (*Pause*) Daddy? Daddy . . . what do we do now?

REVEREND EDDIE *does not respond.* DARRELL *looks at the eggplant, then at the baptismal pool, and at the eggplant again.* HE *makes his decision.* HE *cradles the eggplant in his arms, walks to the edge of the stage and faces the audience. As* HE *speaks,* THE REVEREND EDDIE *begins to sing, very quietly, a few lines of "The Old Rugged Cross."* HE *trails off under* DARRELL's *speech.*

Sweet Jesus . . . you have shown us that . . . even in death . . . there is resurrection. And let it be known . . . that . . . in the second coming of our Lord . . .

sweet Jesus became a man . . . and was baptized in the Holy Ghost . . . died . . . and on that very same day . . . he arose again . . . and was resurrected . . . (*Pause*) as an eggplant. Praise God! Thank you, Jesus! And now . . . let us join together in our final hymn . . . "Faith of Our Fathers" . . .

A pool of light on DARRELL, *holding the eggplant aloft. We hear the taped voice of a male* DRIVER.

DRIVER: Well, ma'am, this is as far as I go.

Sound of car stopping.

BECKY ANN (*Her live voice*): This'll be fine.
DRIVER: That's a real pretty baby.
BECKY ANN: Thank you.
DRIVER: What's its name?
BECKY ANN: Arlene Marie.
DRIVER: I hope you get another ride.

Lights up on BECKY ANN, *carrying an old suitcase, her ukelele slung over her shoulder.*

BECKY ANN: Oh, we won't have no trouble (*Looks at the bundle*) See there, Arlene Marie? He liked you. He saw how special you are. (SHE *sits. We see the sign on the suitcase,* "We'd appreciate a ride") Whew! I feel a lot better now. (*Pause*) This is fun, ain't it? (*She begins to play her ukelele. Her song is punctuated by the baby glowing*)

Doodle li doodle li doo. Hi!
Doodle li doodle li doo. Boo!
Doo doo dooo . . .

As the lights fade, we see the baby glowing, illuminating the face of BECKY ANN.

END OF PLAY

The Colored Museum
George C. Wolfe

About George C. Wolfe

George C. Wolfe was born in Frankfurt, Ky. He holds a B.A. in Directing from Pomona College and an MFA in Dramatic Writing/Musical Theatre from New York University. In 1985 Wolfe's play *Return to Glutten* was performed in Sierra Leone as part of a cultural exchange program sponsored by the State Department. He wrote the book and lyrics for the musical *Paradise!*, which premiered in 1985 at Cincinnati Playhouse in the Park and was subsequently staged in New York by Playwrights Horizons. Wolfe is the librettist on *Queenie Pie*, Duke Ellington's street opera performed at the American Musical Theater Festival in Philadelphia and at the Kennedy Center in Washington, D.C. in 1986. Wolfe has received grants from the Rockefeller Foundation, the National Endowment for the Arts and the National Institute for Music Theater.

About the Play

The Colored Museum premiered in March 1986 at Crossroads Theatre Company in New Brunswick, N.J., as that theatre's winner of the FDG/CBS New Play Award. Artistic director L. Kenneth Richardson directed. Produced by Joseph Papp, the New York Shakespeare Festival production, directed by Richardson, opened at the Public Theater in November 1986 and ran there for nine months. The production subsequently transferred to the Royal Court Theatre, London, as part of the Festival's British exchange program, later moving to the Duke of York Theatre in London's West End. The play, which won the George Oppenheimer/Newsday Award, the Audelco Playwrights Award and the Hull-Warriner Award, is currently being produced by 15 regional theatres across the country. *The Colored Museum* was originally published in the February 1987 issue of TCG's *American Theatre* magazine.

Playwright's Note

The Exhibits: The play, which is performed without an intermission, consists of 11 exhibits:

Git on Board
Cookin' with Aunt Ethel
The Photo Session
Soldier with a Secret
The Gospel According to Miss Roj
The Hairpiece
The Last Mama-on-the-Couch Play
Symbiosis
Lala's Opening
Permutations
The Party

The Cast: an ensemble of five, two men and three women, all black, who play all the characters that inhabit the exhibits. In addition, a girl 5-12 years old appears in *Lala's Opening.*

The Stage: white walls and recessed lighting. A starkness befitting a museum where the myths and madness of black/Negro/colored Americans are stored. Built into the walls are a series of small panels, doors, revolving walls and compartments from which actors can retrieve key props and make quick entrances. A revolve is used, which allows for quick transitions from one exhibit to the next.

Music: All of the music for the show is prerecorded. Only the drummer, who is used in *Git on Board,* and then later in *Permutations* and *The Party,* is live.

The Characters

Git on Board
    MISS PAT
    VOICE OF CAPTAIN
    SLAVES

Cookin' with Aunt Ethel
    AUNT ETHEL

The Photo Session
    GIRL
    GUY

Soldier with a Secret
    JUNIE ROBINSON

The Gospel According to Miss Roj
    MISS ROJ
    WAITER

The Hairpiece
    THE WOMAN
    JANINE
    LAWANDA

The Last Mama-on-the-Couch Play
    NARRATOR
    MAMA
    WALTER-LEE-BEAU-WILLIE-JONES
    LADY IN PLAID
    MEDEA JONES

Symbiosis
    THE MAN
    THE KID

Lala's Opening
    LALA LAMAZING GRACE
    ADMONIA
    FLO'RANCE
    THE LITTLE GIRL
    VOICE OF ANNOUNCER

Permutations
    NORMAL JEAN REYNOLDS

The Party
    TOPSY WASHINGTON
    MISS PAT
    MISS ROJ
    LALA LAMAZING GRACE
    THE MAN (from *Symbiosis*)

The Play

The Colored Museum

Git on Board

Blackness. Cut by drums pounding. Then slides, rapidly flashing before us. Images we've all seen before, of African slaves being captured, loaded onto ships, tortured. The images flash, flash, flash. The drums crescendo. Blackout. And then lights reveal MISS PAT, *frozen.* SHE *is black, pert and cute.* SHE *has a flip to her hair and wears a hot pink miniskirt stewardess uniform.* SHE *stands in front of a curtain which separates her from an offstage cockpit.*

An electronic bell goes "ding" and MISS PAT *comes to life, presenting herself in a friendly but rehearsed manner, smiling and speaking as* SHE *has done so many times before.*

MISS PAT: Welcome aboard Celebrity Slaveship, departing the Gold Coast and making short stops at Bahia, Port-au-Prince and Havana, before our final destination of Savannah.

Hi, I'm Miss Pat and I'll be serving you here in Cabin A. We will be crossing the Atlantic at an altitude that's pretty high, so you must wear your shackles at all times.

(SHE *removes a shackle from the overhead compartment and demonstrates*) To put on your shackle, take the right hand and close the metal ring around your left hand like so. Repeat the action using your left hand to secure the right. If you have any trouble bonding yourself, I'd be more than glad to assist.

Once we reach the desired altitude, the captain will turn off the "Fasten Your Shackle" sign . . . (SHE *efficiently points out the "Fasten Your Shackle" signs on either side of her, which light up)* allowing you a chance to stretch and dance in the aisles a bit. But otherwise, shackles must be worn at all times. *(The "Fasten Your Shackle" signs go off)*

Also, we ask that you please refrain from call-and-response singing between cabins as that sort of thing can lead to rebellion. And, of course, no drums are allowed on board. Can you repeat after me, "No drums." (SHE *gets the audience to repeat)* With a little more enthusiasm, please. "No drums." *(After the audience repeats it)* That was great!

Once we're airborn, I'll be by with magazines, and earphones can be purchased for the price of your first-born male.

If there's anything I can do to make this middle passage more pleasant, press the little button overhead and I'll be with you faster than you can say "Go down, Moses." (SHE *laughs at her "little joke")* Thanks for flying Celebrity and here's hoping you have a pleasant takeoff.

The engines surge, the "Fasten Your Shackle" signs go on, and over-articulate Muzak voices are heard singing as MISS PAT *pulls down a bucket seat and "shackles-up" for takeoff.*

VOICES: Get on board Celebrity Slaveship
Get on board Celebrity Slaveship
Get on board Celebrity Slaveship
There's room for many a more

The engines reach an even, steady hum. Just as MISS PAT *rises and replaces the shackles in the overhead compartment, the faint sound of African drumming is heard.*

MISS PAT: Hi. Miss Pat again. I'm sorry to disturb you, but someone is playing drums. And what did we just say . . . "No drums." It must be someone in coach. But we here in Cabin A are not going to respond to those drums. As a matter of fact, we don't even hear them. Repeat after me. "I don't hear any drums." *(The audience repeats)* And "I will not rebel."

The audience repeats. The drumming grows.

(Placating) OK, now I realize some of us are a bit edgy after hearing about the tragedy on board The Laughing Mary, but let me assure you Celebrity has no intention of throwing you overboard and collecting the insurance. We value you!

(SHE *proceeds to single out individual passengers/audience members)* Why the songs you are going to sing in the cotton fields, under the burning heat and stinging lash, will metamorphose and give birth to the likes of James Brown and the Fabulous Flames. And you, yes *you*, are going to come up with some of the best dances. The best dances! The Watusi! The Funky Chicken! And just think of what *you* are going to mean to William Faulkner.

All right, so you're gonna have to suffer for a few hundred years, but from your pain will come a culture so complex. *And*, with this little item here . . . (SHE *removes a basketball from the overhead compartment*) you'll become millionaires!

There is a roar of thunder. The lights quiver and the "Fasten Your Shackle" signs begin to flash. MISS PAT *quickly replaces the basketball in the overhead compartment and speaks very reassuringly.*

No, don't panic. We're just caught in a little thunderstorm. Now the only way you're going to make it through is if you abandon your God and worship a new one. So, on the count of three, let's all sing. One, two, three . . . "Nobody knows de trouble I seen". . . . Oh, I forgot to mention, when singing, omit the "th" sound. "The" becomes "de." "They" becomes "dey." Got it? Good! "Nobody knows". . . . "Nobody knows . . ."

Oh, so you don't like that one? Well then let's try another: "Summertime, and de livin' is easy". . . . Gershwin. He comes from another oppressed people so he understands. "Fish are jumpin' " . . . come on. "And de cotton is high" "And de cotton is". . . . Sing, dammit!

Lights begin to flash, the engines surge and there is wild drumming. MISS PAT *sticks her head through the curtain and speaks with an offstage* CAPTAIN.

What?

VOICE OF CAPTAIN (*Offstage*): Time warp!

MISS PAT: Time warp! (SHE *turns to the audience and puts on a pleasant face*) The captain has assured me everything is fine. We're just caught in a little time warp. (*Trying to fight her growing hysteria*) On your right you will see the American Revolution, which will give the U.S. of A. exclusive rights to your life. And on your left, the Civil War, which means you will vote Republican until F.D.R. comes along. And now we're passing over the Great Depression, which means everybody gets to live the way you've been living. (*There is a blinding flash of light, and an explosion.* SHE *screams*) Ahhhhhhhhh! That was World War I, which is not to be confused with World War II . . . (*There is a larger flash of light, and another explosion*) Ahhhhh! Which is not to be confused with the Korean War or the Vietnam War, all of which you will play a major role in.

Oh, look, now we're passing over the sixties. Martha and the Vandellas . . . "Julia" with Miss Diahann Carroll . . . Malcolm X . . . those five little girls in Alabama . . . Martin Luther King. . . . Oh no! The Supremes broke up! *(The drumming intensifies)* Stop playing those drums! Those drums will be confiscated once we reach Savannah. You can't change history! You can't turn back the clock! *(To the audience)* Repeat after me. I don't hear any drums! I will not rebel! I will not rebel! I will not re—

The lights go out, SHE *screams, and the sound of a plane landing and screeching to a halt is heard. After a beat, lights reveal a wasted, disheveled* MISS PAT, *but perky nonetheless.*

Hi. Miss Pat here. Things got a bit jumpy back there, but the captain has just informed me we have safely landed in Savannah. Please check the overhead before exiting as any baggage you don't claim, we trash.

It's been fun, and we hope the next time you consider travel, it's with Celebrity.

Luggage begins to revolve onstage from offstage left, going past MISS PAT *and revolving offstage right. Mixed in with the luggage are* TWO MALE SLAVES *and a* WOMAN SLAVE, *complete with luggage and I.D. tags around their necks.*

(With routine, rehearsed pleasantness)
Have a nice day. Bye-bye.
Button up that coat, it's kind of chilly.
Have a nice day. Bye-bye.
You take care now.
See you.
Have a nice day.
Have a nice day.
Have a nice day.

Cookin' with Aunt Ethel

As the SLAVES *begin to revolve off, a lowdown gutbucket blues is heard.* AUNT ETHEL, *a down-home black woman with a bandana on her head, revolves to center stage.* SHE *stands behind a big black pot and wears a reassuring grin.*

AUNT ETHEL: Welcome to *Aunt Ethel's Down-Home Cookin' Show*, where we explores the magic and mysteries of colored cuisine.

Today, we gonna be servin' ourselves up some . . . (SHE *laughs*) I'm not gonna tell you. That's right! I'm not gonna tell you what it is till after you done cooked it. Child, on *The Aunt Ethel Show* we loves to have ourselves some fun. Well, are you ready? Here goes. (SHE *belts out a hard-drivin' blues and throws invisible ingredients into the big, black pot*)

First ya add a pinch of style
And then a dash of flair
Now ya stir in some preoccupation
With the texture of your hair

Next ya add all kinds of rhythms
Lots of feelings and pizazz
Then hunny throw in some rage
Till it congeals and turns to jazz

Now you cookin'
Cookin' with Aunt Ethel
You really cookin'
Cookin' with Aunt Ethel, oh yeah

Now ya add a heap of survival
And humility, just a touch
Add some attitude
Oops! I put too much

And now a whole lot of humor
Salty language, mixed with sadness
Then throw in a box of blues
And simmer to madness

Now you cookin'
Cookin' with Aunt Ethel, oh yeah!

Now you beat it—really work it
Discard and disown
And in a few hundred years
Once it's aged and fully grown
Ya put it in the oven
Till it's black
And has a sheen
Or till it's nice and yella
Or any shade in between

Next ya take 'em out and cool 'em
'Cause they no fun when they hot
And won't you be surprised
At the concoction you got

You have baked
Baked yourself a batch of negroes
Yes you have baked yourself
Baked yourself a batch of negroes

(SHE *pulls from the pot a handful of Negroes, black dolls*) But don't ask me what to do with 'em now that you got 'em, 'cause child, that's your problem. (SHE *throws the dolls back into the pot*) But in any case, yaw be sure to join Aunt Ethel next week, when we gonna be servin' ourselves up some chitlin quiche . . . some grits-under-glass . . . (SHE *sings*)

And a sweet potato pie
And you'll be cookin'
Cookin' with Aunt Ethel
Oh yeah!

On AUNT ETHEL'S *final riff, lights reveal . . .*

The Photo Session

. . . a very glamorous, gorgeous, black COUPLE, *wearing the best of everything and perfect smiles. The stage is bathed in color and bright white light. Disco music with the chant "We're fabulous" plays in the background. As* THEY *pose, larger-than-life images of their perfection are projected on the museum walls. The music quiets and the images fade away as* THEY *begin to speak and pose.*

GIRL: The world was becoming too much for us.
GUY: We couldn't resolve the contradictions of our existence.
GIRL: And we couldn't resolve yesterday's pain.
GUY: So we gave away our life and we now live inside *Ebony Magazine.*
GIRL: Yes, we live inside a world where everyone is beautiful, and wears fabulous clothes.
GUY: And no one says anything profound.
GIRL: Or meaningful.
GUY: Or contradictory.
GIRL: Because no one talks. Everyone just smiles and shows off their cheekbones.

THEY *adopt a profile pose.*

GUY: Last month I was black and fabulous while holding up a bottle of vodka.
GIRL: This month we get to be black and fabulous together.

THEY *dance/pose. The "We're fabulous" chant builds and then fades as* THEY *start to speak again.*

GIRL: There are of course setbacks.
GUY: We have to smile like this for a whole month.
GIRL: And we have no social life.
GUY: And no sex.
GIRL: And at times it feels like we're suffocating, like we're not human anymore.
GUY: And everything is rehearsed, including this other kind of pain we're starting to feel.
GIRL: The kind of pain that comes from feeling no pain at all.

THEY *speak and pose with a sudden burst of energy.*

GUY: But one can't have everything.
GIRL: Can one?
GUY: So if the world is becoming too much for you, do like we did.
GIRL: Give away your life and come be beautiful with us.
GUY: We guarantee, no contradictions.
GIRL AND GUY: Smile/click, smile/click, smile/click.
GIRL: And no pain.

THEY *adopt a final pose and revolve off as the "We're fabulous" chant plays and fades into the background.*

A Soldier with a Secret

Projected onto the museum walls are the faces of black soldiers—from the Spanish-American through the Vietnam War. Lights slowly reveal JUNIE ROBINSON, *a black combat soldier, posed on an onyx plinth.* HE *comes to life and smiles at the audience. Somewhat dimwitted,* HE *has an easygoing charm about him.*

JUNIE: Pst. Pst. Guess what? I know the secret. The secret to your pain. Course, I didn't always know. First I had to die, then come back to life, 'fore I had the gift.

Ya see the Cappin sent me off up ahead to scout for screamin' yella bastards. Course, for the life of me I couldn't understand why they'd be screamin', seein' as how we was tryin' to kill them and they us.

But anyway, I'm off lookin', when all of a sudden I find myself caught smack dead in the middle of this explosion. This blindin', burnin', scaldin' explosion. Musta been a booby trap or something, 'cause all around me is fire. Hell, I'm on fire. Like a piece of chicken dropped in a skillet of cracklin' grease. Why, my flesh was justa peelin' off of my bones.

But then I says to myself, "Junie, if yo' flesh is on fire, how come you don't feel no pain!" And I didn't. I swear as I'm standin' here, I felt nuthin'. That's when I sort of put two and two together and realized I didn't feel no whole lot of hurtin' 'cause I done died.

Well I just picked myself up and walked right on out of that explosion. Hell, once you know you dead, why keep on dyin', ya know?

So, like I say, I walk right outta that explosion, fully expectin' to see white clouds, Jesus, and my mama, only all I saw was more war. Shootin' goin' on way off in this direction and that direction. And there, standin' around, was all the guys. Hubert, J.F., the Cappin. I guess the sound of the explosion must of attracted 'em, and they all starin' at me like I'm some kind of ghost.

So I yells to 'em, "Hey there Hubert! Hey there Cappin!" But they just stare. So I tells 'em how I'd died and how I guess it wasn't my time 'cause here I am, "Fully in the flesh and not a scratch to my bones." And they still just stare. So I took to starin' back.

(The expression on his face slowly turns to horror and disbelief) Only what I saw . . . well I can't exactly to this day describe it. But I swear, as sure as they was wearin' green and holdin' guns, they was each wearin' a piece of the future on their faces.

Yeah. All the hurt that was gonna get done to them and they was gonna do to folks was right there clear as day.

I saw how J.F., once he got back to Chicago, was gonna get shot dead by this po-lice, and I saw how Hubert was gonna start beatin' up on his old lady which I didn't understand, 'cause all he could do was talk on and on about how much he loved her. Each and every one of 'em had pain in his future and blood on his path. And God or the Devil one spoke to me and said, "Junie, these colored boys ain't gonna be the same after this war. They ain't gonna have no kind of happiness."

Well right then and there it come to me. The secret to their pain.

Late that night, after the medics done checked me over and found me fit for fightin', after everybody done settle down for the night, I sneaked over to where Hubert was sleepin', and with a needle I stole from the medics . . . pst, pst . . . I shot a little air into his veins. The second he died, all the hurtin'-to-come just left his face.

Two weeks later I got J.F. and after that Woodrow . . . Jimmy Joe . . . I even spent all night waitin' by the latrine 'cause I knew the Cappin always made a late night visit and pst . . . pst . . . I got him.

(Smiling, quite proud of himself) That's how come I died and come back to life. 'Cause just like Jesus went around healin' the sick, I'm supposed to go around healin' the hurtin' all these colored boys wearin' from the war.

Pst, pst. I know the secret. The secret to your pain. The secret to yours, and yours. Pst. Pst. Pst. Pst.

The lights slowly fade.

The Gospel According to Miss Roj

The darkness is cut by electronic music. Cold, pounding, unrelenting. A neon sign which spells out THE BOTTOMLESS PIT clicks on. There is a lone bar stool. Lights flash on and off, pulsating to the beat. There is a blast of smoke and, from the haze, MISS ROJ *appears.* HE *is dressed in striped patio pants, white go-go boots, a halter and cat-shaped sunglasses. What would seem ridiculous on anyone else,* MISS ROJ *wears as if it were high fashion.* HE *carries himself with total elegance and absolute arrogance.*

MISS ROJ: God created black people and black people created style. The name's Miss Roj . . . that's R-O-J thank you, and you can find me every Wednesday, Friday and Saturday nights at The Bottomless Pit, the watering hole for the wild and weary which asks the questions, "Is there life after Jherri-curl?"

A WAITER *enters, hands* MISS ROJ *a drink and then exits.*

Thanks, doll. Yes, if they be black and swish, the B.P. has seen them, which is not to suggest the Pit is lacking in cultural diversity. Oh no. There are your dinge queens, white men who like their chicken legs dark. (HE *winks at/flirts with a man in the audience*) And let's not forget, "Los Muchachos de la Neighborhood." But the speciality of the house is The Snap Queens. (HE *snaps his fingers*) We are a rare breed.

For, you see, when something strikes our fancy, when the truth comes piercing through the dark, well you just can't let it pass unnoticed. No darling. You must pronounce it with a snap. (HE *snaps*)

Snapping comes from another galaxy, as do all snap queens. That's right. I ain't just your regular oppressed American Negro. No-no-no! I am an extraterrestial. And I ain't talkin' none of that shit you seen in the movies! I have real power.

The WAITER *enters.* MISS ROJ *stops him.*

Speaking of no power, will you please tell Miss Stingy-with-the-Rum, that if Miss Roj had wanted to remain sober, she could have stayed home and drank Kool-Aid. (HE *snaps*) Thank you.

The WAITER *exits.* MISS ROJ *crosses and sits on bar stool.*

Yes, I was placed here on Earth to study the life habits of a deteriorating society, and child when we talkin' New York City, we are discussing the Queen of Deterioration. Miss New York is doing a slow dance with death, and I am here to warn you all, but before I do, I must know . . . don't you just love my patio pants? Annette Funicello immortalized them in *Beach Blanket Bingo,* and I have continued the legacy. And my go-gos? I realize white after Labor Day is very gauche, but as the saying goes, if you've got it flaunt it, if you don't, front it and snap to death any bastard who dares to defy you. *(Laughing)* Oh ho! My demons are showing. Yes, my demons live at the bottom of my Bacardi and Coke.

   Let's just hope for all concerned I dance my demons out before I drink them out 'cause child, dancing demons take you on a ride, but those drinkin' demons just take you, and you find yourself doing the strangest things. Like the time I locked my father in the broom closet. Seems the liquor made his tongue real liberal and he decided he was gonna baptize me with the word "faggot" over and over. Well, he's just going on and on with "faggot this" and "faggot that," all the while walking toward the broom closet to piss. So the demons just took hold of my wedges and forced me to kick the drunk son-of-a-bitch into the closet and lock the door. *(Laughter)* Three days later I remembered he was there. (HE *snaps*)

The WAITER *enters.* MISS ROJ *takes a drink and downs it.*

Another!

The WAITER *exits.*

(Dancing about) Oh yes-yes-yes! Miss Roj is quintessential style. I cornrow the hairs on my legs so that they spell out M-I-S-S R-O-J. And I dare any bastard to fuck with me because I will snap your ass into oblivion.

   I have the power, you know. Everytime I snap, I steal one beat of your heart. So if you find yourself gasping for air in the middle of the night, chances are you fucked with Miss Roj and she didn't like it.

   Like the time this asshole at Jones Beach decided to take issue with my culotte-sailor ensemble. This child, this muscle-bound Brooklyn thug in a skintight bikini, very skintight so the whole world can see that instead of a brain, God gave him an extra-thick piece of sausage. You know the kind who beat up on their wives for breakfast. Snap your fingers if you know what I'm talking about. . . . Come on and snap, child. (HE *gets the audience to snap*) Well, he decided to blurt out when I walked by, "Hey look at da monkey coon in da faggit suit." Well, I walked up to the poor dear, very calmly lifted my hand, and . . . (HE *snaps in rapid succession*) A heart attack, right there on the beach. (HE *singles out someone in the audience*) You don't believe it? Cross me! Come on! Come on!

The WAITER *enters, hands* MISS ROJ *a drink.* MISS ROJ *downs it. The* WAITER *exits.*

(*Looking around*) If this place is the answer, we're asking all the wrong questions. The only reason I come here is to communicate with my origins. The flashing lights are signals from my planet way out there. Yes, girl, even further than Flatbush. We're talking another galaxy. The flashing lights tell me how much time is left before the end.

(*Very drunk and loud by now*) I hate the people here. I hate the drinks. But most of all I hate this goddam music. That ain't music. Give me Aretha Franklin any day. (*Singing*) "Just a little respect. R-E-S-P-E-C-T." Yeah! Yeah!

Come on and dance your last dance with Miss Roj. Last call is but a drink away and each snap puts you one step closer to the end.

A high-rise goes up. You can't get no job. Come on everybody and dance. A whole race of people gets trashed and debased. Snap those fingers and dance. Some sick bitch throws her baby out the window 'cause she thinks it's the Devil. Everybody snap! *The New York Post.* Snap!

Snap for every time you walk past someone lying in the street, smelling like frozen piss and shit and you don't see it. Snap for every crazed bastard who kills himself so as to get the jump on being killed. And snap for every sick muthafucker who, bored with carrying around his fear, takes to shooting up other people.

Yeah, snap your fingers and dance with Miss Roj. But don't be fooled by the banners and balloons 'cause, child, this ain't no party going on. Hell no! It's a wake. And the casket's made out of stone, steel and glass and the people are racing all over the pavement like maggots on a dead piece of meat.

Yeah, dance! But don't be surprised if there ain't no beat holding you together 'cause we traded in our drums for respectability. So now it's just words. Words rappin'. Words screechin'. Words flowin' instead of blood 'cause you know that don't work. Words cracklin' instead of fire 'cause by the time a match is struck on 125th Street and you run to Midtown, the flame has been blown away.

So come on and dance with Miss Roj and her demons. We don't ask for acceptance. We don't ask for approval. We know who we are and we move on it!

I guarantee you will never hear two fingers put together in a snap and not think of Miss Roj. That's power, baby. Patio pants and all.

The lights begin to flash in rapid succession.

So let's dance! And snap! And dance! And snap!

MISS ROJ *begins to dance as if driven by his demons. There is a blast of smoke and when the haze settles,* MISS ROJ *has revolved off and in place of him is a recording of Aretha Franklin singing "Respect."*

The Hairpiece

As "Respect" fades into the background, a vanity revolves to center stage. On this vanity are two wigs, an Afro wig circa 1968 and a long, flowing wig, both resting on wig stands. A black WOMAN *enters, her head and body wrapped in towels.* SHE *picks up a framed picture and, after a few moments of hesitation, throws it into a small trash can.* SHE *then removes one of her towels to reveal a totally bald head. Looking into a mirror on the "fourth wall,"* SHE *begins applying makeup.*

    The wig stand holding the Afro wig opens her eyes. Her name is JANINE. SHE *stares in disbelief at the bald* WOMAN.

JANINE *(Calling to the other wig stand)*: LaWanda. LaWanda girl, wake up.

The other wig stand, the one with the long, flowing wig, opens her eyes. Her name is LAWANDA.

LAWANDA: What? What is it?

JANINE: Check out girlfriend.

LAWANDA: Oh, girl, I don't believe it.

JANINE *(Laughing)*: Just look at the poor thing, trying to paint some life onto that face of hers. You'd think by now she'd realize it's the hair. It's all about the hair.

LAWANDA: What hair! She ain't go no hair! She done fried, dyed, dechemicalized her shit to death.

JANINE: And all that's left is that buck-naked scalp of hers, sittin' up there apologizin' for being odd-shaped and ugly.

LAWANDA *(Laughing with* JANINE*)*: Girl, stop!

JANINE: I ain't sayin' nuthin' but the truth.

LAWANDA AND JANINE: The bitch is bald! *(*THEY *laugh)*

JANINE: And all over some man.

LAWANDA: I tell ya, girl, I just don't understand it. I mean, look at her. She's got a right nice face, a good head on her shoulders. A good job even. And she's got to go fall in love with that fool.

JANINE: That political quick-change artist. Everytime the nigga went and changed his ideology, she went and changed her hair to fit the occasion.

LAWANDA: Well at least she's breaking up with him.

JANINE: Hunny, no!

LAWANDA: Yes child.

JANINE: Oh, girl, dish me the dirt!

LAWANDA: Well, you see, I heard her on the phone talking to one of her girlfriends, and she's meeting him for lunch today to give him the ax.

JANINE: Well it's about time.

LAWANDA: I hear ya. But don't you worry 'bout a thing, girlfriend. I'm gonna tell you all about it.

JANINE: Hunny, you won't have to tell me a damn thing 'cause I'm gonna be there, front row, center.

LAWANDA: You?

JANINE: Yes, child, she's wearing me to lunch.

LAWANDA (Outraged): I don't think so!

JANINE (With an attitude): What do you mean, you don't think so?

LAWANDA: Exactly what I said, "I don't think so." Damn, Janine, get real. How the hell she gonna wear both of us?

JANINE: She ain't wearing both of us. She's wearing me.

LAWANDA: Says who?

JANINE: Says me! Says her! Ain't that right, girlfriend?

The WOMAN *stops putting on makeup, looks around, sees no one, and goes back to her makeup.*

I said, ain't that right!

The WOMAN *picks up the phone.*

WOMAN: Hello ... hello ....

JANINE: Did you hear the damn phone ring?

WOMAN: No.

JANINE: Then put the damn phone down and talk to me.

WOMAN: I ah ... don't understand.

JANINE: It ain't deep so don't panic. Now, you're having lunch with your boyfriend, right?

WOMAN (Breaking into tears): I think I'm having a nervous breakdown.

JANINE (Impatient): I said you're having lunch with your boyfriend, right!

WOMAN (Scared, pulling herself together): Yes, right ... right.

JANINE: To break up with him.

WOMAN: How did you know that?

LAWANDA: I told her.

WOMAN (Stands and screams): Help! Help!

JANINE: Sit down. I said sit your ass down! (*The* WOMAN *does*) Now set her straight and tell her you're wearing me.

LAWANDA: She's the one that needs to be set straight, so go on and tell her you're wearing me.

JANINE: No, tell her you're wearing me.

There is a pause.

LAWANDA: Well?

JANINE: Well?

WOMAN: I ah . . . actually hadn't made up my mind.

JANINE (*Going off*): What do you mean you ain't made up you mind! After all that fool has put you through, you gonna need all the attitude you can get and there is nothing like attitude and a healthy head of kinks to make his shit shrivel like it should!

    That's right! When you wearin' me, you lettin' him know he ain't gonna get no sweet-talkin' comb through your love without some serious resistance. No-no! The kink of my head is like the kink of your heart and neither is about to be hot-pressed into surrender.

LAWANDA: That shit is so tired. The last time attitude worked on anybody was 1968. Janine girl, you need to get over it and get on with it. (*To the* WOMAN) And you need to give the nigga a goodbye he will never forget.

    I say give him hysteria! Give him emotion! Give him rage! And there is nothing like a toss of the tresses to make your emotional outburst shine with emotional flair.

    You can toss me back, shake me from side to side, all the while screaming, "I want you out of my life forever!!!" And not only will I come bouncing back for more, but you just might win an Academy Award for best performance by a head of hair in a dramatic role.

JANINE: Miss Hunny, please! She don't need no Barbie doll dipped in chocolate telling her what to do. She needs a head of hair that's coming from a fo' real place.

LAWANDA: Don't you dare talk about nobody coming from a "fo' real place," Miss Made-in-Taiwan!

JANINE: Hey! I ain't ashamed of where I come from. Besides, it don't matter where you come from as long as you end up in the right place.

LAWANDA: And it don't matter the grade as long as the point gets made. So go on and tell her you're wearing me.

JANINE: No, tell her you're wearing me.

The WOMAN, *unable to take it, begins to bite off her fake nails, as* LAWANDA *and* JANINE *go at each other.*

LAWANDA: Set the bitch straight. Let her know there is no way she could even begin to compete with me. I am quality. She is kink. I am exotic. She is common. I am class and she is trash. That's right. T-R-A-S-H. We're talking three strikes and you're out. So go on and tell her you're wearing me. Go on, tell her! Tell her! Tell her!

JANINE (*Simultaneously*): Who you callin' a bitch? Why, if I had hands I'd knock you clear into next week. You think you cute. She thinks she's cute just 'cause that synthetic mop of hers blows in the wind. She looks like a fool and you look like an even bigger fool when you wear her, so go on and tell her you're wearing me. Go on, tell her! Tell her! Tell her!

The WOMAN *screams and pulls the two wigs off the wig stands as the lights go to black on three bald heads.*

The Last Mama-on-the-Couch Play

A NARRATOR, *dressed in a black tuxedo, enters through the audience and stands center stage.* HE *is totally solemn.*

NARRATOR: We are pleased to bring you yet another Mama-on-the-Couch play. A searing domestic drama that tears at the very fabric of racist America. (HE *crosses upstage center, sits on a stool and reads from a playscript*) Act One. Scene One.

MAMA *revolves on stage left, sitting on a couch reading an oversized Bible. There is a window stage right.* MAMA's *dress, the couch and drapes are made from the same material. A doormat lies down center.*

Lights up on a dreary, depressing but with middle-class aspirations tenement slum. There is a couch, with a Mama on it. Both are well worn. There is a picture of Jesus on the wall . . . (*A picture of Jesus is instantly revealed*) and a window which looks onto an abandoned tenement. It is late spring. Enter Walter-Lee-Beau-Willie-Jones.

SON *enters through the audience.*

He is Mama's thirty-year-old son. His brow is heavy from three hundred years of oppression.

MAMA (*Looking up from her Bible, speaking in a slow manner*): Son, did you wipe your feet?

SON (*An ever-erupting volcano*): No, Mama, I didn't wipe me feet! Out there, every day, Mama, is the Man. The Man, Mama. Mr. Charlie! Mr. Bossman! And he's wipin' his feet on me. On me, Mama, every damn day of my life. Ain't that enough for me to deal with? Ain't that enough?

MAMA: Son, wipe your feet.

SON: I wanna dream. I wanna be somebody. I wanna take charge of my life.

MAMA: You can do all of that, but first you got to wipe your feet.

SON (*As* HE *crosses to the mat, mumbling and wiping his feet*): Wipe my feet . . . wipe my feet . . . wipe my feet . . .

MAMA: That's a good boy.

SON (*Exploding*): Boy! Boy! I don't wanna be nobody's good boy, Mama. I wanna be my own man!

MAMA: I know son, I know. God will show the way.

SON: God, Mama! Since when did your God ever do a damn thing for the black man. Huh, Mama, huh? You tell me. When did your God ever help me?

MAMA (*Removing her wire-rim glasses*): Son, come here.

SON *crosses to* MAMA, *who slowly stands and with an exaggerated stage slap, backhands* SON *clear across the stage. The* NARRATOR *claps his hands to create the sound for the slap.* MAMA *then lifts her clenched fists to the heavens.*

Not in my house, my house, will you ever talk that way again!

The NARRATOR, *so moved by her performance, erupts in applause and encourages the audience to do so.*

NARRATOR: Beautiful. Just stunning.

HE *reaches into one of the secret compartments of the set and gets an award which* HE *ceremoniously gives to* MAMA *for her performance.* SHE *bows and then returns to the couch.*

Enter Walter-Lee-Beau-Willie's wife, the Lady in Plaid.

Music from nowhere is heard, a jazzy pseudo-abstract intro as the LADY IN PLAID *dances in through the audience, wipes her feet and then twirls about.*

LADY IN PLAID: She was a creature of regal beauty
who in ancient time graced the temples of the Nile
with her womanliness.
But here she was, stuck being colored
and a woman in a world that valued neither.

SON: You cooked my dinner?

LADY IN PLAID (*Oblivious to* SON): Feet flat, back broke,
she looked at the man who, though he be thirty,
still ain't got his own apartment.
Yeah, he's still livin' with his Mama!
And she asked herself, was this the life
for a Princess Colored, who by the
translucence of her skin, knew the
universe was her sister.

The LADY IN PLAID *twirls and dances.*

SON (*Becoming irate*): I've had a hard day of dealin' with the Man. Where's my damn dinner? Woman, stand still when I'm talkin' to you!

LADY IN PLAID: And she cried for her sisters in Detroit
who knew, as she, that their souls belonged
in ancient temples on the Nile.
And she cried for her sisters in Chicago
who, like her, their life has become
one colored hell.

SON: There's only one thing gonna get through to you.

LADY IN PLAID: And she cried for her sisters in New Orleans
and her sisters in Trenton and Birmingham,
and
Poughkeepsie and Orlando and Miami Beach
and
Las Vegas, Palm Springs.

As SHE *continues to call out cities,* HE *crosses offstage, returns with two black dolls, then crosses to the window.*

SON: Now are you gonna cook me dinner?

LADY IN PLAID: Walter-Lee-Beau-Willie-Jones, no! Not my babies. (SON *throws them out the window.* SHE *lets out a primal scream*) He dropped them!!!!

The NARRATOR *breaks into applause.*

NARRATOR: Just splendid. Shattering.

The NARRATOR *crosses to* MAMA *and after an intense struggle with her, takes the award from her and gives it to the* LADY IN PLAID, *who is still suffering primal pain.*

LADY IN PLAID: Not my babies . . . not my . . . (*Upon receiving the award,* SHE *instantly recovers*) Help me up, sugar. (SHE *bows and crosses to stand behind the couch*)

NARRATOR: Enter Medea Jones, Walter-Lee-Beau-Willie's sister.

MEDEA *moves very ceremoniously, wiping her feet, then speaking and gesturing as if* SHE *just escaped from a Greek tragedy.*

MEDEA: Ah, see how the sun kneels to speak
her evening vespers, exalting all
in her vision, even lowly tenement
long abandoned.

Mother, wife of brother, I trust
the approaching darkness finds you
safe in Hestia's bosom.

Brother, why wear the face of a man
in anguish. Can the garment of thine
feelings cause the shape of your
countenance to disfigure so?

SON (*At the end of his rope*): Leave me alone, Medea.

MEDEA (*To* MAMA): Is good brother still going on and on and on
about He and the Man.

MAMA AND LADY IN PLAID: What else?

MEDEA: Ah brother, if with our thoughts and
words we could cast thine oppressors
into the lowest bowels of wretched
hell, would that make us more like the
gods or more like our oppressors.

No, brother, no, do not let thy rage
choke the blood which anoints thy
heart with love. Forgo thine darkened
humor and let love shine on your
soul, like a jewel on a young maiden's hand.

(*Dropping to her knees*)
I beseech thee, forgo thine
anger and leave wrath to the gods!

SON: Girl, what has gotten into you.

MEDEA: Julliard, good brother. For I am no
longer bound by rhythms of race or
region. Oh, no. My speech, like my
pain and suffering, have become
classical and therefore universal.

LADY IN PLAID: I didn't understand a damn thing she said, but girl you usin' them
words.

LADY IN PLAID *crosses and gives* MEDEA *the award.* EVERYONE *applauds.*

SON (*Trying to stop the applause*): Wait one damn minute! This my play. It's about
me and the Man. It ain't got nuthin' to do with no ancient temples on the
Nile and it ain't got nuthin' to do with Hestia's bosom. And it ain't got nuthin'
to do with you slappin' me across no room. (*His gut-wrenching best*) It's about
me. Me and my pain! My pain!

THE VOICE OF THE MAN: Walter-Lee-Beau-Willie, this is the Man. You have been convicted of overacting. Come out with your hands up.

SON *starts to cross to the window.*

SON: Well now that does it.
MAMA: Son, no, don't go near that window. Son, no!

Gunshots ring out and SON *falls dead.*

(*Crossing to the body, too emotional for words*) My son, he was a good boy. Confused. Angry. Just like his father. And his father's father. And his father's father's father. And now he's dead.

Seeing SHE'*s about to drop to her knees, the* NARRATOR *rushes and places a pillow underneath her just in time.*

If only he had been born into a world better than this. A world where there are no well-worn couches and no well-worn Mamas and nobody overemotes.
     If only he had been born into an all-black musical. (*A song intro begins*) Nobody ever dies in an all-black musical.

MEDEA *and* LADY IN PLAID *pull out church fans and begin to fan themselves.* MAMA *sings a soul-stirring gospel.*

Oh why couldn't he
Be born
Into a show with lots of singing
And dancing

I say why
Couldn't he
Be born

LADY IN PLAID: Go ahead hunny. Take your time.
MAMA: Into a show where everybody
     Is happy
NARRATOR AND MEDEA: Preach! Preach!
MAMA: Oh why couldn't he be born with the chance
     To smile a lot and sing and dance
     Oh why
     Oh why

Oh why
Couldn't he
Be born
Into an all-black show
Woah-woah

The CAST *joins in, singing doo-wop gospel background to* MAMA'S *lament.*

Oh why
Couldn't he
Be born
(He be born)
Into a show where everybody
Is happy

Why couldn't he be born with the chance
To smile a lot and sing and dance
Wanna know why
Wanna know why

Oh why
Couldn't he
Be born
Into an all-black show
A-men

A singing/dancing, spirit-raising revival begins.

Oh, son, get up
Get up and dance
We say get up
This is your second chance

Don't shake a fist
Just shake a leg
And do the twist
Don't scream and beg
Son Son Son
Get up and dance

Get
Get up
Get up and

Get up and dance—All right!
Get up and dance—All right!
Get up and dance!

WALTER-LEE-BEAU-WILLIE *springs to life and joins in the dancing. A foot-stomping, hand-clapping production number takes off, which encompasses a myriad of black-Broadwayesque dancing styles—shifting speeds and styles with exuberant abandonment.*

(*Bluesy*) Why couldn't he be born into an all-black show
CAST: With singing and dancing
MAMA: Black show

MAMA *scats and the dancing becomes manic and just a little too desperate to please.*

CAST: We gotta dance
We gotta dance
Get up get up get up and dance
We gotta dance
We gotta dance
Gotta dance!

Just at the point the dancing is about to become violent, the CAST *freezes and pointedly, simply sings.*

If we want to live
We have got to
We have got to
Dance . . . and dance . . . and dance . . .

As THEY *continue to dance with zombie-like frozen smiles and faces, around them images of coon performers flash as the lights slowly fade.*

Symbiosis

The Temptations singing "My Girl" are heard as lights reveal a black MAN *in corporate dress standing before a large trash can throwing objects from a Saks Fifth Avenue bag into it. Circling around him with his every emotion on his face is* THE KID, *who is dressed in a late-sixties street style. His moves are slightly heightened. As the scene begins the music fades.*

MAN (*With contained emotions*):

My first pair of Converse All-Stars. Gone.

My first Afro comb. Gone.

My first dashiki. Gone.

My autographed pictures of Stokely Carmichael, Jomo Kenyatta and Donna Summer. Gone.

KID (*Near tears, totally upset*): This shit's not fair man. Damn! Hell! Shit! Shit! It's not fair!

MAN: My first jar of Murray's Pomade.

My first can of Afro-Sheen.

My first box of curl relaxer. Gone! Gone! Gone!

Eldridge Cleaver's *Soul on Ice.*

KID: Not *Soul on Ice!*

MAN: It's been replaced on my bookshelf by *The Color Purple.*

KID (*Horrified*): No!

MAN: Gone!

KID: But—

MAN: Jimi Hendrix's "Purple Haze." Gone.

Sly Stone's "There's A Riot Goin' On." Gone.

The Jackson Five's "I Want You Back."

KID: Man, you can't throw that away. It's living proof Michael had a black nose.

MAN: It's all going. Anything and everything that connects me to you, to who I was, to what we were, is out of my life.

KID: You've got to give me another chance.

MAN: "Fingertips Part 2."

KID: Man, how can you do that? That's vintage Stevie Wonder.

MAN: You want to know how, Kid? You want to know how? Because my survival depends on it. Whether you know it or not, the Ice Age is upon us.

KID (*Jokingly*): Man, what the hell you talkin' about. It's ninety-five damn degrees.

MAN: The climate is changing, Kid, and either you adjust or you end up extinct. A sociological dinosaur. Do you understand what I'm trying to tell you? King Kong would have made it to the top if only he had taken the elevator. Instead he brought attention to his struggle and ended up dead.

KID (*Pleading*): I'll change. I swear I'll change. I'll maintain a low profile. You won't even know I'm around.

MAN: If I'm to become what I'm to become then you've got to go. . . . I have no history. I have no past.

KID: Just like that?

MAN (*Throwing away a series of buttons*): Free Angela! Free Bobby! Free Huey, Duey, and Louie! U.S. out of Vietnam. U.S. out of Cambodia. U.S. out of Harlem, Detroit, and Newark. Gone! . . . *The Temptations Greatest Hits!*

KID (*Grabbing the album*): No!!!

MAN: Give it back, Kid.

KID: No.

MAN: I said give it back!

KID: No. I can't let you trash this. Johnny man, it contains fourteen classic cuts by the tempting Temptations. We're talking "Ain't Too Proud to Beg," "Papa Was a Rolling Stone," "My Girl."

MAN (Warning): I don't have all day.

KID: For God's sake, Johnny man, "My Girl" is the jam to end all jams. It's what we are. Who we are. It's a way of life. Come on, man, for old times sake. (HE sings)

I got sunshine on a cloudy day
Bum-da-dum-da-dum-da-bum
And when it's cold outside
(Speaking) Come on, Johnny man, you ain't "bummin'," man.
I got the month of May
(Speaking) Here comes your favorite part. Come on, Johnny man, sing.
I guess you say
What can make me feel this way
My girl, my girl, my girl
Talkin' 'bout—

MAN (Exploding): I said give it back!

KID (Angry): I ain't givin' you a muthafuckin' thing!

MAN: Now you listen to me!

KID: No, you listen to me. This is the Kid you're dealin' with, so don't fuck with me!

HE hits his fist into his hand and THE MAN grabs for his heart. THE KID repeats with two more hits, which cause THE MAN to drop to the ground, grabbing his heart.

KID: Jai! Jai! Jai!

MAN: Kid, please.

KID: Yeah. Yeah. Now who's begging who. . . . Well, well, well, look at Mr. Cream-of-the-Crop, Mr. Colored-Man-on-Top. Now that he's making it, he no longer wants anything to do with the Kid. Well, you may put all kinds of silk ties 'round your neck and white lines up your nose, but the Kid is here to stay. You may change your women as often as you change your underwear, but the Kid is here to stay. And regardless of how much of your past that you trash, I ain't goin' no damn where. Is that clear? Is that clear?

MAN (Regaining his strength, beginning to stand): Yeah.

KID: Good. (After a beat) You all right man? You all right? I don't want to hurt you, but when you start all that talk about getting rid of me, well, it gets me kind of crazy. We need each other. We are one . . .

Before THE KID can complete his sentence, THE MAN grabs him around his neck and starts to choke him violently.

MAN (As HE strangles THE KID): The . . . Ice . . . Age . . . is . . . upon us . . . and either we adjust . . . or we end up . . . extinct.

THE KID hangs limp in THE MAN's arms.

(Laughing) Man kills his own rage. Film at eleven. (HE dumps THE KID into the trash can and closes the lid. HE speaks in a contained voice) I have no history. I have no past. I can't. It's too much. It's much too much. I must be able to smile on cue. And watch the news with an impersonal eye. I have no stake in the madness.

     Being black is too emotionally taxing; therefore I will be black only on weekends and holidays. (HE turns to go, but sees the Temptations album lying on the ground. HE picks it up and sings quietly to himself)

I guess you say
What can make me feel this way

HE pauses, but then crosses to the trash can and lifts the lid. Just as HE is about to toss the album in, a hand reaches from inside the can and grabs hold of his arm. THE KID emerges from the can with a death grip on THE MAN's arm.

KID (Smiling): What's happenin'?

Blackout.

Lala's Opening

Roving follow spots. A timpani drumroll. As we hear the voice of the ANNOUNCER, outrageously glamorous images of LALA are projected onto the museum walls.

VOICE OF ANNOUNCER: From Rome to Rangoon! Paris to Prague! We are pleased to present the American debut of the one! The only! The breathtaking! The astounding! The stupendous! The incredible! The magnificient! Lala Lamazing Grace!

Thunderous applause as LALA struts on, the definitive black diva. SHE has long, flowing hair, an outrageous lamé dress, and an affected French accent which SHE loses when SHE's upset.

LALA (Sings): Everybody loves Lala
     Everybody loves me
     Paris! Berlin! London! Rome!

No matter where I go
I always feel at home

Ohhhh
Everybody loves Lala
Everybody loves me
I'm très magnifique
And oh so unique
And when it comes to glamour
I'm chic-er than chic

(SHE *giggles*)
That's why everybody
Everybody
Everybody-everybody-everybody
Loves me

(SHE *begins to reach for higher and higher notes, until* SHE *has to point to her final note.* SHE *ends the number with a grand flourish and bows to thunderous applause*)
Yes, it's me! Lala Lamazing Grace and I have come home. Home to the home I never knew as home. Home to you, my people, my blood, my guts.

My story is a simple one, full of fire, passion, magique. You may ask how did I, a humble girl from the backwoods of Mississippi, come to be the ninth wonder of the modern world. Well, I can't take all of the credit. Part of it goes to Him. (SHE *points toward the heavens*)

No, not the light man, darling, but God. For, you see, Lala is a star. A very big star. Let us not mince words, I'm a fucking meteorite. (SHE *laughs*) But He is the universe and just like my sister, Aretha la Franklin, Lala's roots are in the black church. (SHE *sings in a showy gospel style*)

That's why everybody loves
Swing low sweet chariot
That's why everybody loves
Go down Moses way down in Egypt land
That's why everybody everybody loves
ME!!!

(*Once again* SHE *points to her final note and then basks in applause*) I love that note. I just can't hit it.

Now, before I dazzle you with more of my limitless talent, tell me something, America. (*Musical underscoring*) Why has it taken you so long to recognize my artistry? Mother France opened her loving arms and Lala came running. All over the world Lala was embraced. But here, ha! You spat at Lala. Was I too exotic? Too much woman, or what?

Diana Ross you embrace. A two-bit nobody from Detroit, of all places. Now, I'm not knocking la Ross. She does the best she can with the little she has. (SHE *laughs*) But the Paul la Robesons, the James la Baldwins, the Josephine la Bakers, who was my godmother you know. The Lala Lamazing Graces you kick out. You drive ... (SHE *sings*)

Away
I am going away
Hoping to find a better day
What do you say
Hey hey
I am going away
Away

LALA, *caught up in the drama of the song, doesn't see* ADMONIA, *her maid, stick her head out from offstage. Once* SHE *is sure* LALA *isn't looking,* SHE *wheels onto stage right* FLO'RANCE, LALA's *lover, who wears a white mask with blond hair.* HE *is gagged and tied to a chair.* ADMONIA *places him on stage and then quickly exits.*

Au revoir—je vais parter maintenant
Je veux dire maintenant
Au revoir
Au revoir
Au revoir
Au revoir
A—ma—vie

(*On her last note,* SHE *sees* FLO'RANCE *and, in total shock, crosses to him*) Flo'rance, what the hell are you doing out here, looking like that. I haven't seen you for three days and you decide to show up now? (HE *mumbles*) I don't want to hear it! (HE *mumbles*) I said shut up!

ADMONIA *enters from stage right with a letter opener on a silver tray.*

ADMONIA: Pst!
LALA (*Embarrassed by the presence of* ADMONIA *on stage,* SHE *smiles apologetically at the audience*): Un momento. (SHE *pulls* ADMONIA *to the side*) Darling, have you lost your mind coming onstage while I'm performing. And what have you done to Flo'rance? When I asked you to keep him tied up, I didn't mean to tie him up. (ADMONIA *gives her the letter opener*) Why are you giving me this? I have no letters to open. I'm in the middle of my American debut. Admonia, take Flo'rance off this stage with you! Admonia!

ADMONIA *is gone.* LALA *turns to the audience and tries to make the best of it.*

That was Admonia, my slightly overweight black maid, and this is Flo'rance, my amour. I remember how we met, don't you Flo'rance. I was sitting in a café on the left Bank, when I looked up and saw the most beautiful man staring down at me.

"Who are you," he asked. I told him my name . . . whatever my name was back then. And he said, "No, that cannot be your name. Your name should fly, like Lala." And the rest is la history.

Flo'rance molded me into the woman I am today. He is my Svengali, my reality, my all. And I thought I was all to him, until we came here to America, and he fucked that bitch. Yeah, you fucked 'em all. Anything black and breathing. And all this time, I thought you loved me for being me. (SHE *holds the letter opener to his neck)*

You may think you made me, but I'll have you know I was who I was, whoever that was, long before you made me what I am. So there! (SHE *stabs him and breaks into song)*

Oh, love can drive a woman to madness
To pain and sadness
I know
Believe me I know
I know
I know

(SHE *sees what* SHE*'s done and is about to scream but catches herself and tries to play it off)* Moving right along.

ADMONIA *enters with a telegram on a tray.*

ADMONIA: Pst.
LALA *(Anxious/hostile)*: What is it now?

ADMONIA *hands* LALA *a telegram.*

(Excited) Oh, la telegram from one of my fans and the concert isn't even over yet. Get me the letter opener. It's in Flo'rance.

ADMONIA *hands* LALA *the letter opener.*

Next I am going to do for you my immortal hit song, "The Girl Inside." But first we open the telegram. (SHE *quickly reads it and is outraged)* What! Which pig in la audience wrote this trash? *(Reading)* "Dear Sadie, I'm so proud. The show's wonderful, but talk less and sing more. Love, Mama."

First off, no one calls me Sadie. Sadie died the day Lala was born. And secondly, my mama's dead. Anyone who knows anything about Lala Lamazing Grace knows that my mother and Josephine Baker were French patriots together. They infiltrated a carnival rumored to be the center of Nazi intelligence, disguised as Hottentot Siamese twins. You may laugh but it's true. Mama died a heroine. It's all in my autobiography, *Voilà Lala!* So whoever sent this telegram is a liar!

ADMONIA *promptly presents her with another telegram.*

This had better be an apology. *(To* ADMONIA*)* Back up, darling. *(Reading)* "Dear Sadie, I'm not dead. P.S. Your child misses you." What? (SHE *squares off at the audience)* Well, now, that does it! If you are my mother, which you are not. And this alleged child is my child, then that would mean I am a mother and I have never given birth. I don't know nothin' 'bout birthin' no babies! (SHE *laughs)* Lala made a funny.

So whoever sent this, show me the child! Show me!

ADMONIA *offers another telegram.*

(To ADMONIA*)* You know you're gonna get fired! (SHE *reluctantly opens it)* "The child is in the closet." What closet?

ADMONIA: Pst.

ADMONIA *pushes a button and the center wall unit revolves around to reveal a large black door.* ADMONIA *exits, taking* FLO'RANCE *with her, leaving* LALA *alone.*

LALA *(Laughing):* I get it. It's a plot, isn't it. A nasty little CIA, FBI kind of plot. Well let me tell you muthafuckers one thing, there is nothing in that closet, real or manufactured, that will be a dimmer to the glimmer of Lamé the star. You may have gotten Billie and Bessie and a little piece of everyone else who's come along since, but you won't get Lala. My clothes are too fabulous! My hair is too long! My accent too French. That's why I came home to America. To prove you ain't got nothing on me!

The music for her next song starts, but LALA *is caught up in her tirade, and talks/screams over the music.*

My mother and Josephine Baker were French patriots together! I've had brunch with the Pope! I've dined with the Queen! Everywhere I go I cause riots! Hunny, I am a star! I have transcended pain! So there! *(Yelling)* Stop the music! Stop that goddam music.

The music stops. LALA *slowly walks downstage and singles out someone in the audience.*

Darling, you're not looking at me. You're staring at that damn door. Did you pay to stare at some fucking door or be mesmerized by my talent? *(To the whole audience)* Very well! I guess I am going to have to go to the closet door, fling it open, in order to dispel all the nasty little thoughts these nasty little telegrams have planted in your nasty little minds. *(Speaking directly to someone in the audience)* Do you want me to open the closet door? Speak up, darling, this is live. *(Once SHE gets the person to say "yes")* I will open the door, but before I do, let me tell you bastards one last thing. To hell with coming home and to hell with lies and insinuations!

    (SHE goes into the closet and after a short pause comes running out, ready to scream, and slams the door. Traumatized to the point of no return, SHE tells the following story as if it were a jazz solo of rushing, shifting emotions) I must tell you this dream I had last night. Simply magnifique. In this dream, I'm running naked in Sammy Davis Junior's hair. *(Crazed laughter)*

    Yes! I'm caught in this larger-than-life, deep, dark forest of savage, nappy-nappy hair. The kinky-kinks are choking me, wrapped around my naked arms, thighs, breast, face. I can't breathe. And there was nothing in that closet!

    And I'm thinking if only I had a machete, I could cut away the kinks. Remove once and for all the roughness. But then I look up and it's coming toward me. Flowing like lava. It's pomade! Ohhh, Sammy!

    Yes, cakes and cakes of pomade. Making everything nice and white and smooth and shiny, like my black/white/black/white/black behiney.

    Mama no!

    And then spikes start cutting through the pomade. Combing the coated kink. Cutting through the kink, into me. There are blood lines on my back. On my thighs.

    It's all over. All over . . . all over me. All over for me. *(SHE accidentally pulls off her wig to reveal her real hair. Stripped of her "disguise" SHE recoils like a scared little girl and sings)*

Mommy and Daddy
Meet and mate
The child that's born
Is torn with love and with hate
She runs away to find her own
And tries to deny
What she's always known
The girl inside

The closet door opens. LALA runs away, and a LITTLE BLACK GIRL emerges from the closet. Standing behind her is ADMONIA. The LITTLE GIRL and LALA are in two isolated pools of light and mirror each other's moves until LALA reaches past her reflection and the LITTLE GIRL comes to LALA and THEY hug. ADMONIA joins them as LALA sings. Music underscores.

What's left is the girl inside
The girl who died
So a new girl could be born

Slow fade to black.

Permutations

Lights up on NORMAL JEAN REYNOLDS. SHE *is very southern/country and very young.* SHE *wears a simple faded print dress and her hair, slightly mussed, is in plaits.* SHE *sits, her dress covering a large oval object.*

NORMAL: My mama used to say, God made the exceptional, then God made the special and when God got bored, he made me. Course she don't say too much of nuthin' no more, not since I lay me this egg. (SHE *lifts her dress to uncover a large, white egg lying between her legs*)

Ya see it all got started when I had me sexual relations with the garbage man. Ooowee, did he smell.

No, not bad. No! He smelled of all the good things folks never shoulda thrown away. His sweat was like cantaloupe juice. His neck was like a ripe-red strawberry. And the water that fell from his eyes was like a deep, dark, juicy-juicy grape. I tell ya, it was like fuckin' a fruit salad, only I didn't spit out the seeds. I kept them here, deep inside. And three days later, my belly commence to swell, real big like.

Well my mama locked me off in some dark room, refusin' to let me see the light of day 'cause, "What would the neighbors think." At first I cried a lot, but then I grew used to livin' my days in the dark, and my nights in the dark ... (SHE *hums*) And then it wasn't but a week or so later, my mama off at church, that I got this hurtin' feelin' down here. Worse than anything I'd ever known. And then I started bleedin', real bad. I mean there was blood everywhere. And the pain had me howlin' like a near-dead dog. I tell ya, I was yellin' so loud, I couldn't even hear myself. Noooooooo! Noooooo! Carrying on something like that.

And I guess it was just too much for the body to take, 'cause the next thing I remember ... is me coming to and there's this big white egg layin' 'tween my legs. First I thought somebody musta put it there as some kind of joke. But then I noticed that all 'round this egg were thin lines of blood that I could trace to back between my legs.

(*Laughing*) Well, when my mama come home from church she just about died. "Normal Jean, what's that thing 'tween your legs? Normal Jean, you answer me, girl!" It's not a thing, Mama. It's an egg. And I laid it.

She tried separatin' me from it, but I wasn't havin' it. I stayed in that dark room, huggin', holdin' onto it.

And then I heard it. It wasn't anything that coulda been heard 'round the world, or even in the next room. It was kinda like layin' back in the bathtub, ya know, the water just coverin' your ears . . . and if you lay real still and listen real close, you can hear the sound of your heart movin' the water. You ever done that? Well that's what it sounded like. A heart movin' water. And it was happenin' inside here.

Why, I'm the only person I know who ever lay themselves an egg before so that makes me special. You hear that, Mama? I'm special and so's my egg! And special things supposed to be treated like they matter. That's why every night I count to it, so it knows nuthin' never really ends. And I sing it every song I know so that when it comes out, it's full of all kinds of feelings. And I tell it secrets and laugh with it and . . . (SHE *suddenly stops and puts her ear to the egg and listens intently*)

Oh! I don't believe it! I thought I heard . . . yes! (*Excited*) Can you hear it? Instead of one heart, there's two. Two little hearts just pattering away. Boom-boom-boom. Boom-boom-boom. Talkin' to each other like old friends. Racin' toward the beginnin' of their lives.

(*Listening*) Oh, no, now there's three . . . four . . . five, six. More hearts than I can count. And they're all alive, beatin' out life inside my egg.

We begin to hear the heartbeats, drums, alive inside NORMAL's *egg.*

Any day now, this egg is gonna crack open and what's gonna come out a be the likes of which nobody has ever seen. My babies! And their skin is gonna turn all kinds of shades in the sun and their hair a be growin' every which-a-way. And it won't matter and they won't care 'cause they know they are so rare and so special 'cause it's not everyday a bunch of babies break outta a white egg and start to live.

And nobody better not try and hurt my babies 'cause if they do, they gonna have to deal with me.

Yes, any day now, this shell's gonna crack and my babies are gonna fly. Fly! Fly! (SHE *laughs at the thought, but then stops and says the word as if it's the most natural thing in the world*) Fly.

Blackout.

The Party

Before we know what's hit us, a hurricane of energy comes bounding into the space. It is TOPSY WASHINGTON. *Her hair and dress are a series of stylistic contradictions which are hip, black and unencumbered. Music, spiritual and funky, underscores.*

TOPSY (*Dancing about*): Yoho! Party! Party! Turn up the music! Turn up the music!

Have yaw ever been to a party where there was one fool in the middle of the room, dancing harder and yelling louder than everybody in the entire place? Well, hunny, that fool was me!

Yes, child! The name is Topsy Washington and I love to party. As a matter of fact, when God created the world, on the seventh day, he didn't rest. No child, he P-A-R-T-I-E-D. Partied!

But now let me tell you 'bout this function I went to the other night, way uptown. And baby when I say way uptown, I mean way-way-way-way-way-way-way-way uptown. Somewheres between 125th Street and infinity.

Inside was the largest gathering of black/Negro/colored Americans you'd ever want to see. Over in one corner you got Nat Turner sippin' champagne out of Eartha Kitt's slipper. And over in another corner, Bert Williams and Malcolm X was discussing existentialism as it relates to the shuffle-ball-change. Girl, Aunt Jemima and Angela Davis was in the kitchen sharing a plate of greens and just goin' off about South Africa.

And then Fats sat down and started to work them eighty-eights. And then Stevie joined in. And then Miles and Duke and Ella and Jimi and Charlie and Sly and Lightnin' and Count and Louie!

And then everybody joined in. I tell you all the children was just all up in there, dancing to the rhythm of one beat. Dancing to the rhythm of their own definition. Celebrating in their cultural madness.

And then the floor started to shake. And the walls started to move. And before anybody knew what was happening, the entire room lifted up off the ground. The whole place just took off and went flying through space— defying logic and limitations. Just a-spinning and a-spinning and a-spinning until it disappeared inside of my head.

TOPSY *stops dancing and regains her balance and begins to listen to the music in her head. Slowly we begin to hear it, too.*

That's right, girl, there's a party goin' on inside of here. That's why when I walk down the street my hips just sashay all over the place. 'Cause I'm dancing to the music of the madness in me.

And whereas I used to jump into a rage anytime anybody tried to deny who I was, now all I got to do is give attitude, quicker than light, and then go on about the business of being me. 'Cause I'm dancing to the music of the madness in me.

As TOPSY *continues to speak,* MISS ROJ, LALA, MISS PAT, *and* THE MAN *from Symbiosis revolve on, frozen like soft sculptures.*

And here, all this time I been thinking we gave up our drums. But, naw, we still got 'em. I know I got mine. They're here, in my speech, my walk, my hair, my God, my style, my smile and my eyes. And everything I need to get over in this world, is inside here, connecting me to everybody and everything that's ever been.

So hunny, don't waste your time trying to label or define me.

The SCULPTURES *slowly begin to come to life.* THEY *mirror/echo* TOPSY's *words.*

TOPSY AND SCULPTURES: . . . 'Cause I'm not what I was ten years ago or ten minutes ago. I'm all of that and then some. And whereas I can't live inside yesterday's pain, I can't live without it.

All of a sudden, madness erupts on the stage. The SCULPTURES *begin to speak all at once. Images of black/Negro/colored Americans begin to flash—images of them dancing past the madness, caught up in the madness, being lynched, rioting, party-ing, surviving. Mixed in with these images are all the characters from the exhibits. Through all of this* TOPSY *sings. It is a vocal and visual cacophony which builds and builds.*

LALA: I must tell you about this dream I had last night. Simply magnifique. In this dream I'm running naked in Sammy Davis Junior's hair. Yes. I'm caught in this larger-than-life, deep, dark tangled forest of savage, nappy-nappy hair. Yes, the kinky-kinks are choking me, are wrapped around my naked arms, my naked thighs, breast, and face, and I can't breathe and there was nothing in that closet.

MISS ROJ (*Simultaneously*): Snap for every time you walk past someone lying in the street smelling like frozen piss and shit and you don't see it. Snap for every crazed bastard who kills himself so as to get the jump on being killed. And snap for every sick muthafucker who, bored with carrying about his fear, takes to shooting up other people.

THE MAN (*Simultaneously*): I have no history. I have no past. I can't. It's too much. It's much too much. I must be able to smile on cue and watch the news with an impersonal eye. I have no stake in the madness. Being black is too emo-tionally taxing, therefore I will be black only on weekends and holidays.

MISS PAT (*Simultaneously*): Stop playing those drums. I said stop playing those damn drums. You can't stop history. You can't stop time. Those drums will be con-fiscated once we reach Savannah, so give them up now. Repeat after me: I don't hear any drums and I will not rebel. I will not rebel!

TOPSY (*Singing*): There's madness in me
And that madness sets me free
There's madness in me
And that madness sets me free
There's madness in me
And that madness sets me free

There's madness in me
And that madness sets me free
There's madness in me
And that madness sets me free

My power is in my . . .
EVERYBODY: *Madness!*
TOPSY: And my colored contradictions.

The SCULPTURES *freeze with a smile on their faces as we hear the voice of* MISS PAT.

VOICE OF MISS PAT: Before exiting, check the overhead as any baggage you don't
claim, we trash.

Blackout.

END OF PLAY

About TCG

Theatre Communications Group is the national organization for the nonprofit professional theatre. Since its founding in 1961, TCG has developed a unique and comprehensive support system that addresses the artistic and management concerns of theatres, as well as institutionally based and freelance artists nationwide.

TCG provides a national forum and communications network for a field that is as aesthetically diverse as it is geographically widespread. Its goals are to foster the cross-fertilization of ideas among the individuals and institutions comprising the profession; to improve the artistic and administrative capabilities of the field; to enhance the visibility and demonstrate the achievements of the American theatre by increasing public awareness of the theatre's role in society; and to encourage the development of a mutually supportive network of professional companies and artists that collectively represent our "national theatre."

TCG's centralized services today encompass some 30 programs, including job referral services, management and research services, publications, literary services, conferences, and a wide range of other information and advisory services. These programs facilitate the work of thousands of actors, artistic and managing directors, playwrights, literary managers, directors, designers, trustees and administrative personnel, as well as a constituency of more than 270 theatre institutions across the country.

TCG gratefully acknowledges the generous support of individual contributors and the following corporations, foundations and government agencies: Actors' Equity Foundation, Alcoa Foundation, ARCO Foundation, AT&T Foundation, Citicorp/Citibank, Columbia Pictures Industries, Consolidated Edison Company of New York, Eleanor Naylor Dana Charitable Trust, Dayton Hudson Foundation, Exxon Corporation, The William and Mary Greve Foundation, Home Box Office, Inc., The Andrew W. Mellon Foundation, Mobil Foundation, Inc., National Broadcasting Company, National Endowment for the Arts, New York Life Foundation, New York State Council on the Arts, The Pew Charitable Trusts, Philip Morris Incorporated, The Rockefeller Foundation, The Scherman Foundation, Shell Oil Company Foundation, The Shubert Foundation, Inc., Consulate General of Spain and The Xerox Foundation.